W9-BRQ-369

"*Hard Facts, Dangerous Half-Truths, and Total Nonsense* delivers a clear and compelling approach to management and leading successful organizations. A great gift to leaders determined to be viable, relevant, and effective in a tenuous future."

—*Frances Hesselbein, Chairman, Leader to Leader Institute*

"Pfeffer and Sutton marshal bountiful evidence to demolish a number of the most cherished and ingrained superstitions in all of management. And even better, they provide a suite of practical tools for profiting from evidence-based management. If you want to unlock the secrets to outperforming your superstitious competitors, this book is your key."

—*Roger Martin, Dean, Rotman School of Management,*
University of Toronto, and former Global Co-head of
Monitor Company

"Virtually every organization, public or private, lives or dies on the bottom line of execution. The powerful insights of *Hard Facts, Dangerous Half-Truths, and Total Nonsense* point out that the road to profitability and better execution is all too often littered with more myth than evidence. To understand these perspectives is to turn roadblocks into building blocks."

—*Rudy Crew, Superintendent, Miami-Dade County Public Schools,*
Former Chancellor, New York City Department of Education

Hard Facts, Dangerous Half-Truths, and Total Nonsense

Profiting from Evidence-Based Management

Jeffrey Pfeffer
Robert I. Sutton

Harvard Business School Press
Boston, Massachusetts

Copyright 2006 Jeffrey Pfeffer and Robert I. Sutton
All rights reserved
Printed in the United States of America
10 09 08 07 06   5 4 3 2

No part of this publication may be reproduced, stored in or introduced into a
retrieval system, or transmitted, in any form, or by any means (electronic, mechanical, photocopying, recording, or otherwise), without the prior permission
of the publisher. Requests for permission should be directed to permissions@hbsp
.harvard.edu, or mailed to Permissions, Harvard Business School Publishing,
60 Harvard Way, Boston, Massachusetts 02163.

978-1-59139-862-2 (ISBN 13)

   Library of Congress Cataloging-in-Publication Data
Pfeffer, Jeffrey.
   Hard facts, dangerous half-truths, and total nonsense : profiting from
evidence-based management / Jeffrey Pfeffer, Robert I. Sutton.
      p. cm.
   Includes bibliographical references.
   ISBN 1-59139-862-2
  1. Industrial management—Decision making. I. Sutton, Robert I. II. Title.
   HD30.23.P468 2006

                                                    2005030854

ACC Library Services
   Austin, Texas

mum requirements of the
:nces—Permanence of Paper
ג.

Contents

To Kathleen and Marina,

The Loves of Our Lives

Preface

Our last book, *The Knowing-Doing Gap*, struck a chord with lots of people. In many companies there were experienced, intelligent, motivated people who, both individually and collectively, knew what to do but couldn't or wouldn't act on that knowledge. We identified the main causes of knowing-doing gaps and how organizations could avoid or reverse such impediments to action. We also found that the problem was not confined to for-profit companies. We heard story after story from people in educational research and school administration about how decades of research on teaching and learning was neglected in the practices actually enacted in schools. As we write this preface in the fall of 2005, we see the problem playing out once again. The terrible devastation and human suffering caused by hurricane Katrina, which nearly obliterated New Orleans and much of the nearby Gulf Coast, and the halting, disorganized initial rescue efforts reflect the failure to implement what was known and even planned for months and years ago both to mitigate the effects of the storm and to speed up recovery efforts. There is no question that the knowing-doing gap persists as a big problem in the private and public sector.

After writing *The Knowing-Doing Gap* we soon encountered a different and somewhat unexpected management problem. People kept telling us about the wonderful things they were doing to implement knowledge—but those things often clashed with, and at times were the opposite of, what we knew about organizations and people. Upon probing, we soon discovered that many managers had been prompted by a seminar, book, or consultants to do things that were at odds with the best evidence about what works. We began to call this the "doing-knowing" problem—doing without knowing, or at least knowing enough.

We became fascinated with why this problem existed, and what might be done about it. We also became fascinated with certain half-truths that we kept hearing again and again, ideas and principles that are partly right at times, but are flawed and misleading often enough to get organizations into serious trouble. Beliefs like "the best organizations have the best people," "strategy is destiny," and "great leaders are in control and ought to be" have an element of truth, but when treated as the whole truth and applied to every decision and design of every program and practice, they cause severe damage to companies; management careers; and employee loyalty, effort, and mental health. Meanwhile, we witnessed attempts to introduce evidence-based practice into education, efforts that—despite the best intentions—were often met with resistance that undermined learning and wasted billions of dollars. We also followed the rise in evidence-based medicine because a number of our former students are physicians with a heavy research emphasis in their practice and work. We began to wonder if there were principles that might apply across domains and make decisions and actions wiser. In fact, in the National Institute of Health's publication *Keeping Patients Safe*, there is a chapter entitled "Evidence-Based Management."

So off we went, to study organizations, read, think, and to the surprise of no one who knows us, to argue and debate about the best logic, evidence, and management practices. The result is this book. It is a call for evidence-based management, a case for its potential impact, and a guide on how to use it. *Hard Facts, Dangerous Half-Truths, and Total Nonsense* identifies some of the barriers to implementing evidence-based management and presents steps that leaders can take to overcome those barriers, with an emphasis on how to manage in light of the most dangerous half-truths that bedevil organizations.

We emerged from this exercise with a renewed appreciation for how difficult it is to manage and lead an organization, and how much time and effort managers must devote to learning their craft. We also gained a stronger appreciation for how evidence-based management can help managers and leaders do a better job of learning and practicing their profession, and make these difficult jobs a bit less taxing and more successful. There are no simple, easy answers, but there *are* answers: better ways of thinking about business knowledge and more fact-based ways of understanding management practices. This book shares our insights and the results of our research, thought, reading, and yes, argument and debate, with you.

Part One

Setting
the Stage

Why Every Company Needs Evidence-Based Management

O N THE DAY Synoptics and Wellfleet Communications merged to form Bay Networks, the company's revenue was about equal to its major competitor, Cisco Systems. If you haven't heard of Bay Networks, don't be surprised. This merger between two firms, similar in size and headquartered on opposite coasts of the United States, failed by any measure. Bay Networks fell on hard times economically, was left in the dust technologically by Cisco and others, and was finally purchased by Nortel—another troubled networking company that suffered operating problems as a result of botched mergers. Mergers often come to a bad end. Remember Conseco—the insurance and financial services company that purchased Green Tree Lending, a company that financed the purchase of mobile homes by non-prime borrowers? Conseco wound up in bankruptcy and CEO Stephen Hilbert was fired. Or how about Mattel, the famous toy company? In an attempt to diversify beyond its Barbie franchise, Mattel made an ill-fated acquisition of the Learning Company, a technology-based education firm. The deal cost Mattel a lot of money, led to a substantial decline in its stock market value, and effectively ended the corporate career of CEO Jill Barad. And remember the ill-fated Daimler-Chrysler, American Online–Time Warner, and Hewlett-Packard–Compaq mergers?

This is not a new or surprising phenomenon—the list of failed mergers is long and provides fodder for much media attention.[1] Study after study shows that most mergers—some estimates are 70 percent or more—fail to deliver their intended benefits and destroy economic value in the process. A recent analysis of 93 studies covering more than 200,000 mergers published in peer-reviewed journals showed that, on average, the negative effects of a merger on shareholder value become evident less than a month after a merger is announced and persist thereafter.[2]

Corporate leaders who want to practice evidence-based management might begin by recognizing that the odds are against them in undertaking a merger and, as a consequence, resist the urge to merge. More thoughtful leaders might do what Cisco Systems has done—figure out the factors associated with successful and unsuccessful mergers and then actually use those insights to guide behavior. In 1993 Cisco CEO John Chambers and his senior team decided they needed to ramp up their growth and break into new and emerging networking technologies on a continuous basis, in part through acquisition. So Cisco embarked on a policy of aggressively acquiring new technologies and companies. Between 1993 and 1998, it acquired on average one firm per quarter, and since 1998 this pace has continued, if not intensified.[3] Yet a *Fortune* article on bad mergers noted that "infrastructure giant Cisco has digested 57 companies without heartburn."[4]

The difference between Cisco and so many other companies has little to do with either luck in finding the right things to buy or the charisma and charm of its senior management that somehow made the mergers work. Cisco's success stems from its systematic examination of evidence about what went right and went wrong in other companies' mergers, as well as its own. Cisco figured out that mergers between similar-sized companies rarely work, as there are frequently struggles about which team will control the combined entity (think Daimler-Chrysler or Dean Witter–Morgan Stanley). Cisco's leaders also determined that mergers work best when companies are geographically proximate, making integration and collaboration much easier (think Synoptics and Wellfleet Communication, which were not only about equal in size, but 2,500 miles apart), and they also uncovered the importance of organizational cultural compatibility for merger success, a lesson lost on many other firms.

But Cisco, as we've noted, is an exception. Siebel, the customer relationship management software firm, is yet another company that has botched numerous acquisitions: for instance, purchasing an industrial sales training company and driving its revenues from about $75 million to $10 million in less than five years. Siebel's business development executive admitted that all of the company's acquisitions have failed and noted that an internal study indicated that "cultural conflicts" were the cause in every case.[5] Cisco, by contrast, works relentlessly to understand the crucial dimensions of its culture versus its target's to determine if there is a match. Cisco has walked away from deals when the requisite cultural fit was missing.

Finally, and perhaps most importantly, Cisco has developed and uses a merger integration process to ensure that the people (what they are really buying) stay with the company, feel at home, and can use their knowledge to make key contributions. Integration activities are carefully planned and rapidly implemented to help guarantee that problems do not have a chance to arise. The company also keeps refining its merger integration process as well as the business development process to identify merger candidates, learning over time how to make its already impressive acquisition capability even better.[6]

Cisco's experience and its lessons, as well as lessons from other successful and unsuccessful acquisitions, are neither difficult to understand nor secret— they have been written about extensively. You might think companies would learn from all this experience and make fewer bad merger decisions. You also might think in a world of presumed "hypercompetition" where companies spend billions each year on consultants, more billions on intranets and chief knowledge officers, and more fortunes on training—all in an effort to acquire and use knowledge at a time when companies and their leaders are seeking every possible competitive edge and when business leaders are mightily rewarded with both money and status for success—that management decisions would be based on the best evidence, that managers would systematically learn from experience, and that organizational practices would reflect sound principles of thought and analysis.

But if you thought any of that, you would be wrong. Business decisions, as many of our colleagues in business and your own experience can attest, are frequently based on hope or fear, what others seem to be doing, what senior leaders have done and believe has worked in the past, and their dearly held ideologies—in short, on lots of things other than the facts. Although evidence-based practice may be coming to the field of medicine and, with more difficulty and delay, the world of education, it has had little impact on management or on how most companies operate. If doctors practiced medicine the way many companies practice management, there would be far more sick and dead patients, and many more doctors would be in jail.

Yet there is good news for leaders and companies in all this recalcitrance. As we will show you, practicing evidence-based management is neither arcane nor extraordinarily difficult—and it can produce superior results. It can also generate sustained competitive advantage, because since so few organizations and their leaders do it, the likelihood of imitation is not high.

Before we talk about what evidence-based management is and how to practice it, we need to show why and how you and your organization should halt some common ways of making decisions that are so accepted and widely recommended that they are rarely questioned—yet are deeply flawed. Even if you don't otherwise adopt an evidence-based approach, your company will suffer less harm by putting aside these suspect practices. So, we begin by telling you what evidence-based management is *not* and what you should avoid doing, before we tell you what evidence-based management *is* and how to practice it.

Poor Decision Practices, and How to Recognize and Avoid Them

The catalogue of poor decision practices is immense, but we focus here on three of the most common and, in our experience, most harmful to companies.

Casual Benchmarking

There is nothing wrong with learning from others' experience—vicarious learning, as contrasted with direct experience, is an important way for both people and organizations to learn how to navigate a path through the world. After all, it is a lot cheaper and easier to learn from the mistakes, setbacks, and successes of others than to treat every management challenge as something no organization has ever faced before. So benchmarking—using other companies' performance and experience to set standards for your own company—makes a lot of sense. In the end, good or bad performance is defined and measured largely in relation to what others are doing.

The problem lies with the way that benchmarking is usually practiced: it is far too "casual." The logic behind what works at top performers, why it works, and what will work elsewhere is barely unraveled, resulting in mindless imitation. Consider a pair of quick examples. When United Airlines decided in 1994 to compete with Southwest in the intra-California marketplace, the company tried to imitate Southwest. United put its gate staff and flight attendants in casual clothes; it flew only Boeing 737s; it gave the service a different name, "Shuttle by United," and used separate planes and crews; it stopped serving food; it increased the frequency of its flights and reduced the scheduled time planes spent on the ground, copying Southwest's legendary quick turnarounds. Southwest, however, wound up with a higher market share in California than it had before United launched its imitation.[7] The Shuttle failed and is now shuttered.

When U.S. automobile companies decided to embrace total quality management and emulate Toyota, the world leader in automobile manufacturing, many copied its factory-floor practices. They installed pull-cords that stopped the assembly line if defects were noticed, just-in-time inventory systems, and statistical process control charts. Yet even today, decades later, U.S. automakers for the most part still lag behind Toyota in productivity—the hours required to assemble a car—and many trail in quality and design features as well. Similar failures have plagued retailers' efforts to copy Nordstrom's sales commission system to achieve higher service levels, and the numerous organizations that attempted to mimic General Electric's forced-curve performance-ranking system.

In these and scores of other examples, a pair of fundamental problems render casual benchmarking ineffective. The first is that people copy the most visible, obvious, and frequently least important practices. Southwest's success is based on its culture and management philosophy, the priority it places on its employees (Southwest did not lay off one person following the September 11 meltdown in the aviation industry), not on how it dresses its gate agents and flight attendants, which planes it flies, or how it schedules them. Similarly, the secret to Toyota's success is not a set of techniques but its *philosophy*—the mind-set of total quality management and continuous improvement it has embraced—and the company's relationship with workers that has enabled it to tap their deep knowledge. As a wise executive in one of our classes said about imitating others, "We have been benchmarking the wrong things. Instead of copying what others *do*, we ought to copy how they *think*."

This executive was partly right but did not go far enough. The second problem is that companies often have different strategies, different competitive environments, and different business models—all of which make what they need to do to be successful different from what others are doing. Something that helps one organization can damage another. This is true particularly for companies that borrow practices from other industries, but often is true for organizations even within the same industry.

The fundamental problem is that few companies, in their urge to copy—an urge often stimulated by consultants who, much as bees spread pollen across flowers, take ideas from one place to the next—ever ask the basic question of *why* something might enhance performance. Before you run off to benchmark mindlessly, spending effort and money that results in no pay-off, or worse yet, in problems that you never had before, ask yourself:

- Is the success you observe by the benchmarking target *because of* the practice you seek to emulate? Southwest Airlines is the most success-ful airline in the history of that industry. Herb Kelleher served as CEO during most of Southwest's history and remains the chairman to this day. Kelleher drinks a lot of Wild Turkey bourbon. So does that mean that if your CEO starts drinking as much Wild Turkey as Kelleher, your company will dominate its industry? Get the point?

- *Why* is a particular practice linked to performance improvement—what is the logic? If you can't explain the underlying logic or theory of why something should enhance performance, you are likely engag-ing in superstitious learning and may be copying something that is irrelevant or even damaging.

- What are the downsides and disadvantages to implementing the prac-tice, even if it is a good idea? Are there ways of mitigating these prob-lems, perhaps ways your target uses that you aren't seeing?

Doing What (Seems to Have) Worked in the Past

Suppose you went to a doctor who said, "I'm going to do an appendec-tomy on you." When you asked why, the doctor answered, "because I did one on my last patient and it made him better." We suspect you would high-tail it out of that office, because you know that the treatment ought to fit the disease, regardless of whether or not the treatment helped the previous patient. Strangely enough, that logical thought process happens less than we might care to admit in most companies.

Consider a couple of industry examples. In a compensation committee meeting of a small software company that we worked with, the committee chair, a successful and smart executive, recommended the compensation policies he had employed at his last firm. He even suggested that his former head of human resources call the head of HR at this company to facilitate precise imitation. The fact that the two companies were of dramatically dif-ferent sizes, used different distribution methods, and sold to different mar-kets and customers somehow didn't faze him or many fellow committee members. This company isn't alone: how many of you are using performance appraisal forms that your executives brought with them from another com-pany? And then there is the case of the same strategy and approach being used regardless of the situation. Al Dunlap—the notorious Chainsaw Al—did layoffs (and it turns out, accounting fraud) in all of his companies, including Scott Paper and Sunbeam. Similarly, executives who believe that any unit that isn't ranked number one or two in its market needs to be sold typically carry that approach to new jobs. The aphorism that nothing predicts future behavior better than past behavior is especially true for executives who develop a template and use it again and again in every situation.

There is nothing wrong with learning from experience and developing proficiency at certain strategies and tactics. We ought to learn from experience—and use that experience to get better at what we do and develop specialties and talents that we can execute with consummate skill. The problems come when the new situation is different from the past and when what we "learned" was right in the past may have been wrong, or incomplete, in the first place.

In the software company example, the chair's recommended system—individual incentive pay with big rewards for making sales—would have undermined the consultative sales process that was essential for selling this company's particular product. The layoffs used routinely by Al Dunlap and so many other executives often don't work. Blindly copying the same approach without considering the underlying business problems is just plain dumb.[8] And lots of companies have gotten into trouble by importing, without sufficient thought, performance management and other measurement practices from past experience at other companies.

As in benchmarking, asking some simple questions and acting on their answers can help avoid the bad results that come from mindlessly repeating the past:

- Are you sure that the practice that you are about to repeat is associated with the past success? Be careful to not confuse success that has occurred *in spite of* some policy or action with success that has occurred *because of* that action.

- Is the new situation—the business, the technology, the customers, the business model, the competitive environment—so similar to past situations that what worked in the past will work in the new setting?

- *Why* do you think the past practice you intend to use again has been effective? If you cannot unpack the logic of why things have worked, it is unlikely you will be able to determine whether or not they will work this time.

Following Deeply Held Yet Unexamined Ideologies

The third flawed and widespread basis for decisions often does the most damage because it is the most difficult to change. It happens when people are overly influenced by deeply held ideologies or beliefs—causing their organization to adopt some management practice not because it is based on sound logic or hard facts but because managers "believe" it works, or it matches their (sometimes flawed) assumptions about what propels people and organizations to be successful.

The use and defense of stock options as a compensation strategy is a great example of belief trumping evidence, to the detriment of organizations. In the early years of the new millennium, there was an unprecedented wave of corporate bankruptcies and financial scandals. Senior executives lied about their company's performance, even as they sold stock and left pension funds and other investors holding worthless paper. Experts and evidence now place a large part of the blame for financial scandals on the excessive use of stock options and stock-based compensation.

Carol Bowie, director of governance research services at the Investor Responsibility Research Center, concluded, "At the very least, options tended to promote a short-term focus . . . and at worst they promoted fraudulent activity to manipulate earnings."[9] Roy Satterthwaite, a beneficiary of the options craze while a vice president at Commerce One, noted that options not only fueled long work weeks but they skewed people's decision priorities, leading to an excessive focus on cutting deals and growing revenues, the numbers the market seemed to focus on.[10] Satterthwaite confessed that options "motivated us to a selfish, short-term view" and did not create long-term value. Nor is the evidence about stock options and their effects just anecdotal. One study comparing 435 companies that had to restate their financial statements with companies that did not found that the higher the proportion of the senior executives' pay in stock options, the more likely the company was to have restated its earnings.[11] A study by Moody's, the bond rating service, concluded that incentive pay packages can "create an environment that ultimately leads to fraud."[12]

Even the logic behind the use of options as managerial incentive is flawed once you consider what behaviors are actually rewarded. Roger Martin, dean of the University of Toronto's business school and one of the cofounders of the strategy consulting firm Monitor, noted the problems of mixing the measuring and rewarding of performance in an expectations market—the stock market—with the measuring and rewarding of performance in the real market of sales, earnings, and productivity. As he noted, in the National Football League, players would never be permitted to profit from beating the point spread—the expectations market—because it would encourage all kinds of nefarious activity. Martin argued that "stock-based compensation is an incentive to increase expectations, not performance. The easiest way to do that is to hype the stock."[13]

There is, in fact, little evidence that equity incentives of any kind, including stock options, enhance organizational performance. One review of more than 220 studies concluded that equity ownership had no consistent effects on financial performance.[14] Another massive study and review of research on executive compensation published by the National Bureau of Economic Research reported that most schemes designed to align managerial and shareholder interests failed to do so; instead, executive compensation practices just operated as devices to enrich senior managers, who usually received most of the stock options.[15]

Yet executives, particularly those in high technology, remain uninterested in and unconvinced by the logic and the evidence, waging political battles to avoid expensing stock options on their income statements and maintaining that stock options are not only helpful but essential for building their companies. The evidence notwithstanding, many executives maintain that options create an ownership culture that encourages 80-hour workweeks, frugality with the company's money, and a host of personal sacrifices designed to make the options more valuable. T. J. Rodgers, chief executive of Cypress Semiconductors, is typical. He has maintained that without options, "I would no longer have employee shareholders, I would just have employees."[16]

Stock options are more crucial to success, and perhaps less likely to produce false hype, in small, privately held start-up companies. The entrepreneurship fueled by options helps new companies get off the ground. Cash is at a premium in most start-ups, and the chance to strike it rich attracts talent that otherwise would remain out of reach. Yet, despite such virtues, unwavering belief in stock options that is so pervasive among the leaders of high-technology companies is not based on sound evidence or logic.

And stock options are just one case where vehement beliefs rather than logic and evidence guide management ideas and actions. A series of studies demonstrates that people, especially those who write for and read the business press, believe in the first-mover advantage—that the first company to enter an industry or market will have an edge over competitors. Existing empirical evidence is actually mixed and unclear as to whether such an advantage exists, and many of the "success stories" purported to support the

first-mover advantage turn out to be false—Amazon.com, for example, was
not the first company to start selling books on the Web. The more that people
read the business press, the more strongly they believe in first-mover advantage. But nonbusinesspeople usually believe in it as well, apparently because
of cultural beliefs that favor being first, and giving either group—experienced or naïve—contradictory evidence does not cause them lose their faith
in the first-mover advantage. Beliefs rooted in ideology or in cultural values
are quite "sticky"—they resist disconfirming evidence and persist in affecting
judgments and choice, regardless of whether or not they are true.[17]

To avoid succumbing to using belief or ideology over evidence, ask yourself:

- Is my preference for a particular management practice solely or mostly
  because it fits with my intuitions about people and organizations?

- Am I requiring the same level of proof and the same amount of data
  regardless of whether or not the issue is one I believe in?

- And, most important, are my colleagues and I allowing our beliefs to
  cloud our willingness to gather and consider data that may be pertinent to our choices?

What Is Evidence-Based Management?

When Andy Grove, former Intel chairman and CEO, got prostate cancer, he as-
siduously tracked down all the data he could comparing treatment options and
their risks and benefits, gathering the best available evidence to guide his medical decisions.[18] That's what we would expect from a well-trained engineer and
scientist. Grove, however, like many of his Silicon Valley friends, continues to
insist on the benefits of options and doesn't cite evidence for his views—even
though with other business decisions, Grove sticks closely to the facts.

The contradictory behavior is instructive. Many companies and leaders
show little interest in subjecting their business practices and decisions to the
same scientific rigor they would use for technical or medical issues. It is a
pity, because we actually know a lot about how to make organizations and
people more effective. Every day there are opportunities for companies to
use better information to gain an advantage over the competition. Doing so
simply entails using evidence-based management.

If taken seriously, evidence-based management can change how every manager thinks and acts. First and foremost, it is a way of seeing the world and

thinking about the craft of management. Evidence-based management proceeds from the premise that using better, deeper logic and employing facts to the extent possible permits leaders to do their jobs better. Evidence-based management is based on the belief that facing the hard facts about what works and what doesn't, understanding the dangerous half-truths that constitute so much conventional wisdom about management, and rejecting the total nonsense that too often passes for sound advice will help organizations perform better.

Evidence-Based Medicine: A Model for Evidence-Based Management

Our interest in evidence-based *management* was inspired and, to some extent, guided by the evidence-based *medicine* movement. The belief that physicians' actions should be guided by solid research goes back at least 200 years. Bloodletting was used routinely until 1836 when French physician Pierre Louis conducted one of the first clinical trials in medicine. Louis compared pneumonia patients whom he treated with aggressive bloodletting and those he treated without it. Louis found that bloodletting was linked to far more deaths, which helped convince physicians to halt the practice. Unfortunately, this knowledge came too late for George Washington, the first president of the United States, who died two days after a doctor treated his sore throat by draining almost five pints of blood.[19]

Dr. David Sackett is often described as the founder of the modern evidence-based medicine movement. Sackett has worked with colleagues at McMaster University in Canada to train physicians in evaluating research and developing methods for screening out all but the best research—his team screens out 98 percent of published articles. Nonetheless, a remarkably high percentage of medical decisions still reflect the often-obsolete practices that a doctor learned in medical school, the ingrained traditions of a hospital or region, and the power (or lack of it) of physicians in a given specialty. Other reasons that many doctors don't use the best evidence remind us of why managers might not either: they trust their clinical experience more than research, there is too much evidence for any person to absorb, and those who try to keep up with the advances in knowledge often aren't trained to distinguish strong research from weak. Plus, doctors face an endless supply of vendors who muddy the waters by exaggerating the benefits and downplaying the risks of using their products. You may recall Merck's tactics for selling Vioxx, where salespeople were instructed to play "dodgeball"—to avoid initiating discussions and to deflect physician's questions about research establishing a link between the painkiller and heart disease.[20]

The evidence-based medicine movement has its critics, especially physicians who worry that clinical judgment will be replaced by search engines and who fear that bean counters from health maintenance organizations will veto expensive or experimental techniques. But while the use of evidence in medicine is still far from where it should be, the movement has made much progress and appears to help doctors provide better patient care. Teaching hospitals that embrace evidence-based medicine try to overcome the impediments to its use by providing training, technologies, and work practices to take the critical results of the top studies to the bedside. The *Evidence-Based Medicine Journal* now has a hefty 70,000 subscribers. Initial studies also suggest that physicians trained in evidence-based techniques are better informed than their peers, even 15 years after graduating from medical school.[21]

Evidence-based medicine and evidence-based management require a mind-set with two critical components: first, willingness to put aside belief and conventional wisdom—the dangerous half-truths that many embrace—and instead hear and act on the facts; second, an unrelenting commitment to gather the facts and information necessary to make more informed and intelligent decisions, and to keep pace with new evidence and use the new facts to update practices.

Substituting Facts for Conventional Wisdom

In almost every field there are accepted truths, or conventional wisdom, that guide decisions and actions. And in almost every field, including medicine, many practitioners and their advisers are unwilling or unable to observe the world systematically because they are trapped by their beliefs and ideologies. Their observations are contaminated by what they expect to see, or because they aren't logical enough in their thinking. The result is that much conventional wisdom is wrong. Organizations can gain competitive advantage if they take the trouble to substitute facts for common lore and to test conventional wisdom against the data. The following pair of organizations illustrates how this is done.

The gaming or "casino entertainment" industry is rife with conventional wisdom, some so widespread that it is known outside the industry as well. One deeply held belief is that the key to success is attracting the high rollers, people who drop lots of money at the card tables or the roulette wheels. Another belief is that casinos must offer discounted hotel rooms and meals, or even give away lodging to entice people into the casino, where they will spend money on gambling, restaurants, and entertainment. Other beliefs include:

- Building family-friendly places with rides, like mini-Disneylands, attracts customers, particularly families, to gaming venues.

- Building lavish—and expensive—facilities that look like Venice, Paris, or the New York skyline is the best way to draw customers away from other casinos.

- Increasing the "hold" (the money the casino retains from slot machines) will drive people out of your casino.

- Advertising on radio and television is among the best ways to build customer traffic and revenue.

When Gary Loveman was appointed chief operating officer of Harrah's in 1998, taking a leave from his position as an associate professor at Harvard Business School, he knew little about the details of casino operations, interior design, or architecture. Loveman had consulted for Harrah's and had studied the retail industry. He arrived with a professor's commitment to rigorous analysis and fact-based decisions. Loveman soon made these such a part of the company's culture that, as he commented when we talked to him, there were three ways to get fired at Harrah's: steal, harass women, or institute a program or policy without first running an experiment. Casinos produce lots of data—on things like revenues, occupancy, profitability, and staff turnover. Loveman was determined to use those data, and to collect more information by constantly running small experiments, to uncover facts that would help the company make more money.

Loveman and his colleagues soon discovered that much of the conventional wisdom in the industry was wrong and changed company practices to reflect what they learned. Rather than relying on extensive media advertising, Harrah's uses direct mail—promotions aimed at targeted customers to tempt them to spend more of their gaming dollars at a Harrah's casino and to persuade them to return if they haven't visited in a while. Harrah's learned that its most profitable customers were locals, often older retired or semi-retired people, who visited the casino frequently to play for entertainment. These people weren't as interested in discounted rooms as in meals and complimentary chips. In one experiment, Harrah's offered a control group the typical promotional package worth $125 (a free room, two steak dinners, and $30 worth of free chips); customers in the experimental group were only offered $60 worth of free chips. The $60 offer generated more gambling revenue than the $125 offer, at a reduced cost.[22]

Harrah's figured out that families with small children, a target audience for many competitors, generally have little discretionary time or money, so were not profitable to court. The company also discovered that spending money on employee selection and retention, including giving people realistic job previews, enhancing training, and bolstering the quality of frontline supervision, reduced turnover and produced more committed employees. Harrah's was able to reduce staff turnover by almost 50 percent as a result. Loveman and his colleagues reasoned, using academic research on service effectiveness, that more experienced, committed, and better-managed employees would improve customer service, which in turn would bolster guest satisfaction and, ultimately, their willingness to return. This attention to employees, plus Harrah's investment in data warehousing and analytics that permitted the company to track and analyze guest behavior, had a far bigger payoff than throwing money at facilities.

With $50 billion going through Harrah's slot machines each year, Loveman insisted on running experiments to see if holds could be varied, for instance, according to the machine's location, without affecting play. Conventional industry wisdom dictated that you could not vary the payouts at all, but Loveman didn't accept it. As he asked a group of Stanford students, how can price (which is what the hold really is) be completely inelastic when one woman can buy a black dress for $1,000 at a designer store and another woman can buy a similar black dress for $100 at Target, and both can be equally satisfied with their purchase? Harrah's discovered that you could increase the hold, generating additional money that fell straight to the bottom line.

Harrah's has done very well since Loveman's arrival; profits keep growing and so does the stock price. Loveman is now CEO and chairman following the retirement of Phil Satre, the CEO with the courage and foresight to offer him the COO job. What now seems obvious about the gaming business was far from obvious when he began. And note that Harrah's competitors, for the most part, have not copied the company's philosophy of fact-based decision making, nor have they stopped relying on conventional wisdom to run their businesses.

Using facts rather than conventional wisdom can even help surmount market forces, as the Oakland Athletics baseball team illustrates. A primary tenet of classical economics is that a competitive market efficiently determines the value of both labor and goods, so price is an accurate indicator of quality. That would mean that the talent a major league team has at its disposal should be closely related to its payroll, since more talented players should command higher salaries. Conventional wisdom in baseball says that raw talent is the only thing that matters. And although the size of teams' payrolls is linked to performance, the relationship is surprisingly weak. One study found no significant differences between the amount of money that strong versus weak teams spent on players' salaries between 1997 and 2001. That same study revealed a wide difference in labor costs among teams. In 2001, the average team paid approximately $630,000 in salary for each game it won, with the cost per game won ranging from a low of $225,000 for the Minnesota Twins to a high of over $1 million per win for the Boston Red Sox.[23] In August 2005, an analysis showed that the New York Yankees and Kansas City Royals had spent about $4.8 million per game won—reflecting the inflation in salaries since 2001—while the Cleveland Indians spent about $800,000 per game won, about one-sixth as much, and the Oakland Athletics spent just $1.1 million per win.[24]

The differences arise because some general managers, and Billy Beane of the Oakland Athletics is Exhibit A, have analyzed the factors that drive success—many going against conventional wisdom—and use these insights in a sort of informational arbitrage to outperform their salary budgets. This evidence has caused the A's to reject familiar truisms about the kind of talent and skills that winning teams use, for example that "hitting in the clutch," sacrifice bunts, and stolen bases are crucial to team performance. During games, the team is managed in ways that encourage players to do what they have been selected and trained to do, while ignoring rules of thumb that aren't supported by the facts. For example, in 2002 the A's had fewer sacrifice bunts and steals than any major league club, despite the general belief in baseball that these tactics win games. Another piece of conventional wisdom that the A's and other salary-efficient teams have eschewed is the idea that you need to hire big-name stars to be successful. The problem with this half-truth is that past performance does not guarantee future results, and marquee players are often older and injury prone. So, "middle-market teams have been given an opening to use the tools of baseball's information revolution—video, injury reports, obscure statistics—to find players on the rise, while the big spenders often sign stars whose best games might be behind them."[25]

Between 1999 and 2002, the Yankees paid over three times what the A's paid for the average player on their roster. The Yankee payroll was $130 million in 2002; that of the A's, just $40 million. Yet the difference in performance between the two teams was surprisingly small considering the vast difference in salaries. The Yankees made the championship playoffs in 2000, 2001, and 2002, but so did the A's. The Yankees did go all the way to the

World Series in 2000 and 2001, and won it in 2000. But during the 2002 regular season, the A's and the Yankees each won 103 games. Just think what the A's might have accomplished with the combination of evidence and unlimited budget.

Being Committed to Fact-Based Decision Making

Sometimes, unlike major league baseball where reams of data are gathered—or even Harrah's, where the operation itself and its information system regularly generate data—the facts required for decision making are not readily at hand. That is not an excuse for continuing to rely solely on casual benchmarking, past experience, ideology, and conventional wisdom to guide what your organization does now and in the foreseeable future. Companies that practice evidence-based management are committed to doing the best they can with what they have at the time, while taking steps to gather new and possibly more useful information. These companies are relentless in assessing the utility of either new or old measures, and above all, in being ideologically committed to making decisions based on the evidence—both quantitative and qualitative. Consider three examples.

Enterprise Rent-A-Car is the largest car rental company in the United States, with revenues in 2005 of about $8 billion. When Andy Taylor took over the leadership of this privately owned company from his father in the early 1980s, it was making about $76 million in revenue—so they have grown about a hundredfold in twenty years. With 6,000 locations in five countries, a focus on providing outstanding customer service is a large part of the company's success. Customers are asked, "How satisfied were you with your last rental experience?" on a five-point scale. Only the percentage of people responding they were completely satisfied—answering five on the five-point scale—are counted. The company's evidence shows that people who give that answer are three times more likely to rent from Enterprise again. As a manager, if you are even one point below average on that question, you can't get promoted. By focusing on this question, which has been validated through internal studies as most predictive of future behavior (they started with a number of others, including whether or not customers would recommend Enterprise to a friend), the company has driven the mean response up over time. Plus, they have greatly reduced the variance in responses. Unusual among companies, Enterprise pays attention to the variation in responses, as it believes "you are only as good as your weakest link."

Enterprise does not rely on their employees to pass out surveys because of the attendant temptations to cheat or bias the results (like the BMW mechanic who handed Robert Sutton a survey and pleaded for a five on a five-point scale, because otherwise he would get in trouble). Instead, Enterprise hired an objective, third-party surveying firm to randomly select and survey 25 to 30 of its customers from each branch each month—about 150,000 surveys total. Enterprise also constantly runs experiments—for instance, on its advertising and pricing—and evaluates them quantitatively to learn how to improve its operations and success.

Or take an example from a different industry. In October 1999, when Kent Thiry joined DaVita, a $2 billion operator of kidney dialysis centers, the company was in default on its bank loans, could barely meet payroll, and teetered close to bankruptcy. A big part of the turnaround effort involved educating the facility administrators, a large proportion of whom were nurses, to use data to guide their decisions. This was accomplished by spending some $5 million a year on DaVita University, along with various DaVita meetings and academies, to explain the business to people throughout the organization. The senior management team and the company's chief information officer, Harlan Cleaver, have been relentless in building and installing systems that help leaders at all levels understand how well they are doing and make sure they have the information they need to run the company. Thiry's motto is "no brag, just facts," and COO Joe Mello has a degree in industrial engineering from Georgia Tech. When Thiry stands up at a DaVita academy, a meeting of about 400 frontline employees from throughout the company, and states that the company has the best quality of treatment in the industry, that assertion is demonstrated with specific, quantitative comparisons, and he ends the presentation with the statement "no brag, just facts."

A large part of the company's culture involves a commitment to quality of patient care. Reports and meetings always begin with data on the effectiveness of their dialysis treatments and patient health and well-being. Each facility administrator also gets an eight-page report every month that shows a number of measures of the quality of care, which are summarized in a DaVita Quality Index (DQI). This emphasis on evidence extends to management issues, so administrators also get information on operations including treatments per day, employee retention, the retention of higher-profit private-pay patients, and resource-utilization measures, including labor hours per treatment and controllable expenses. The data enable the administrators to compare their facilities to others within the same region, as well as to DaVita as a whole.

The most interesting thing about these monthly reports is what *isn't yet* included. Joe Mello explains that if the company decides that a particular measure is important, but is not yet able to collect it, it is included on the report anyway with the notation "not available." Mello notes that the persistent appearance of an important measure that is missing motivates his people to figure out ways and systems for gathering it. For instance in scheduling labor, a critical efficiency issue, things get messed up by patients who are voluntary no-shows or are in the hospital, on vacation, or absent for other reasons. On the June 2005 report, there is a place for this measure to be reported with the notation "not available." Many impressive aspects of the DaVita culture have contributed to its success in driving voluntary turnover down by 50 percent, raising patient care quality to the best in the industry, and producing exceptional financial results. But the emphasis on evidence-based decision making and a culture that reinforces speaking the truth about how things are going is a crucial component.

Yahoo!, Inc. is also skilled at running experiments and learning from them, as well as building a culture that emphasizes evidence-based management. Usama Fayyad, chief data officer at Yahoo!, points out that because its home page gets literally millions of hits an hour, the company can design rigorous experiments that yield results in an hour or less—randomly assigning, say, one or two hundred thousand visitors to the experimental group and several million to the control group. Fayyad's background was in running a company that had a data-mining product and provided data-mining and analysis services to big companies. Yahoo! was one of his clients. He now leads Yahoo!'s efforts to conduct experiments and use the results to enhance company revenues and profits. Much of this can be done very quickly; sometimes, results can be seen within minutes of tweaking something on the homepage or in Yahoo! Mail. This means there is often no reason to spend time discussing which variation to explore or what design opportunities to pursue—it is often cheaper, easier, and faster to simply try all of them and learn what actually works. Yahoo! typically runs 20 or so experiments at any time, manipulating things like colors, placement of advertisements, and location of text and buttons. These little experiments can have big effects, like the one run by Nitin Sharma, which showed that simply moving the search box from the side to the center of the home page would produce enough additional "click-throughs" to bring in about $20 million more in advertising revenue a year.

This approach seems obvious in hindsight. Yes, Yahoo! gets loads of visitors, and yes, that means Yahoo! has an opportunity to vary the experience in many ways and gather information quickly on what entices visitors to stay and to spend money—things that drive revenue and profits. Yet seizing this opportunity requires a mind-set that says, "Instead of debating which screen design looks best, or which placement of content and which choice of specific content works best, we're going to try it all and see what works." Trust us, we have been associated with lots of companies with Web sites and have seen few of them run experiments and analyze the results. In fact, this observation—of a willingness to debate endlessly rather than try some things and learn from what actually works—applies to domains ranging from sales to manufacturing.

Fayyad himself confirmed this insight about the neglect of an experimenting, data-driven mind-set when he talked about his experience at the DMX group, the consulting spin-off from DigiMine, the company he had cofounded. In meeting with *Fortune* 500 CEOs, he often received a favorable reception when he described what could be done in the domain of business intelligence. But as he told us, "When it came to meeting a lot of the *Fortune* 500 leaders, we'd have these meetings and they'd really engage and all that. And what I learned is that to the CEO of the company, they had no way of understanding what data could mean to them. They thought of it as another service, part of the infrastructure, stuff that IBM does."[26]

What to Do When There Are No Sound Data Available

The examples we have described may seem daunting to companies facing enormous uncertainties and complexities, often without information systems and infrastructures that make much evidence available in a timely fashion. Even when companies have little or no data, however, there are things executives can do to rely more on evidence and logic and less on guesswork, fear, belief, or hope. For starters, qualitative data, especially field trips to test existing assumptions, can be powerful tools for gathering useful evidence quickly. We once worked with a large computer company that was having trouble selling its computers at retail stores. Senior executives kept blaming their marketing and sales people for doing a lousy job, and dismissed their complaints that it was hard to get customers to buy a lousy product, until one weekend when members of the senior team went out to stores and tried to buy their computers. Every executive encountered salespeople who tried to dissuade them from buying the firm's computers, citing the excessive price, weak feature set, clunky appearance, and poor customer service.

Even before gathering any data, however, you can assess ideas that you are using or thinking about using: unpack the assumptions that underlie the proposed policy, practice, or intervention, and confront those assumptions with your collective wisdom and experience to see if they seem sensible. If they are, proceed; if they are not, don't bother. Table 1-1 presents a set of diagnostic questions to answer before experimenting with some approach.

We can make this process concrete with an exercise that we often do with executives. Consider merit pay for teachers. As most readers know, because U.S. public schools often are viewed as doing a poor job and education is a hot political issue, schools face constant pressure to change their management approaches to improve performance, which is usually assessed by standardized reading, math, and science scores. The extensive research on schools, learning, and test scores is rarely used to design such reforms.

In most public schools teachers are unionized, but unionized or not, their pay is determined almost exclusively by seniority, years of total teaching experience, and credentials. Pay is rarely based on results or performance, which clashes with what is thought to prevail in the private sector and annoys voters and business leaders who lament that there are no carrots or sticks to properly motivate teachers. Consequently, in the late 1990s there was a great push to implement some form of merit pay, a push that continues to this day.

It turns out that merit pay for teachers is an idea that is almost 100 years old and has been subject to much research. In one study conducted in 1918, "48 percent of U.S. school districts sampled used compensation systems that they called merit pay."[27] Before telling you the results of all of that research, however, we can illustrate how you can figure out if merit pay will or won't

TABLE 1-1

Questions to ask before trying a business idea or practice

What assumptions does the idea or practice make about people and organizations? What would have to be true about people and organizations for the idea or practice to be effective?

Which of these assumptions seem reasonable and correct to you and your colleagues? Which seem wrong or suspect?

Could this idea or practice still succeed if the assumptions turned out to be wrong?

How might you and your colleagues quickly and inexpensively gather some data to test the reasonableness of the underlying assumptions?

What other ideas or management practices can you think of that would address the same problem or issue *and* be more consistent with what you believe to be true about people and organizations?

work, and the conditions under which it will or won't, simply by listing the assumptions inherent in virtually all teacher pay-for-performance plans:

- Teacher motivation is *a*, perhaps *the*, determinant of student learning and achievement. (Because merit pay is focused on teachers and administrators—not, for instance, on parents or even students—the presumption must be that teachers and other school personnel are the primary causal agents in learning.)

- Learning can be measured *reliably and accurately* by a test given once a year, or less. (Success, as defined by these plans, is almost always assessed by standardized test scores.)

- Teachers are motivated largely, or at least significantly, by financial incentives; so pay for performance will induce greater and more effective effort.

- Teaching is a solo activity—there is little interdependence with others in the school. (Many plans reward only individual teachers; there is no incentive to cooperate or share with others; and some plans reward teachers for hoarding knowledge in a competition with peers.)

Do these assumptions seem plausible? Think about it. Can you imagine a person saying, "I am motivated a lot by money, so I think teaching first graders is the career for me"? And how important do you think teacher motivation is to student achievement, compared to teacher skill (and skill is not affected by incentives), parental involvement, the community where the children live, the quality of the facilities and resources, school culture, and parental education and income? Is peer support and learning from colleagues important in affecting teacher performance? What are the consequences of measuring and rewarding student performance on a set of standardized tests?

You don't have to read the evidence from literally decades of research to spot the problems with merit pay for schoolteachers. That evidence shows that merit-pay plans seldom last longer than five years and that merit pay consistently fails to improve student performance.[28] The very logic of merit pay for teachers suggests that it won't do what it is intended to do, or do it very well. Moreover, the signal that all that matters is student test scores and the provision of rewards for improving those scores provides an incentive for some teachers to game the system. After all, if you want to enhance students' performance on a test, one way to accomplish this is by giving students the test or the answers in advance. Research on cheating by teachers and students by economists Brian Jacob and Steven Levitt led directly to the firing of several principals and teachers in Chicago. Their research also showed that cheating was quite sensitive to the size of the incentive provided for enhancing student scores.[29] Anthony Bryk, a prestigious educational researcher, tells us that the problems with the implementation of merit pay don't surprise him or his colleagues because the same problems emerged when merit-pay systems were implemented in the 1980s. Bryk jokes, "It is like policy makers suffer from amnesia."[30]

We have found that a thoughtful consideration of the assumptions that underpin interventions is often sufficient to reproduce the insights gained from piles of empirical research. That doesn't mean you shouldn't try to access such research or gather your own data, but it does mean that in the absence of available data, sometimes careful, structured analysis can get you almost to the same place.

The Focus on Dangerous Half-Truths

As we've seen in numerous industries ranging from gaming to baseball to education, failure to find and follow the best logic and evidence leads to relying on conventional wisdom that is frequently incorrect or incomplete, and as a consequence, downright hazardous to organizational health. *Hard Facts, Dangerous Half-Truths, and Total Nonsense* shows how managers can avoid these pitfalls and gain competitive advantage in three intertwined ways. First, as we've shown in this chapter, managers and their companies can profit by using evidence-based management as way of thinking. Second, chapter 2 will show how to use simple but powerful standards for judging which advice and practices advocated in the vast marketplace for business ideas are sound, which are suspect, and which are total nonsense. These standards for judging the logic and evidence behind the advice given by authors, gurus, consultants, and academics clash with the standards that currently reign in the marketplace—but are far more consistent with the fundamentals of logical reasoning and the scientific method. And third, this book will help you apply the mind-set of evidence-based management by questioning six widely accepted and applied, but flawed and incomplete, beliefs about managing people and organizations.

These ideas are dangerous half-truths because they have much currency and many advocates, yet are often applied in the wrong ways and at the wrong times. Certainly, beliefs that are total nonsense do harm and must be debunked by practicing evidence-based management. We focus far more attention on dangerous half-truths, however. Even greater damage is done by beliefs that are partly right and apply at certain times, but when treated as completely true and applied in full force to every decision and every action, undermine performance, destroy management careers, and ruin employee well-being. Half-truths are more difficult to debunk than total nonsense because arguments can always be mustered about times and places they are correct—and then generalized to the wrong settings and times. Half-truths also require subtle skills and more complete knowledge to navigate properly because—rather than resorting to appealing but simplistic sound bites and slogans—leaders need to know when these ideas are right and when they are wrong in order to guide organizational decisions and actions. We will consider dangerous half-truths about work-life integration, managing talent, structuring rewards, setting strategy, managing change, and leadership—and will show how to manage in light of the best logic and evidence about each half-truth.[31]

Chapter 3 examines perhaps the most basic half-truth—"work is fundamentally different from the rest of life and should be." Some readers might not experience the difficulty of living in separate worlds, or the ripple effects of living with someone who struggles to balance the world of work with the rest of life. Yet all the evidence we have gathered, including our own experiences, show that this is a vexing problem and is getting worse. The half-truth that these are and should be separate domains is fundamental because so much else follows from it. The organizational practices that we believe are best for managing talent and for implementing rewards, and even our views of good leadership, are quite different than what we observe—or at least aspire to—in our families, churches, synagogues, mosques, and communal organizations. That is because we do things, think about things, and tolerate things at work that are different than what we would do, or even attempt to get away with, in other domains.

Member selection (who is admitted and who gets to stay) and how people are rewarded once inside are two of the most important and time-consuming processes in any organization. Chapter 4 shows why the idea that "the best organizations have the best people" is a half-truth, with particular attention to the "war for talent" imagery that was embraced during the dot-com boom and lives on in conferences on talent management and programs to attract and retain high potentials. As you will see, many of these much ballyhooed talent management practices reflect assumptions that don't stand up to sound logic and, despite vehement claims by experienced and expensive consultants, clash with the best evidence. Chapter 5 examines one of the most deeply held half-truths in the business world, that "financial incentives drive company performance." We see so many organizations treat financial incentives as the solution to every problem—including problems caused by financial incentives in the first place. We review the assumptions that guide interventions and show that, although financial incentives propel behavior, the best evidence shows that using them to solve many problems leads organizations to stray from their goals and undermines performance.

The remaining three half-truths move up to the organizational level of analysis, focusing on the challenges of managing the enterprise. Chapter 6 questions whether and when "strategy is destiny" and makes an evidence-based case that excessive faith in strategic decision making is hazardous to an organization's health. There is enormous emphasis on strategy in the business world, reflecting the belief that if companies get their strategy right, everything else will be fine. It turns out that this is not quite true, and that having the right strategy may provide less competitive advantage than many of the most respected and highly paid senior executives, gurus, and management consultants believe. There is also strong interest in the challenges of organizational change, in part because to implement a chosen strategy, organizations often need to change their product lines, adopt new technologies, and merge with other companies. Chapter 7 examines the faulty evidence and logic behind the mantra "change or die." This is a dangerous half-truth because many changes actually increase rather than decrease the chances of failure, so delaying and avoiding some changes can help an organization, even when those changes seem to mesh with the strategy. This chapter also takes on a related half-truth, that change is difficult and takes a long time. We show that this isn't always the case and describe what organizations can do to speed change. Chapter 8 considers what leaders are expected to do versus what they actually can and should do. In a world of heroic leaders, who so often do things that don't turn out to be very heroic, no book that considers dangerous half-truths would be complete without examining the fundamental, and partly flawed, belief that "great leaders are in control of their companies" and whether and when leaders ought to be in control.

We focus on these half-truths because leaders who understand why each belief is flawed, and who think hard about the evidence for and against each, can develop more effective and sophisticated approaches to running their organizations. And we don't simply show why each of these beliefs is at least half-wrong; we explain how and what organizations can do to prosper in light of the best evidence about these beliefs.

Making the Difficult Job of Managing a Little Easier

It is one thing to argue that organizations would perform better if leaders knew and applied the best evidence. It is another thing to do it. We appreciate how hard it is for working managers and executives to do their jobs. The demands for decisions are relentless, information is incomplete, and even the very best executives make many mistakes and face constant criticism and second guessing from people both inside and outside their companies. In that respect, managers are like physicians who face one decision after another. It isn't possible for even the very best physician—or manager—to make the right decision each time. Hippocrates, the famous Greek who wrote the physician's oath, described this plight well: "life is short and the art long, the occasion instant, experiment perilous, decision difficult."[32]

These constraints mean that it would be naïve to claim that evidence-based management, or any other mind-set or practice, can improve every managerial decision and action. But evidence and data do matter. There are better and worse ways to think about solving organizational problems, and many organizations and their leaders fail to use the best data or the best logic to navigate what are admittedly tough issues.

This raises the question of *why* evidence-based management isn't used more. We believe that managers are seduced by far too many half-truths: ideas that are partly right but also partly wrong and that damage careers and companies over and over again. Yet managers routinely ignore or reject solid evidence that these truisms are flawed. The problem isn't just that executives face a lack of time, knowledge, or data. It is worse than that. As we dug into the market for business knowledge, we identified a clear, albeit largely unspoken, set of deeply flawed standards for judging managerial knowledge and writing that are ingrained and remarkably counterproductive. Before evidence-based management can become a reality, many of the current ways of gathering and assessing business knowledge need to be described, understood, and rejected—and then replaced with better standards and guidelines. The next chapter shows how and why so many of the current standards for judging business ideas and management practices are flawed and then goes on to provide some alternative ways of approaching the marketplace for ideas more consistent with the concepts of evidence-based management. These better standards can help leaders figure out which advice to follow and—even more importantly—which to ignore.

2

How to Practice Evidence-Based Management

Instead of being interested in what is *new*, we
ought to be interested in what is *true*.

Pfeffer's Law

If you think that you have a new idea, you are wrong.
Someone probably already had it. This idea isn't original
either; I stole it from someone else.

Sutton's Law

THE QUEST for information and research-based insight is an obsession in the capital markets. There is a veritable industry of analysts, investment bankers, portfolio managers, and investors who seek any informational advantage, which is one reason that academics who study finance—such as Nobel Prize winners Myron Scholes, William Sharpe, and Michael Spence—have been recruited to work on Wall Street and with money managers. The value of evidenced-based investment decisions also explains why acting on private information—insider trading—is regulated so tightly, and why U.S. companies are forbidden from releasing information to elite groups of investors and analysts. Instead, they must make conference calls and announcements simultaneously available to the general public. Quantitative research on capital markets abounds, and companies such as Vanguard, Fidelity, Barclays Global Investors, and hundreds more have used it to develop investment products and strategies.

The potential payoff for using valid evidence is even greater when it comes to *managing* organizations. Capital markets are among the most efficient in the world, so it is hard to gain an enduring information advantage. Innovations such as junk bonds, indexed mutual funds, and derivatives, for example, were copied with lightning speed. Imitation is much slower and less effective in the world of management practices, in part because such practices depend on tacit knowledge and implementation skill, on knowing not just *what* to do but *how* to do it. And management practices and logic resist copying because of the power of precedent and ideology that we described in the last chapter. Consider how long Southwest Airlines had its business model and an amazing record of unparalleled profitability in the airline industry pretty much to itself before JetBlue and a few others began to seriously copy it. Or witness the failure of competitors to catch Toyota in productivity, quality, or time to market with new product innovations, even though Toyota gives tours to competitors, and the fundamentals of its system have been described in numerous writings.[1]

We have found that most managers actually *try* to act on the best evidence. They follow the business press, buy business books, hire consultants, and attend seminars featuring business experts. Companies do sometimes benefit from these efforts. Yet there is surprisingly little rigorous use or serious appreciation of evidence-based management. Why? And what practical guidelines can we offer to help managers practice evidence-based management? This chapter addresses those questions. But first we consider key impediments to implementing evidence-based management and how to overcome them. Then we offer guidelines and ways of thinking to help organizations turn these ideas into action.

Obstacles on the Road to Implementing Evidence-Based Management

Implementing evidence-based management is a journey, not a quick-fix technique, and along the road you will encounter hindrances and obstacles. It is our job to tell you about some of the most pernicious potential roadblocks and provide suggestions about how to avoid and overcome them, or at least mitigate their effects.

Using Data Changes Power Dynamics

A former student who worked at Netscape reported that James Barksdale, a former CEO of that company, once remarked at a meeting at the company something to the effect of: "If the decision is going to be made by the facts, [then] anyone's facts, as long as they are relevant, are equal. If the decision is going to be made on the basis of people's opinions, then mine [he was the CEO at the time] counts for a lot more." What that anecdote illustrates is that facts and evidence are great levelers of hierarchy. Therefore, some of the resistance to evidence-based practice arises because, when done right, it does change power dynamics, replacing formal authority, reputation, and intuition with data. One pundit, referring to evidence-based medicine, called it replacing warriors with accountants.[2]

Adopting evidence-based management could send similar reverberations through the corporate world. Senior leaders are often seen as heroes and venerated for their wisdom and decisiveness. CEOs and their brethren could lose stature as their intuitions are replaced, at least at times, by judgments based on evidence available to virtually any educated person with access to the data. But as recent research by Rakesh Khurana suggests, less heroic CEOs and leaders who operate on the basis of the best data and insights might actually fuel better organizational performance.[3]

The implication is that leaders need to make a fundamental decision: do they want to be told they are always right, or do they want to lead organizations that actually perform well? When Gary Loveman of Harrah's told a group of Stanford students that he frequently made mistakes, that he was willing to listen to all the facts and analysis, and that his facts and insights were not privileged over anyone else's, this was not some politically correct posture. Loveman is a very competitive person, and he wants Harrah's to win—and winning requires mustering the truth and the best information for making decisions, not deferring to people based on title, rank, or anything else. That sort of egalitarian culture was supposedly the norm in the Silicon Valley—and is still evident at places such as Google, with its more academic and long-term orientation.

But egos loom large even in high-technology companies, and evidence often cuts inflated egos down to size. There is a clear implication in all of this for selecting leaders—avoid at all costs the people who think they know everything. They don't. But worse than that, they are unlikely to embrace any facts that disagree with their preconceptions. This is why one of our favorite sayings is, "When two people always agree, one of them is unnecessary."

This is a principle both of us have applied when advising leaders how to interact with others, helping companies hire new people, or looking for a coauthor to work with.

People Often Don't Want to Hear the Truth

The phrase *don't shoot the messenger* contains an enormous amount of truth, namely that delivering bad news is not something that typically wins you many friends. People like to deliver good news, regardless of its validity, in large part because most people seem to prefer hearing good news. The important insight here is that a lie takes two parties—the person who tells the lie and quite frequently the listener who signals in a number of ways that she or he wants to be lied to.

As Gary Loveman explained to us, say he goes to a casino that isn't doing well. If the leadership at the facility tells him that they understand the problem and know how to fix it, he can fly off feeling good that things will get better. If instead they tell him that they've tried a bunch of things, basically everything they can think of, and the casino is still losing out to the competition, Loveman and his team have to actually fix the problem, possibly deliver bad news to their bosses, the board of directors, and can't go off into the sunset content and secure. But the important thing is that they *can* fix it, because they've been given the facts. Building a culture of truth telling and acting on the hard facts requires an enormous amount of self-discipline in order to not only be willing to hear the truth, however unpleasant, but to actually encourage people to deliver bad news. Kent Thiry, the CEO of DaVita, told us that senior managers at his company actively seek out problems and bad news. That's because the good news doesn't require any decisions or action; it's the bad news that creates the need to do something to fix the failure. And you can't fix things or bring advice and talent to bear on problems unless you know about them.

There is really only one way around this reluctance to confront the hard facts, and that is to consciously and systematically understand the psychological propensity to want to both deliver and hear good news and to actively work against it. To practice evidence-based management you first need to know the real truth. And it's better to know the truth early, when situations can be remedied, than later when it may be too late to do much.

The Marketplace for Business Ideas Is Messy and Inefficient

There is yet another barrier to practicing evidence-based management, and that is the sorry state of the business idea marketplace. The sad fact is that any sane manager, consultant, or change agent who wades into the market for business knowledge is soon overwhelmed by vast amounts of clashing and misleading advice. The business-idea marketplace is plagued by several intertwined problems that confront anyone who seriously tries to practice evidence-based management.

First, there is simply too much information for any single person to consume. There are at least a hundred magazines and newspapers devoted to business issues.[4] There are at least 30,000 business books in print[5] and approximately 3,500 new ones are published *each year*.[6] Second, disparate and disconnected recommendations about management practice are seldom woven together in a way that makes remembering them or thinking about them easy, or maybe even possible. Consider for instance *Business: The Ultimate Resource*, an encyclopedic tome that weighs over eight pounds and runs 2,172 oversized pages. *Business* claims "it will become the 'operating system' for any organization or anyone in business." This claim is faulty because a good operating system fits together in a seamless and logical manner. Unfortunately, this collection of over 150 essays and articles reads like a nearly random collection of disconnected bits of advice. No discernable effort is made to connect any of these bits. *Business* offers advice on a dizzying array of topics from creating a fun place to work, to calculating working capital, to creating powerful brands, to designing a website. Beyond that, the reader is given almost no information about what evidence, theory, or logic (if any) supports the thousands of "do's" and "don'ts" listed, making it impossible to judge the quality of all that advice.[7]

Third, the advice managers get from the vast and ever-expanding supply of business books, articles, gurus, and consultants is remarkably inconsistent. Consider the following clashing recommendations, drawn directly from popular business books: Hire a charismatic CEO; hire a modest CEO.[8] Embrace complexity theory; strive for simplicity.[9] Become a strategy-focused organization; don't waste much time on strategic planning because it is of little value.[10] The deeper you look, the more confusing and bewildering it all becomes. Table 2-1 illustrates just a small sample of the conflicting advice managers obtain from the business book marketplace.

Even worse, because good advice is frequently hard to distinguish from bad, managers are constantly enticed to believe in and implement flawed business practices. This happens partly because consultants and others who sell ideas and techniques are *always* rewarded for getting work, only *sometimes* rewarded for doing good work, and *hardly ever* rewarded for whether their advice actually enhances performance.[11] The incentives are often even

TABLE 2-1

Whom should you believe? Clashing business book titles

In Search of Excellence: Lessons from America's Best-Run Companies	The Myth of Excellence: Why Great Companies Never Try to Be the Best at Everything
Charisma: Seven Keys to Developing the Magnetism That Leads to Success	Leading Quietly: An Unorthodox Guide to Doing the Right Thing
Leading the Revolution: How to Thrive in Turbulent Times by Making Innovation a Way of Life	Managing for the Short Term: The New Rules for Running a Business in a Day-to-Day World
Love Is the Killer App: How to Win Business and Influence Friends	Business Is Combat: A Fighter Pilot's Guide to Winning in Modern Business Warfare
The Peaceable Kingdom: Building a Company Without Factionalism, Fiefdoms, Fear and Other Staples of Modern Business	Capitalizing on Conflict: Strategies and Practices for Turning Conflict to Synergy in Organizations
Managing by Measuring: How to Improve Your Organization's Performance Through Effective Benchmarking	Managing with Passion: Making the Most of Your Job and Your Life
The Quest for Authentic Power: Getting Past Past Manipulation, Control, and Self-Limiting Beliefs	What Would Machiavelli Do? The Ends Justify the Meanness
Thinking Inside the Box: The 12 Timeless Rules for Managing a Successful Business	Out of the Box: Strategies for Achieving Profits Today and Growth Tomorrow through Web Services
Built to Last: Successful Habits of Visionary Companies	Corporate Failure by Design: Why Organizations Are Built to Fail

more perverse than that, because if a client company's problems are only partly solved, that leads to more work for the consulting firm. The senior executive of a human resources consulting firm, for example, told us that because pay for performance programs almost never work that well, you usually get asked back again and again to repair the programs your clients bought from you. Similarly, while we were writing our last book, a senior partner in a large consulting firm commented that the business process reengineering work his firm had done was one of the best things that had ever happened. First the firm made a lot of money doing the reengineering consulting; then it made even more money from the same clients because it turned out that many of the "unnecessary" people removed during reengineering efforts had in fact been doing necessary work. The result was that his own consultants were then hired to do that same work—of course, at a far higher wage rate than the people they replaced.

If you think our charge is too harsh, ask your favorite consulting firm what evidence they have that their advice or techniques actually work—and pay attention to the evidence they offer using some of the guidelines we will provide a little later on in this chapter. A few years ago, senior Bain consultant Darrell Rigby began conducting the only survey we have encountered on the use and persistence of various management techniques and practices.[12] As Rigby told us, it struck him as odd that you could get good information on products such as toothpaste and cereal but there was almost no information about interventions that companies were spending literally millions of dollars to implement. Even the Bain survey, noteworthy as it is, measures only the presence and persistence of various programs and subjective assessments of them.

Yet another flaw with the marketplace for business ideas is that it is filled with sloppy analogies that somehow win managers over. Two of our favorites are: those that have been used to justify forced curve ranking systems, made famous by General Electric; and the *business is war* or combat analogy, which has been used to argue for harsh steps toward the competition and occasionally, toward one's own people (who are viewed as "necessary evils"). Jack Welch, the former CEO of GE, made the argument for forced curve ranking, a quite controversial management practice, this way: people get graded in school, so why shouldn't they get graded at work? This leads to the (reasonable) implication that grades in school are typically assigned on a comparative basis.[13] First of all—and ironically, given the use of this analogy—the evidence strongly suggests that students learn better when they are *not* graded and certainly not when they are graded on a curve.[14] But setting that fact aside, consider a crucial difference between school and work. In school, there is relatively little interdependence in performance—if you learn chemistry and your colleagues don't, it does not affect you in any way. Learning is a matter of you, individually, mastering the particular subject matter. Cooperation or teamwork in school, at least on tests, is called *cheating*. By contrast, work organizations are typically filled with interdependent action, where your ability to accomplish something is crucially dependent on the help and cooperation of others. So, if grading on the curve causes competition and conflict, the consequences will be vastly different for interdependent as opposed to noninterdependent systems.

Following the business as war analogy can be similarly misleading. The analogy implies that you would always aim to hobble and destroy competitors and avoid cooperating with other firms in your industry. If such logic had been followed, however, the Napa Valley might never have become such a prestigious winegrowing region. When Robert Mondavi started his winery in 1966, he worked to enhance the reputation and quality of *every* Napa winery, not just his own. Such cooperation set the stage for the famous "Judgment in Paris" in 1976, where prestigious French wine critics consistently mistook the California wines for French and ranked the California wines higher. Although no Mondavi wines were tasted, California winemakers from Chateau Montelena (the top white) and Stag's Leap (the top red) were quick to thank Mondavi for helping them succeed. Indeed, both winners—Mike Grgich and Warren Winiarski—had worked for Mondavi before leaving with his blessing to start their own wineries. Mondavi's generosity paid off: he and his company profited when the prices of *all* Napa wines skyrocketed after the 1976 "Judgment."[15] Yet if you read a Harvard case by strategy researcher Michael Porter about Robert Mondavi Winery, it only considers how Mondavi competes with other California winemakers like Kendall-Jackson and Gallo. Apparently, Porter's narrow focus on the useful but incomplete "competitive strategy" analogy led him to avoid noticing (or mentioning) the cooperation that benefited Mondavi's company as he enjoyed the reputational spillover from the Napa Valley's growing prestige.[16]

Use Sound Logic and Analysis

So, what is an executive who is committed to implementing evidence-based management to do? We have two broad categories of recommendations. First, familiarize yourself with analytical and logical issues so that you can be a more sophisticated and informed consumer of business ideas and research. And second, develop a different set of criteria for evaluating business writing and research. We consider each of these suggestions in turn.

Using sound logic and analysis does *not* mean you have to take a course in statistics or the scientific method. It just means you need to pay close attention to problems in exposition, logic, and inference that are reasonably obvious once identified and that bedevil much of what passes for business research. For instance, some popular business books, such as *The War for Talent*, collect information on the independent variables, in this case practices for managing talent, *after* the time period covered by the data on the performance that talent management presumably causes.[17] This is not the only book that has this problem of causal order. But it is important to recognize that in most discussions of causality, the cause needs to occur *before* the effect.

Or consider a big problem that plagues managers who try to learn from experience as well as many business writers who draw lessons from currently successful companies. What both the managers and the writers don't seem to realize is that crucial evidence is lost if they ignore the practices and strategies used by failed companies. As a consequence, the steps taken by failed companies are consistently undersampled.[18] It is hard to overstate the breadth of this problem, and how much it distorts the conclusions that people reach. For example, in 1922 the U.S. tire industry had 274 firms, but by 1936 the number of companies was down by 80 percent, to 49.[19] Today only two U.S.-owned tire companies are still standing. One study estimated that there were 2,197 automobile producers in the United States between 1885 and 1981; less than 1 percent still exist.[20] Yet few study the histories and practices used by all those "losers" and how they differ from surviving companies.

Studying and imitating only surviving companies, especially the most successful ones, can lead to flawed and dangerous conclusions about what are the best and safest practices. For instance, companies that use risky, unusual practices perform either much better or much worse than average, especially compared to those that do what most other companies do. But "if only the best, not the worst, performers are observed, performance will seem to be associated with strategies that are far more likely to kill a company than to result in superior performance."[21] Similarly, concentrating resource allocations on a narrow range of products, strategies, and markets will expose companies to greater risk than a strategy of diversification, because they will have put all of their eggs in fewer baskets. But if we just observe the survivors and top performers—those that have managed to concentrate their efforts and resources in precisely the right way—it will appear as if concentrated, focused strategies win out most of the time, even though the exact opposite is usually true. The only way to avoid learning such flawed lessons is to devote more attention to studying companies that fail and why they fail, not just those that succeed.

It is also useful to get in the habit of running small experiments and thinking about the inferences you are drawing from your observations and from the data your organization is constantly generating. In medical research, two main research methodologies are used to generate knowledge. The gold standard is the double-blind, placebo-controlled study, in which patients in one group are randomly assigned to get a treatment, patients in another group are randomly assigned to get a placebo, and neither doctors nor patients know who is in which group, so prior expectations don't affect the results. It is often impossible, however, to use such studies. For example, it would be unethical to randomly assign nonsmoking teenagers to conditions where they did and did not start smoking. The alternative, less rigorous approach is to use surveys or observations to measure behaviors like exercise, vitamin consumption, or smoking; assess health outcomes with medical records; and use statistical techniques to relate the behavior and outcomes, controlling for as many alternative explanations as possible.

Similarly, in management it often isn't feasible to use experiments, especially double-blind designs. People will often know, for instance, if they are getting certain incentives or not. Yet field experiments are valuable, as we showed with examples from Harrah's and Yahoo! in chapter 1, and field experiments are to be found in some of the most compelling and useful academic research. As one example, a randomized field experiment with Israeli soldiers confirmed the *Pygmalion Effect*, that high or low performance expectations can become self-fulfilling. When drill instructors were tricked into believing that certain randomly selected soldiers would achieve superior performance, those soldiers subsequently performed far better on tasks like firing weapons and reading maps than soldiers in control conditions who did not have the higher performance expectations. This experiment and numerous other studies show that leaders often get the performance they expect from subordinates.[22] In other field experiments, incentives have been used in some parts of an organization and not others, as have changes to make jobs more challenging and to compare open and closed offices.[23]

A big barrier to using experiments to build management knowledge is that companies tend to adopt practices in an all or nothing way—either the CEO is behind it so everyone does it, or at least claims to do it, or it isn't tried at all. This tendency to do things everywhere or nowhere severely limits a company's ability to learn by trying things in some places but not in others, much as firms routinely do when test-marketing a product or evaluating an advertising campaign. In particular, multisite organizations like restaurants, hotels, and manufacturers with multiple plants can learn by experimenting in selected sites and comparing the results to control locations.

The wisdom of starting with a small experiment is illustrated by research we did years ago with the Southland Corporation, which operates and franchises 7-Eleven stores. Southland executives were enamored with Peters and Waterman's *In Search of Excellence*, which exhorted managers to "be close to the customer" and develop a "service obsession." This infatuation was translated into a companywide effort to improve customer service, which aimed to get every clerk in every store in North America to offer a greeting, smile, eye contact, and a *thanks* to every customer. Millions of dollars of management bonuses were linked to these courtesy measures and, in 1987, Southland held the "Thanks a Million" contest where 17 store managers who won regional courtesy contests qualified to enter a drawing for $1 million. The contest culminated in a slick media event hosted by game show host Monty Hall of *Let's Make a Deal* fame. Debra Wilson, a store manager from Plano, Texas, won the million bucks.

This was good fun, but was it worth the money? We worked with Larry Ford, then Southland's director of field research, to do research (including a randomized experiment with 15 stores) to discover if courteous clerks fueled sales. Unfortunately, executives hadn't bothered to try any pilot studies or experiments before spending all that money on courtesy programs, although Ford urged them to do so. We ultimately found little if any evidence that courtesy increased store sales. Yes, it was possible to increase courtesy. We used training and coaching during our 10-week field experiment to increase the percentage of customers who received greetings from 33 percent to 58 percent and smiles from 32 percent to 49 percent. But the main finding, including results from large-scale studies by Ford's group, was that clerks in stores with more sales were actually *less* courteous. Apparently, the crowding and long lines in busy stores made clerks and customers grouchy. This research ultimately helped convince executives to scale back courtesy programs and realize that, for most 7-Eleven customers, good service meant getting out of the store fast, not fake smiles and insincere social amenities. Southland could have saved millions by doing some pilot studies first.

In management research, studies that use surveys or data from company records to correlate practices with various performance outcomes are far more common than experiments. Such *nonexperimental* research is useful, but care is required to control statistically for alternative explanations, which arise in even the best studies. Managers who consume such knowledge need to understand the limitations and think critically about the results. Anyone who ever had a statistics class knows that correlation is not causation, but it is surprising how often purveyors of business knowledge are fooled or try to fool customers. We admire Bain's consulting and have made favorable comments here about their research. We do wonder, however, why they put a table on their home page that brags: "Our Clients Outperform the Market 3 to 1."[24] The smart people at Bain know this correlation doesn't prove or even imply that their advice transformed clients into top performers. For starters, top performers may simply have more money for hiring consultants. Indeed, any claim that Bain deserves credit for such performance is conspicuously absent. Perhaps they are hoping that visitors will momentarily forget what they learned in their statistics classes.

Although quantitative data are important, it is crucial to also learn from clinical practice and observation, and to understand that management, like medicine, is both an art and a science. We reject the notion that only quantitative data are acceptable for evidence-based management. As Einstein put it, "Not everything that can be counted counts, and not everything that counts can be counted." By focusing only on what can be quantified, we can lose sight of what matters most. John Steinbeck explained the limits of quantification in *The Log from the Sea of Cortez*, his book about a scientific expedition:

> *The Mexican Sierra has "XVII-15-IX" spines on the dorsal fin. These can be easily counted. But if the sierra strikes hard so that our hands are burned, if the fish sounds and nearly escapes and finally comes over the rail, his colors pulsing and his tail beating the air, a whole new relational reality comes into being—an entity which is more than the sum of the fish plus the fisherman. The only way to count the spines of the sierra unaffected by this second relational reality is to sit in a laboratory, open an evil smelling jar, remove a stiff colorless fish from the formalin solution, count the spines, and write the truth "D.XVII-15-IX." There you have recorded a reality that cannot be assailed—probably the least important reality concerning either the fish or yourself.*
>
> *It is good to know what you are doing. The man with the pickled fish has set down one truth and has recorded in his experience many lies. The fish is not that color, that texture, that dead, nor does he smell that way.*[25]

When used correctly, stories and cases are powerful tools for building management knowledge. Many quantitative studies are published on developing new products, but few compare to Tracy Kidder's Pulitzer Prize–winning *Soul of a New Machine* for capturing how engineers develop products and how managers can contribute to—or undermine—their success. Gordon McKenzie's *Orbiting the Giant Hairball* is the most charming and useful book on corporate creativity we know. *Hairball*, for example, argues that teasing is "a disguised form of shaming" and illustrates how it stifles creativity and damages people, a hypothesis confirmed by recent experiments.[26] We are enthusiastic about such writings because they are engaging, bolster other (often quantitative) research, and suggest new practices that companies can try.

Some Guidelines for Evaluating Management Ideas and Knowledge

Our first set of suggestions dealt with learning enough about the logic of analysis to put claims and data to the test. Our second set of suggestions addresses a different but related problem: the existing standards for assessing management knowledge are deeply flawed and often completely dysfunctional.

To partially remedy this problem, we propose six standards for generating, evaluating, selling, and applying business knowledge. Table 2-2 contrasts these new (or more precisely old, but less common) standards with current standards. Unfortunately, although deeply flawed, the reigning standards are reinforced by the actions of virtually every major player in the marketplace for business knowledge. Those who generate such knowledge—gurus, consultants, and academics—need to think harder about whether anyone can comprehend or use their wares. They need to stop pretending that proven—or debunked—old ideas are shiny new cures. And they need to ground their recommendations in better evidence. The business press, purveyor of so many

TABLE 2-2

Current standards versus evidence-based management

Current practice	Evidence-based management
Treat old ideas as if they are brand-new.	Treat old ideas like old ideas.
Glorify, celebrate, and apply breakthrough ideas and studies.	Be suspicious of breakthrough ideas and studies—they almost never happen.
Celebrate brilliant individuals like management gurus, thought leaders, and star performers.	Celebrate communities of smart people and collective brilliance, not lone geniuses or gurus.
Emphasize only the virtues of the research methods and the management practices you use. Don't mention drawbacks or uncertainties.	Emphasize the virtues *and* drawbacks (and uncertainties) of your research and proposed practices.
Use success and failure stories about companies, teams, and people to uncover best and worst practices.	Use success and failure stories to illustrate practices supported by other evidence, not necessarily as valid evidence.
Use popular ideologies and theories to generate and justify management practices. Ignore or reject all clashing evidence (no matter how strong).	Take a neutral approach to ideologies and theories. Base management practices on the best evidence, not what is in vogue.

practices, needs to reduce its fixation on individual heroes and *what's new*, and talk more about *what's true*. Finally, as those who buy and use such knowledge, and impose it on others, managers will have the greatest say over if and how evidence-based approaches spread. Yes, dear managers, you are already beleaguered with other burdens. But you and your companies can reap great benefits—and ultimately save much time and money—by becoming more sophisticated at judging ideas in the plethora of books, seminars, and advice that rains down on you.

We didn't write *Hard Facts, Dangerous Half-Truths, and Total Nonsense* just to identify incomplete and flawed beliefs that shape organizational action. An even more important aim is to help teach managers, and those who write for and advise them, how to make better judgments about the virtues and flaws of the evidence they generate and encounter. Toward this end, we use the principles in table 2-2 to critique influential studies and writings throughout the rest of this book. We do name the works and authors, and do make pointed judgments about imperfections and excessive claims. But our aim isn't to pick on any particular person or idea; rather it is to help readers become more savvy consumers and producers of management knowledge.

1. Treat Old Ideas As If They Are Old Ideas

The management ideas marketed by consultants, publishers, and the business press are often treated like laundry detergent—the only thing they are interested in is what's new and presumably improved. This pursuit of novelty for its own sake may be charming and profitable when applied to fashion, dress, and popular culture or food, but is costly and destructive when used to guide management practice. Consider exhibit A, the quality movement at the Ford Motor Company: "Twenty years ago, when an invasion of Japanese imports threatened the American automobile industry, the Ford Motor Company led a quality revival based on the management philosophy of W. Edwards Deming, who was controversial then and is out of fashion now. The results of the movement . . . were stunning at Ford. After racking up $3 billion in losses between 1979 and 1982 . . . by 1986 Ford had become the most profitable American auto company."[27]

Yet, once implemented total quality management was yesterday's news, an old idea. And making cars was so yesterday. Under Jacques Nasser, the CEO at the time who was subsequently fired, Ford pursued innovation and "revolution." It was lauded in *Fast Company*—because the business press is enamored with novelty—for its emphasis on doing new things: "[A manager's] team recommended that Ford enter the parts-recycling business, start a for-profit driver education program, and develop a chain of branded maintenance and repair shops. The company has done all three."[28]

There is nothing wrong with innovation, encouraging creativity, or for that matter, introducing new products and services, except that in this case Ford lost its focus on quality. Costs and defects increased, competitors developed superior designs, and sales slipped. By 2001 Ford was in the same fix it had been in two decades earlier. The solution: re-embrace an old idea, quality, but this time under the Six Sigma banner so that it would presumably look "new." A *New York Times* business reporter concluded, "Had Ford stuck with Total Quality Management, it might have avoided many of the problems that have plagued it recently."[29] But how could it? Sticking with old ideas is boring. Managers, and for that matter, academics and the business press, pursue novelty often for its own sake.[30]

Perhaps sticking with proven practices is boring, but we need to acknowledge—even glorify—old ideas if we want to debunk bad management practices and improve good ones. After all, isn't bland old excellence a better fate than an exciting new failure? It sounds ironic, but even creativity is mostly sparked by old ideas. Both major creative leaps and incremental improvements come from fiddling with ideas from other places and blending them in new ways. Better ideas result when people act like "nothing is invented here" and seek new uses for others' ideas.[31] This holds for even the most creative companies like Apple, 3M, IDEO, Genentech, Google, Capital One, and Cirque du Soleil. Unfortunately, too many companies are plagued by the *not invented here syndrome*, where people insist on using homegrown ideas, especially ideas that can be ballyhooed as new and different. There are, after all, substantial rewards for pretending that the same old ideas are brand-new. Managers can impress bosses with cutting edge ideas. Consultants can sell clients unique services. Gurus can land lucrative book contracts and speaking fees by peddling the next big thing. And journalists can sell newspapers and magazines by giving readers the latest scoop.

These incentives fuel a bizarre collective amnesia. The same things are "discovered," or at least reported, over and over, which wastes much effort and time. The *Harvard Business Review* has published at least three articles on incentive pay and organizational performance in the past decade. Each makes a similar point: compensating people for only individual performance creates more problems than it solves, so rewards should emphasize organizational, not just individual, performance. Alfie Kohn wrote about this idea in 1993, Jeffrey Pfeffer did it 1998, and Egon Zehnder did it yet again in 2001. Not one of these articles refers to the prior article, because *HBR* policy precludes footnotes and—based on our experience in publishing seven *HBR* articles—discourages references to prior work.[32]

How do we break free from this cycle where again and again business writers, experts, and managers act like old ideas are brand-new? The short answer is to treat old ideas as old ideas. The longer answer is more complex, but some simple steps would help. People who spread management knowledge can tell us where they got their ideas. They can also review past work to avoid reinventing the past. Although footnotes are not right for all publications, as they slow and distract readers, there are alternatives. We are consistently impressed with how the *Economist* and *New Yorker* weave references to past work into the text, especially in Malcolm Gladwell's deft *New Yorker* contributions.[33]

No matter how it is done, people who spread ideas ought to acknowledge key sources, as it discourages clothing old ideas as new and encourages writers and managers to build on and blend existing ideas. Doing so isn't just intellectually honest and polite. It leads to better ideas. The 17th-century physicist Sir Isaac Newton is often credited as saying, "If I have seen farther, it is by standing on the shoulders of giants." Of course Newton didn't invent this saying. The originator is impossible to find, but versions of it go back at least 1,000 years before Newton's time. Our favorite is, "A dwarf standing on the shoulder of a giant may see farther than the giant himself."[34]

2. Be Suspicious of "Breakthrough" Ideas and Studies

Related to the desire for *new* is the desire for *big*—the big idea, the big study, the big innovation. Unfortunately, they rarely if ever happen. Even in the physical sciences, close examination of so-called breakthroughs nearly always reveals painstaking, incremental work that finally is recognized as a big insight. For instance, the development of the integrated circuit was the work of numerous people in a variety of companies interacting over a number of years, even though one or a few people often got most of the public credit.[35] Yet many managers still yearn for breakthroughs and hordes of purveyors pretend to bring them the magic they crave.

The result of this search for the big thing is what we saw at a large bank: the idea of the moment. The former CEO of this bank fancied himself (and was) quite an intellectual. He was always learning about new techniques, hoping each would be *the* concept to propel the bank to the next performance level. The bank shifted from one program to another and managers learned to brace themselves for the next flavor of the month. When a new initiative was announced, veterans did nothing, recognizing that by the time their inaction was noticed, the CEO would be on to the next big thing. We repeatedly talked to and heard of managers who perfected the art of pretending to use the latest flavor, while making no actual changes in how they or their people worked. The upshot was that the company churned through talking about one idea after another, but had little else to show for it.

The temptation to search for the silver bullet, that breakthrough study or concept, occurs far more often in the world of management than in academic research. We constantly travel between academia and the real world of practicing managers and their advisers. Breakthroughs hardly ever seem to happen in academic research, even though thousands of studies are published in peer-reviewed journals each year. Academics hesitate to place too much weight on any one study, preferring to find patterns across many studies and to base conclusions on the weight of the evidence. In contrast, managers face an onslaught of writers, gurus, and consultants who claim or imply one breakthrough after another. Even when people who do a study or coin a phrase don't call it a breakthrough, the press often reinterprets modest progress (or none at all) as "shocking" and "revolutionary" ideas. In 2001 through 2005, the February issue of *Harvard Business Review* has published lists of "Breakthrough Ideas for Today's Business Agenda," described as "bold and unsettling new ideas."[36] We've had three of our ideas selected for the list. One of our *HBR* articles that was selected for the list in 2002, Sutton's "The Weird Rules of Creativity," really isn't a breakthrough. The publicity was nice, but embarrassing because these rules were actually derived from past, sometimes quite old, research. And in 2005 Pfeffer's "breakthrough idea" was evidence-based management, which might be unsettling to some people, but we are the first to admit it isn't new. As Stanford's James March—among the most renowned organizational theorists—put it, "Most claims of originality are testimony to ignorance and most claims of magic are testimony to hubris."[37]

3. Celebrate and Develop Collective Brilliance, Not Lone Geniuses or Gurus

The business world is among the few places where the term *guru* apparently has primarily positive connotations. In religion and politics, gurus are portrayed as extraordinary but often dangerous leaders, who attract fanatical disciples who bend to their wishes, even when doing so harms themselves and others. Yet despite the occasional cynical article or book, gurus are still portrayed in largely positive terms by the press, where they are routinely listed, rank ordered, and gossiped about. *What's the Big Idea?* by Thomas Davenport and Laurence Prusak uses press mentions, Google Internet searches, and citations in academic journals to rank the top 100 business gurus (Michael Porter was number one and Tom Peters was number two). In 2001 and 2002, *Business 2.0* not only listed top gurus like Tom Peters and Larry Bossidy, they inserted cardboard "Business Guru Trading Cards" for each, with a color picture and information including star power (from one to four stars), fees, the guru's "big idea," and a "little known fact."

Certainly, people who have good ideas and communicate them well can help organizations. But a focus on gurus masks how business knowledge is and ought to be developed and used. Knowledge isn't generated by lone geniuses who magically produce brilliant new ideas in their gigantic brains. This is a dangerous fiction. Writers and consultants need to be more careful about describing the teams and communities of researchers who develop ideas. Even more important, implementing practices, accomplishing organizational change, and executing strategy require the coordinated actions of many people. This is partly because commitment to an idea or program is amplified when people feel ownership for it. Learning also happens faster when people take an active role in developing a practice or program. Sitting and listening to even the most insightful speaker does none of this—there is no ownership of the ideas and no involvement in building a solution, so little information is retained and less is learned about how to actually use the ideas.

Moreover, gurus too often oversimplify management challenges. The common implication that business practices can be installed like a new machine is especially dangerous. As Wharton's Russell Ackoff put it, "Gurus provide ready made solutions, but educators provide ways that one can find solutions for oneself . . . The output of a guru is a closed system of thought, closed to external influences and not subject to change; the output of an educator is an open system of thought, open to external influences and subject to change."[38] Leading a revolution, reengineering, adopting Six Sigma, or becoming strategy focused can help some companies, but no approach is right for everyone. Those of us who hawk business knowledge need to come clean. We need to deny that we have magic answers. We need to confess that we are just suggesting ideas that might make managers' hard jobs a bit easier. We also need to follow those few gurus who rebuke dangerous oversimplification. Consider C. K. Prahalad, who (with Gary Hamel) wrote the blockbuster *Competing for the Future* and ranks high on many guru lists. A few years back, he ended an engaging 45-minute speech to a huge audience by warning, "Don't forget, if someone tells you they have the answer, they probably don't understand the question."[39]

4. Emphasize Virtues *and* Drawbacks

No drug is without side effects. Most surgical procedures have risks and even when performed perfectly may have downsides. Doctors are getting better at explaining risks to patients and, in the best circumstances, enabling them to join in a decision process where risks and potential problems are considered. This rarely happens in management, where too many solutions are presented as costless and universally applicable, with little acknowledgment of potential pitfalls. Yet all management practices and programs have strong and weak points, and even the best have costs. This doesn't mean companies shouldn't implement things like Six Sigma or balanced scorecards, just that they should recognize the hazards. That way, managers won't become disenchanted when known setbacks occur, or worse yet, abandon a valuable program or practice.

Last year, one of us (Sutton) gave a speech at a company that is renowned for innovation. The company had spent the prior year implementing a Six Sigma program to improve efficiency and customer satisfaction. Sutton mentioned during his speech that process improvement programs like Six Sigma and TQM had been shown to drive out errors and improve efficiency, but also to stifle innovation.[40] A self-described "internal quality guru" and "quality evangelist" came up after the talk and argued that Six Sigma could be used to improve any process, including creativity. This guru kept insisting this was so, even though (after working in the field for 10 years) he couldn't name a single instance where Six Sigma or Total Quality Management programs had improved innovation. Sutton finally asked, "Can you think of *any* drawbacks to using Six Sigma or TQM?" There was a long silence until the guru said, "Other than irrational fear and resistance, I can't think of any."

This evangelist illustrates how business knowledge is routinely sold. Unlike medicine, where physicians are ethically obligated to reveal risks and drawbacks, advocates of business practices rarely describe risks, problems that arise even in successful cases, or occasions when their wares are likely to be ineffective. A few exceptions illustrate a better approach. Consider J. Richard Hackman's article "On the Coming Demise of Job Enrichment," published at the height of a management fad in the 1970s, a fad based largely on Hackman's research. Hackman was troubled because he could only find published success stories about companies that had redesigned work to be more motivating and meaningful. Yet in his experience most redesign efforts were failing. Hackman warned managers that enrichment programs were time-consuming and expensive to implement; they couldn't simply be installed like a new machine. He predicted that job enrichment would be just another failed fad (a prediction that partly came true) if companies didn't start diagnosing work systems before trying to enrich jobs, kept pretending that jobs had changed when they hadn't, and did not change the organization (especially incentives and supervision) to support enriched work.[41]

The lesson is that, although some "experts" will make less money in the short term, business knowledge will advance and cynicism about "flavors of the month" will wane if those who peddle business practices routinely admit flaws and uncertainties. This means, among other things, admitting that their wares are the best they can build right now and, like all good ideas, will require constant modification as more is learned along the way.

5. Use Success (and Failure) Stories to Illustrate Sound Practices, Not as a Valid Research Method

One of the most common research methods entails sorting teams or organizations into "high" and "low" performers, and then digging into their pasts with interviews, questionnaires, and published press reports that rely on fuzzy and flawed human memory. These recollections are used to explain the differences between winners and losers, and to identify which practices to use (what winners did) and which to avoid (what losers did). A related, and even more suspect, method is to gather recollections from and about only winners, and to assume that similarities explain success—even though (unstudied) losers may have acted the same way. *In Search of Excellence* used precisely this approach— which may explain why a study by Michael Hitt and Duane Ireland found no significant performance differences between Peters and Waterman's "excellent" companies and a representative sample of *Fortune* 1000 companies.[42]

Academic researchers also make extensive use of retrospective success and failure stories, although they usually offer ritualistic apologies. But such apologies don't prevent what is learned from being based on suspect evidence. Many influential studies, for example, have asked managers to identify one successful and one unsuccessful past product development effort, and then to recall differences between the two. These studies find dramatic differences between winners and losers. Successful efforts are remembered as having more top management support, more competent engineers, superior planning and execution, more frequent interaction between key players, and on the whole using a process that was superior to failed efforts in nearly every way.[43]

There is an enormous problem with inferences based on recollection. In 1911, Ambrose Bierce's *The Devil's Dictionary* defined *recollect* as "to recall with additions something not previously known,"[44] foreshadowing much research on human memory.[45] It turns out that eyewitness accounts are notoriously unreliable. We humans have terrible memories, regardless of how confident we are in our recollections. In particular, we remember very different things when we are anointed winners versus losers, and what we recall has little to do with what happened. Barry Staw, for example, assigned 20 teams of MBAs to work on a financial puzzle game. These three-person teams used a company's annual report to predict its sales and stock price a year later. Staw then gave them false performance feedback. Ten teams were told their predictions were almost perfect; the other 10 were told their estimates were far off target. In reality, there were no significant differences between how well teams in the two groups predicted performance. Yet these false beliefs led to profound differences in what members recalled. The 30 winners reported that their teams were more motivated, more cohesive, more open to others' ideas, had more constructive conflict, and had greater ability compared to what the 30 losers remembered about their teams. This research and similar studies showing that false information causes winning team members to recall having more effective leaders demonstrate that winners and losers tell predictable stories, no matter what actually happened. So using reports from winners or losers to find ways to turn your company or team into a winner is questionable at best.[46]

We aren't advocating a ban on success and failure stories. Vivid cases grab our attention, show us what to do, and inspire us to do it. The challenge is to tell more true stories. This means that storytellers (and listeners too) must remind themselves that once they know who wins and who loses, they will believe predictable things that are not necessarily true. It also means that we can learn more by studying what people do in real time rather than by studying what they remember doing. And when we do tell and hear tales of triumph and despair, if we want to learn despite our biases, we might look for *failures embedded in success stories* and *successes embedded in failure stories*. This could mean, for example, that we should look back at what Enron and WorldCom did *right* rather than what they did *wrong!*

6. Take a Neutral, Dispassionate Approach to Ideologies and Theories

Ideology is among the more widespread, potent, and vexing impediments to using evidence-based management. People routinely ignore evidence about management practices that clash with their political convictions or idiosyncratic personal histories. Simon and Garfunkel were right when they sang, "A man hears what he wants to hear and disregards the rest." Academics and other thought leaders may worship and believe in their own theories so fervently that it renders them incapable of learning from new evidence. This happens partly because people "see what they believe." It also happens because theories can become self-fulfilling: when we act as our pet theories suggest we should, we can produce the very behavior we expect in ourselves and those around us. So, if we expect people to be untrustworthy, we will closely monitor their behavior, which makes it impossible to develop trust. After all, how can I know if you can be trusted unless I provide you an opportunity to show you can be trusted? And experimental evidence shows that when people are placed in situations where authority figures expected them to cheat, more of them do in fact cheat.[47]

Many economists, including Gary Becker and Oliver Williamson, believe that human beings act primarily to enhance their individual self-interest. The assumption that people are wired to be selfish isn't just used to explain the power of financial incentives; economists use it to explain why people fall in love, get married (including why they may or may not prefer polygamy), and have children. Yet these economists ignore evidence that being selfish—or not—is learned, not a hardwired human trait.[48] Indeed, economists appear to teach students to be selfish. Research by Cornell's Robert Frank and his colleagues showed that the percentage of students choosing unethical options on an honesty test increased dramatically among students taking microeconomics courses, but not among students in astronomy classes. Other researchers asked students to recommend a plumber for a film club from offers that varied by how much money the plumber charged and how much money the student would get if the recommended plumber were hired. They found that "economists are more corruptible than others." Such studies suggest that self-interest is learned and varies widely across people, groups, and countries. Yet most economic theories still rest on the assumption that everyone is selfish. The lesson is that even people trained to do rigorous research are still prone to reject and ignore evidence that contradicts their most precious beliefs.[49]

Another example of how ideology trumps evidence comes from education. At the moment, U.S. schools are applying and enforcing the most stringent performance standards ever, especially holding students, teachers, and administrators accountable for performance. It is hard to argue against high standards. But when an ideal is applied without regard to evidence about which tough practices work and which don't, performance suffers. For instance, there is great pressure to end *social promotion*, advancing a child to the next grade even if his or her work isn't up to par—in other words, to start flunking more kids who don't meet certain standards. Social promotion was ended in Chicago in 1996 at Mayor Daley's urging, in New York in 1999 at Mayor Giuliani's insistence, and in numerous other cities including Baltimore and Philadelphia. Former president Bill Clinton's 1999 State of the Union address called for an end to social promotion, because "when we promote a child from grade to grade who hasn't mastered the work, we do the child no favors." And President Bush is just as vehement as Clinton was about eliminating social promotion.

On the surface, it is hard to argue with Clinton's conclusion. But it is a half-truth. Clinton's statement is partly right because when students fail to meet minimum standards during the school year, going to summer school before starting the next grade may enhance test scores. And advancing kids who can't perform at the next grade level certainly creates frustration and may lower motivation of kids who put forth the effort to meet standards. But ending social promotion harms students and schools, and the strongest negative effects are found in the best, most rigorous studies. At least 55 studies show that when flunked students are compared to socially promoted students, flunked students perform worse and drop out of school at higher rates. One of the most careful studies found that, after controlling for numerous alternative explanations including race, gender, family income, and school characteristics, students held back one grade were 70 percent more likely to drop out of high school. Holding students back also leaves schools crowded with older students, and costs skyrocket as more teachers and other resources are needed because the average student spends more years in school.[50] Clinton, Bush, Giuliani, and many other politicians ignored the overwhelming evidence that ending social promotion would fail, even though renowned educational researcher Robert Hauser warned in 1999: "We should know that a new policy works before trying it out on a large scale. In its plan to end social promotion the administration appears to have [included] . . . an enforcement provision—flunking kids by the carload lot—about which the great mass of evidence is strongly negative. And this policy will hurt poor and minority children most of all."[51]

Hauser's predictions came true. New York eliminated social promotion in 1999, but reinstated it in 2002 because the numbers of holdovers mounted to 43,000 and reached a disastrous 100,000 by 2004. This drove up costs, forcing the elimination of numerous programs, including those for helping underachievers. There was also no evidence that flunking students helped them learn more. This was not a new lesson: the exact same problems happened when New York City ended social promotion 20 years earlier.[52] Yet as of this writing, Mayor Bloomberg is once again moving to eliminate social promotion in New York.

Why can't smart people like Mayor Bloomberg and Mayor Daley learn from such clear evidence? Because learning is difficult when leaders or anyone else is driven by ideology rather than evidence.

Wisdom: The Most Important Thing

The guidelines developed here can help managers and their advisers to do a better job evaluating and applying business knowledge. But something else, something broader, is more important than any single guideline for reaping the benefits of evidence-based management: the *attitude* people have toward business knowledge. The idea that wisdom is reflected in the attitude people have toward what they know, not in how *much* or how *little* they know, goes back at least to Plato's writings. Plato described Socrates' visit to "a man with a high reputation for wisdom." Socrates "gave a thorough examination of this person" and concluded:

> *[I] formed the impression that although in many people's opinion, and especially his own, he appeared to be wise, in fact, he was not ... I reflected as I walked away, well I certainly am wiser than this man. It is only too likely that neither of us has any knowledge to boast of, but he thinks that he knows something which he does not know, whereas I am quite conscious of my ignorance. At any rate it seems that I am wiser than him to this small extent, that I do not think that I know what I do not know.*

The power of Plato's ancient insight persists because wisdom (or the lack of it) shapes how people think, feel, and act in so many ways. Psychologists including John Meacham and Robert Sternberg have studied the nuances of wisdom, especially how being wise is different from being smart. One of their most important insights is that, as Plato's quote suggests, wisdom means "knowing what you know and knowing what you don't know," especially striking a balance between arrogance (assuming you know more than you do) and insecurity (believing that you know too little to act). This attitude enables people to act on their present knowledge while doubting what they know. It means they can do things now, as well as keep learning along the way.[53]

The attitude of wisdom pervades the standards we've proposed for consumers and purveyors of business knowledge in this chapter. To illustrate, we urged people to compensate for their limited knowledge by building on old ideas and to join communities of smart people rather than relying only on their own insights. Our perspective implies that the unacknowledged ignorance or arrogance behind most apparent breakthroughs stems from an absence of wisdom. And we emphasized that embracing an ideology or theory can be comforting, but can make it difficult for devotees to acknowledge flaws in their ideas—let alone to seek, accept, and learn from criticism. In essence, practicing evidence-based management means adopting beliefs and designing settings that enable people to keep acting with knowledge while doubting what they know, and to openly acknowledge the imperfections in even their best ideas along the way.

To return to evidence-based medicine, pioneer David Sackett's reaction to the accolades he has received demonstrates the attitude of wisdom. He worries openly that people will treat his ideas as gospel rather than an initial effort that must be constantly revised and challenged. Sackett even despises when people call him an expert on evidence-based medicine since "[he] dislikes the concept of experts and expertise because so-called experts can't help but be biased toward their own published views." Dr. Sackett has gone to extreme lengths to convey that he is not a lone genius, that he was part of a team at McMaster University that developed modern evidence-based medicine, and so doesn't deserve to be singled out as the guru. Sackett refused an invitation to be inducted into the Canadian Medical Hall of Fame, and only relented after they allowed him to accept the honor on behalf of all of his colleagues. Sackett's words and deeds not only demonstrate the right attitude for sparking constant improvement in medical knowledge, they provide a model for management researchers and writers.[54]

Unfortunately, there are few David Sacketts in the management idea marketplace. Modesty is in short supply and absolutes abound—in recommendations as to what to do, in conclusions about what affects individual and organizational performance, and in beliefs about what is true and what is false. There is little wonder then that half-truths fill management lore, causing all sorts of problems for those who are seduced by their appeal. That's why investigating, understanding, and deciding what to do about some of the most important dangerous half-truths is so crucial for implementing evidence-based management. We turn to that task next.

Part Two

Dangerous Half-Truths About Managing People and Organizations

3

Is Work
Fundamentally
Different from the
Rest of Life and
Should It Be?

L IBBY SARTAIN rose to become executive vice president for people at
Southwest Airlines, is now running human resources at Yahoo!, and
wrote a book sharing her wisdom, *HR from the Heart*.[1] Despite Sartain's massive talent, things were not always easy in her early years. After
finishing her MBA in the mid-1970s, Sartain was turned down for one job
because, she was told, "You smile too much."[2] Later, when working at
Mary Kay Cosmetics, Sartain decided to leave after a well-intentioned boss
advised, "You're so much fun to be around, and I really enjoy working with
you. But when you laugh out loud in the hall, people are going to think
you're not very professional. You just need to tone it down a little bit."[3] Sartain could have done what many us do every day: "toned down her act" and
been more somber person at work, thereby becoming a different—if less authentic—person on the job. Instead, she elected to find a place that wanted
her infectious laugh and enthusiasm, and so she wound up with a successful
career at Southwest Airlines. As her experience shows, most organizations

expect people to take themselves more seriously at work than in other parts of life. Laughing loudly and being overtly expressive is okay at home or when visiting friends but is often frowned on in corporate life and, as we've discovered at times, at the Stanford Business School, too.[4]

We suspect that few readers are surprised by Sartain's story. After all, most organizations press their people to look, talk, and act in ways that differ from what they do in other spheres of their lives and often from who they really are. Sometimes it seems that surviving and thriving in organizational life requires the skills of a great actor—the ability to play a role that is not necessarily you. Whether and when encouraging people to be and behave differently helps or harms organizations and their people is another matter entirely.

We begin our discussion of dangerous half-truths with this one because it is so pervasive and can be so damaging. The presumption that work is and should be separate from the rest of life, with different standards for motivating and judging human action, runs through many of the other half-truths we unpack in this book. Take incentives, the cornerstone of so many celebrated management practices. Do you always need to offer money and other bribes to get people to act the right way? Are people who get more of those goodies always the best human beings? These two beliefs are rarely questioned when applied to work settings, but seem suspect and simplistic when we think about our families, children, friends, communities, and religious groups. We don't expect friends to need incentives to have dinner with us or offer help. We don't rate Mother Theresa or Gandhi as failures because they died with little money in their personal bank accounts. How we manage and develop people also is taken for granted to be different in work organizations than in our regular lives. We doubt that parents who use a GE-style forced curve reward system at home would talk about it, let alone be offered huge speaking fees and book advances for bragging about how they devoted most of their time and money to their star children and only modest attention to their ordinary and inferior children. And we don't know of any parents who fire children who aren't up to snuff.

We also start with this half-truth—that work is different and separate from the rest of life and should be—because, perhaps even more than the others we'll discuss, the belief that work is and should be separate from the rest of life is so pervasive. It is widely seen as:

- Conventional wisdom about the *right* way to manage

- A fact of life that describes nearly all organizations

- Difficult, perhaps impossible, to sidestep or change because of over-whelming constraints, including financial costs, legal risks, competitive pressures, and societal expectations about what good people and organizations ought to say and do

So we begin with the presumption that work is and should be separate from the rest of life not just to show how to avert the damage caused by this dangerous half-truth. We do it to get you in the habit of thinking differently about how you manage and recognizing that choices are available to you and your organization. Organizations are rarely condemned to keep doing what everyone else does, even when everyone acts and talks as if escape seems impossible.

What Is Supposedly Different About Work?

Managers, consultants, academics, and lawyers routinely treat work as fundamentally different from the rest of life. They talk as if the workplace, be it virtual or face-to-face, is a separate land governed by distinct, narrow, and sometimes downright oppressive rules about what people ought to do and how they ought to be. Many pretend that the moment a human being crosses the magical threshold from nonwork to work, different behavioral and social forces come into play. Even in some of the most enlightened workplaces, the psychological contract is that, in exchange for money, some security, and status, people must conform to major constraints on what they think, say, feel, and do. In less enlightened places, the assumptions and restrictions are even more extreme, oppressive, and irrational.

Your Time Is Our Time, Even When You Work All the Time

In most places, when you come through the door your other responsibilities and obligations—to family, to community, and even to yourself—are supposed to be put aside, and you are supposed to focus solely on the organization and its well-being. The idea seems to be that people and concerns important to you cease to exist once you enter the workplace. Companies try to stop people from taking care of personal matters at work, limiting or forbidding everything from personal phone calls, to socializing with friends, to using office machines for personal projects. These days organizations are cracking down on *cyber-slacking*, sending personal e-mail, surfing the Web for entertainment, or doing personal business like stock trading or signing the kids up for summer camp. In a memorandum dated April 21, 2003, which we received anonymously from a clearly disgruntled employee, AppealTech, an appellate printing company in New York City, told employees that "no one is to access his or her personal email accounts from the office . . . No one is to access his or her personal computers from the office . . . Personal deliveries may no longer be received at the office unless you have no other alternative. If this is the case, please discuss your personal situation with me."

To enforce such rules, many companies are deploying software to help uncover and punish behavior they consider to be waste and abuse. One vendor of such software brags, "Spector CNE adds a whole new dimension to Internet monitoring. Now you can record everything your employees do online, including instant messages, chats, e-mails sent and received, Web sites visited, applications launched, network connections established and bandwidth consumed, files downloaded, files copied to removable media, and keystrokes typed."[5]

The irony is that even as employees are expected to keep personal matters out of the workplace, they are expected to spend more and more of their time at work. This is a long-term trend in the United States, Canada, and New Zealand, where the hours worked by the average adult increased over 15 percent between 1970 and 2002, including a 20 percent increase in the United States. There is recent evidence, despite falling per capita work hours in European countries between 1970 and 2002—including a 20 percent decline in France—that American-style pressures are now leading to longer hours throughout Europe. And even the French have been working longer hours in recent years.

The pressure to work long hours is extreme in some occupations, such as professional service and high-technology firms, where time spent on the job is seen as a sort of loyalty test or a proof of commitment. U.S. law firms are notorious for pressing partners and associates to work long hours. A partner in one especially hard-driving firm reported he hadn't been home in time for dinner with his children in years. The boss stays late and so he must as well. These pressures are amplified by demanding and difficult clients, who insist that their every whim be catered to *right now*, like the one who complained that his lawyers sometimes take *hours* to answer the e-mails he sends out at 3:00 a.m.

Computer game companies are also notorious for overworking young programmers—"gamers" who live to play and design cool games. At least at first, these young designers are so thrilled about the work (and to be surrounded with fellow "gamers") that they are happy to work for lower salaries than programmers with similar skills and to endure long hours during crunches to meet project deadlines—but most burn out within a few years. Electronic Arts (EA), the world's largest computer gaming company, faced a swirl of controversy when employees sued the company for not paying overtime during crunch time. The bad publicity got worse when the wife of an EA programmer posted an anonymous, and hotly debated, complaint that EA was driving employees to collapse by working them 80-plus-hour weeks, month after month. EA has made adjustments in overtime pay and does have work-life balance programs, but crunch time is still a big part of the job, and having a life outside of work remains a challenge for most game developers.[6]

Worse yet, when people are off work, they really aren't off work anymore. Even enlightened employers press their people to work weekends, take work calls at home, answer e-mails while on vacation, and entertain business guests in the evening. The wife of a successful lawyer once told us that she didn't have any real friends left because her nights and weekends were spent at social events with his clients. Lip service about work-life balance aside, companies routinely treat employees' nonwork lives as less important than work. As Libby Sartain asked us, "How can anyone maintain that work should be separate from the rest of life, when in many places, there is not much life other than work?[7]

Clothes Make the Person

Many organizations require people to dress in distinct and preordained attire at work. There are formal or informal dress codes in many places. Although the famous "white shirt" rule at IBM may be out, it is still the case that most of us dress differently at work. Uniforms are omnipresent in service occupations; it is easy to tell who is a waiter, flight attendant, doctor, baseball player, police officer, or firefighter just by looking. Dress also signals where people stand in the pecking order. As Howard Becker put it after studying medical students, "For the rest of their lives they will spend a good many hours among people who wear uniforms, more often white than not, which tell the place of each in the complicated division of work and the ranking system of the medical world."[8]

Requiring people to dress in narrowly prescribed, often more formal ways also serves as a constant reminder to employees that they are expected to give up their individuality and to cast their own taste and judgment aside in favor of the organization. When everyone follows the same narrow dress code it creates a world in which each person is surrounded with similarly decorated clones, so the unspoken, but not-so-subtle message is, "We are all alike and we all do what we are told."

Some people consciously dress differently for strategic reasons but do so at some risk. Dr. Laura Esserman is not only a breast surgeon and Stanford MBA, she is also the director of the Carol Frank Buck Breast Care Center at the University of California, San Francisco, and a renowned health care practitioner. When she sees patients, Esserman *never* wears a white coat and instead dresses as she usually does—in colorful, even flamboyant, clothes and large, distinctive earrings. As she said, "My patients are already stressed out enough by their disease. I want them to be partners in their care, and the last thing I want to do is to separate myself from them by a doctor's uniform." Her unusual style has helped her gain notoriety and influence. Once when she attended some national medical meeting dressing more conservatively, she got complaints from her colleagues and queries as to "Why are you dressing so boring?"

Putting on a uniform or costume may sound trivial, too weak to snuff out a person's true self. But theory and evidence on everything from Phillip Zimbardo's experiment on mock prison guards to managers in blue power suits suggests that putting on a uniform fuels a psychological process where "individual preferences are replaced by group goals and values."[9] We became acutely aware of such pressures in the 1980s when one of our students worked as an intern at IBM. He tried to conform to IBM's uniform in those days, a blue suit, white shirt, and tie. He rotated among the three ties he had: red, blue, and yellow. Whenever he wore the yellow tie, he was teased about his ugly tie. He didn't realize that the teasing was serious and that it happened because IBM's unofficial dress code banned yellow ties. Then his boss's boss pulled him aside and warned him that only red and blue ties were appropriate at IBM. This intern wasn't only taught a lesson about fashion, he was also taught a lesson about conformity.[10]

Don't Think, You'll Weaken the Team—Just Do What You're Told

Employees are supposed to think differently while at work. They are routinely expected to happily accept less control over their lives and cede both control and decision-making authority to their bosses. Employees who may manage complex personal finances, have multiple hobbies and talents, and run small businesses on the side are still expected to subordinate themselves at work—to do as told, not to ask too many questions, and to not make waves. It is ironic, but often all too true, that companies hire people for their experience and talents and then turn around and convey to people "that's not the way things are done around here" and tell them to follow orders. It is little wonder that so many employees are not engaged with their work and that satisfaction with bosses and employers is, as measured by many surveys, not very high.[11]

Some of the most striking examples we've heard of how talented people are stifled by their employers come from talking to airline pilots and flight attendants. Many have degrees from top colleges and universities, some have degrees in business and law, and many operate successful businesses or professional practices during their off-hours. They are especially knowledgeable about airline economics, the culture and management styles of the major airlines, and the psychology of work. But when they are on the job at places like United Airlines, they are expected to *not* behave like the intelligent, thoughtful people that they are and contribute their ideas to the airline. Rather, senior leaders want them to just do what they are told. When they offer advice, it is rebuffed.

Display Prescribed Feelings, Not Your Real Feelings— Check Your Emotions at the Door

As Libby Sartain's experience shows, organizations often have written or unwritten rules about which feelings employees should convey to customers and to each other—called *display rules* by sociologists. Many organizations go to great lengths to hire, train, monitor, and reward employees so they will express the right feelings and screen out, retrain, and, if need be, remove employees who express the wrong feelings. There are sound business reasons that companies try to control the emotions that employees convey to customers. Friendly service can make a company more attractive to customers and a more fun place to work. That is why both Southwest Airlines and Jet-Blue specify that employees will be hired and fired on the basis of their demeanor to customers and to each other. There are also jobs where employees are paid to annoy and pressure people. Sutton once spent three months watching, being trained as, and working as a bill collector, making calls to people who were late paying their Visa and MasterCard accounts. He learned that effective bill collectors created urgency and alarm in debtors and were trained to be especially gruff with nice people who didn't seem overly concerned, to raise the tension in their voices and make threats like: "Do you ever want to buy a car? Do you ever want to buy a house? If you do, you better pay this bill right now."[12]

The right emotions conveyed to the right people at the right time can increase revenues and strengthen organizational cultures. But there are costs to forcing people to express false emotions. Some studies show that when people constantly express emotions that they do not feel, they become burned out, alienated, and suffer physical and mental health problems.[13] Even more well documented is the Libby Sartain problem. Companies have such narrow definitions of the *right demeanor* that they screen out skilled people who aren't quite smooth, emotionally controlled, or reserved enough—or, conversely, who are too reserved, too quiet, or socially awkward.[14]

Personal style can be given too much weight when companies screen technical employees. Years ago we studied the rise and fall of the Atari corporation, once a wildly successful computer gaming company. When we interviewed Nolan Bushnell, the founder and visionary behind the company before it was sold to Warner Brothers in the late 1970s, he emphasized that he didn't pay attention to how a prospective engineer looked, whether the candidate held eye contact, and other signs of expressed friendliness or happiness. Instead, he just looked at their work because "the best engineers sometimes come in bodies that can't talk."[15]

Love—Maybe Even Friendship—Is a Dirty Word

Social relations are also supposed to be different at work than in other settings—such as with family or friends—mostly more distant and less cordial and intimate. However, when people spend lots of time in close proximity, personal relationships, including romantic relationships, often develop. A 2003 Vault.com survey found that 59 percent of the more than 1,100 respondents admitted to dating a colleague; another 17 percent said they would like to.[16] But many companies have policies forbidding dating among coworkers, and people who wind up moving in with and marrying fellow employees sometimes find that one of them must get a new job. Employers fear legal liability from sexual harassment claims, charges of nepotism and favoritism, and the intrusion of workplace gossip. They want to ensure that work time is not spent flirting with fellow employees, so they try to control interactions between employees, even off the job.

Conflict and Competition Are Desirable in the Workplace

Actions that are praised and rewarded at work are often forbidden, or at least discouraged, in other parts of life. Interpersonal competition is expected, accepted, praised, and routinely encouraged at work. By contrast, sibling rivalry is seen as a problem, not a virtue that brings out the best in people. Former CEO James Halpin of CompUSA told his people, "You should consider your coworker your enemy."[17] We can't imagine a father or mother saying to a child, "You should view your brothers and sisters as your enemies." But work is apparently different. Organizations are often filled with office politics, with people maneuvering for favor and to get ahead, while such behavior is rarely acceptable with family members and friends.

In engaging in political behavior to advance one's career, deception, deceit, and displaying false emotions occur routinely and are seen simply as things done by people who play the organizational power game. One of the most influential economic theories proposes, despite much evidence to the contrary, that such selfish and nasty behavior is just human nature, so it is expected and excusable. Agency theory presumes that people at work seek self-interest with guile, deceit, and cunning.[18] This theory also proposes (again, contrary to evidence) that people are *effort averse*, naturally lazy and prone to shirking. But out of the workplace, lying and presenting false fronts are not ways to win loyal friends and lovers, and people who shirk the responsibilities of friendships and family may find that they have fewer of both in the future.

Rules of Polite, Civilized Behavior Don't Apply at Work

Some bosses bully, intimidate, and belittle others. Underlings are expected to endure abuse that is condemned in other settings. As the *New York Times* put it, "Every working adult has known one—a boss who loves making subordinates squirm, whose moods radiate through the office, sending workers scurrying for cover, whose very voice causes stomach muscles to clench and pulses to quicken."[19] Former CEO Al Dunlap was eventually fired from Sunbeam for accounting fraud, but he was once lauded by the business press as a hero and great leader. Dunlap was notorious for the abuse he heaped on employees. An executive at Dunlap's first meeting with Sunbeam's top team described him: "like a dog barking at you for hours . . . He just yelled, ranted, and raved. He was condescending, belligerent, and disrespectful."[20]

Dunlap's behavior is unfortunately not rare. Richard Grasso, former chairman of the New York Stock Exchange who was swept up in a scandal over his $140 million retirement package, apparently wasn't all that different. "Subordinates who failed to meet his exacting standards received brutal tongue-lashings . . . After seating his victim in a chair, Grasso, his face flushed, would unleash a stream of venom."[21] Nor is such behavior confined to male executives. Dr. Gary Namie, director of the Workplace Bullying and Trauma Institute, reports that women are as likely as men to be the aggressors.[22] Linda Wachner, former CEO of apparel manufacturer Warnaco, "developed a reputation for demoralizing employees by publicly dressing them down for missing sales and profit goals or for simply displeasing her. Often . . . the attacks were personal rather than professional, and not infrequently laced with crude references to sex, race, or ethnicity."[23] Unfortunately, what would be considered abusive behavior in families and other social relationships is accepted and even lauded in work situations more frequently than many of us might admit.

Meaning and Fulfillment Come Elsewhere—Work Is Just About the Job

Books that extol the importance of corporate vision and values notwithstanding, many companies do not worry that much about providing meaning and fulfillment to their people. Work is, after all, a four-letter word. Jobs are done for money, and presumably, not for social and spiritual values. The search for meaning and fulfillment should occur in other domains. Even companies that have mission statements and corporate values often treat such things as ritualistic totems that don't actually affect what goes on in the day-to-day operations.

In part, this is because of the increasing tendency to see companies solely as economic entities whose task is maximizing shareholder value. Most employees have a hard time getting excited about the glories of maximizing shareholder value, particularly when they recognize that many shareholders hold the shares for literally a fraction of a day. The emphasis on financial goals at the expense of providing meaning seems to be increasingly prevalent, at least in the United States, and contributes to the segmented existence that so many people live. Spend a lot of time on the job, but find meaning and fulfillment elsewhere.

Although they usually stop short of saying it outright, managers and purveyors of management knowledge act as if—or find it useful to pretend that—people are transformed into different creatures when they step into their work roles. The message is that employees ought to be trusted less, monitored more; they should dress, smile, and frown in preordained ways; they should be more competitive, self-interested, political, cunning, and perhaps even nasty. And it is okay—even desirable—to treat people as if their skills and ideas are inferior to those of their superiors. There is no question that many people have come to accept that work is different from the rest of their lives, which is one reason why so many look forward to vacations and retirement. The question is whether such segmentation really makes sense as a model for thinking about, managing, and living inside organizations. And is it even possible to separate the domains in a world where technology blurs and destroys the boundaries?

Work Doesn't Have to Be Different from the Rest of Life

One of the most formidable barriers to implementing evidence-based management is the belief that things can't be different because they have always been that way, are that way everywhere, and *must* be that way for good reasons. If people don't know or understand alternative paths, or haven't been enticed or forced to think about such alternatives, they won't make changes, regardless of the evidence. That is why we are big advocates of field trips. Simple things like touring factories, watching people work, watching customers, becoming customers for your own product—or better yet your competitors' products—provide vivid experiences. When people visit other places and see what actually happens, it is harder to ignore the reality of their own senses, compared with more abstract and sanitized reports and PowerPoint presentations.

Similarly, if people don't understand the history of how and why things came about, change is difficult because they don't come to grips with the (often obsolete or suspect) reasons and assumptions behind present practices. Think about the half-truth being considered in this chapter: Work is and should be separate from the rest of life. How did this idea originate and become so pervasive? It is not obvious that subjecting people to roles that clash with their values and demeanor, as Libby Sartain's early employers did, is a sensible practice. It turns out that the current separation of work and nonwork is relatively recent. One hundred and fifty years ago most people worked on farms, in small shops, or in workshops. Work wasn't separate from the rest of life. People lived where they worked—or above where they worked—often worked with family members, and had more control over their work. Life was far from idyllic, as making a living often required more hours and effort than it does today. But it did mean that work and family roles were integrated.

Even today, for many people—such as independent contractors, some of whom work from home, people working in family businesses, entrepreneurs, particularly in smaller start-up companies, and professionals in small private practices—work and the rest of life remain tightly integrated. It is mostly in formal organizations, companies, and public bureaucracies that the distinctions between work and nonwork domains occur.

The emergence of the employment relationship—the idea that you work for someone else for a wage—is what seems to have caused the separation and segmentation of work from the rest of life. Being an employee was a drastic shift in the relationship between people and their work. If you worked for yourself or with family members, there were no agency problems, the stuff of much modern economics and its focus on how to align incentives and maintain control when owners and employees have different and conflicting interests. You worked, and you or your family members reaped the fruits of your labor. The more you worked, the more you got, and the choice between leisure and effort was largely private. Once people worked for strangers rather than for themselves (particularly as piecework became less common), what most employers purchased was time—hours of effort. The result was a struggle for control over the workplace and work arrangements: the tug-of-war that we described between companies and employees. So, I only care if you are surfing the Internet if I pay you to spend your time doing something else. I only care how many hours you bill in a law firm if I keep some of the fruits of your efforts. I only care how much vacation you take, how many sick days you use, and whether you use your work time to provide service for our customers or to enhance your social life if I pay for the lost time and productivity.

Employers constantly struggle with the problem of control, which is why it is a central theme in organization theory, economics, and business history. Each organizational response during the history of this struggle unleashed a chain of effects, often changes that employers eventually realized were hurting themselves and their people, leading them to try different methods for controlling their people. An early response to dealing with mass production employees, for example, was to hire and fire them willy-nilly, tolerate enormous turnover, and treat people as replaceable cogs in a machine. Employers were mainly focused on squeezing as much work out of each employee for as little money as possible. Turnover at Ford Motor Company in its early days exceeded 300 percent annually, reaching 380 percent in December 1913.[24] Things began to change when employers realized the costs of such turnover: the value of on-the-job learning and skills was higher than they first realized. Many employers raised wages, like the famous $5 a day wage that Ford instituted in 1914. Companies also took steps to bring more of employees' lives into the workplace, so they could place people more firmly under control.

The phrase *company town* or *company store* captures one dimension of this process—having people live, work, and shop in isolated areas so if they lost their jobs, they also lost their place to live, schools for their children, and places to buy food. Even in urban areas, companies became more involved in people's lives outside of work. Ford Motor Company, for instance, established a 50-person Sociological Department because Henry Ford argued that he was not just making automobiles, he also wanted to build men in his factories.[25] Department staff spent their days collecting personal information about prospective and current employees to make sure that the *right* men worked at Ford, "checking off information about marital status, religion, citizenship, savings, health, hobbies, life insurance, and countless other questions."[26] Although Ford's intervention was extreme, by the 1920s many companies had adopted management practices called *welfare capitalism*. These practices reflected the belief that employers were not only responsible for employees' wages, retirement, and health; companies were communities with responsibility for the well-being of workers and their families.[27]

This intrusion into workers' lives provoked reactions from labor unions, which were concerned that such personal information was used to spot, screen out, and oust anyone with pro-union attitudes. Governments in the United States and elsewhere were also concerned about employee rights and began questioning company encroachment on workers' lives, basically deciding that they too had the right to control the employment relationship. The state was, and remains today, interested in two policy issues that caused it to limit work hours—safety (people who work long hours get tired, make mistakes, and have accidents, so there are legal limits on hours worked by pilots and truck drivers, for instance) and employment (limiting the hours that people can work, at least without being paid overtime, presumably means more people are hired and total employment increases).

The separation of work and nonwork began to evolve in the early 20th century because some corporations were seen as too paternalistic and intrusive. But it is important to recognize that the degree of separation between work and nonwork and presumed virtues of such separation has waxed and waned over the years. In the early 1980s, William Ouchi's best-seller *Theory Z* argued that U.S. corporations ought to copy their successful Japanese competitors, which included incorporating more of the person into the company and treating employees as more than just economic agents. Ouchi's work reminds us that management practices and customs vary across cultures as well as over time. In Japan, employees lived in company housing, particularly when they were younger and single, took vacations together, and were expected to socialize with each other after work, so there was far less separation of work and nonwork activities. These patterns have eroded somewhat since Ouchi did his research in the 1970s but still describe life in many large Japanese companies. The importance of work compared to other parts of life also varies widely across cultures, and when work is viewed as less important, and therefore worthy of less time, separation is easier to accomplish.

This all means that companies face crucial choices about how to frame the link between work and the rest of their employees' lives. The two strategies are to either press for increasing separation, or conversely, to move toward intertwining the spheres more completely.[28]

The Benefits of Keeping Work Separate from the Rest of Life

If your aim is to bolster organizational performance, there are some sound reasons why work should be divorced from the rest of life, people ought to treat each other differently (and often worse) than in other roles, and employees should present modified and muted versions of themselves at work, even if it means masking or lying about their essential natures. Most companies—and increasingly nonprofit and government organizations as well—face harsh external competition and internal pressures to keep ratcheting up performance. Such imperatives can render actions based on destructive or irrational feelings—or worse yet, a desire to do favors for friends, family, and businesses associates—harmful to long-term success. After all, employees who display their authentic selves can be bad for business. Consider what happened to Yahoo!'s leadership coach Tim Sanders at a DoubleTree hotel in Houston. When Sanders complained that his guaranteed room wasn't saved, a clerk named Mike expressed contempt and told him, "I have nothing to apologize to you for." We are sure that DoubleTree's management would have been horrified by such nastiness (not to mention that Sanders speaks to big groups about it), no matter how authentic Mike's feelings might have been.[29] So there are good reasons why organizations press employees to be different at work, and to treat work and the rest of life as distinct spheres with different rules. We consider three primary benefits.

Reducing Role Conflict

The struggle to balance clashing demands from different roles hurts people and organizations. The stress generated by such juggling acts increases turnover, undercuts productivity, and results in exhaustion and compromised immune systems, which drive up health care costs. One strategy is to keep work separate from other roles in an effort to avoid negative spillover from one domain to the other. In general, reducing role conflict is a good thing. The damage caused by clashing demands from one's role as a family member or parent versus one's role as an employee have been well documented. The evidence shows that "a considerable proportion of employed parents (i.e., 40 percent) experience problems in combining work and family demands" and that the prevalence of work interfering with home is experienced three times more often than home demands interfering with work.[30] Not surprisingly, many studies show that work-family conflicts undermine job satisfaction.[31]

Companies respond to role conflict, including work-family conflict, in many ways. The most common response is to do nothing, except to tell employees that they must meet work demands and that reconciling their jobs with family responsibilities, civic activities, or hobbies are the employee's responsibility—and should not compromise job performance. The idea is that because work ought to be separate from the rest of life, employers have no obligation—and perhaps not even the right—to shape what people do outside of work. A Towers Perrin-Hudson Institute survey of 658 American companies found that out of a list of 19 possible programs and activities, which included things like on-site daycare, sick-child care, extended maternity leave, and adoption leave, the average company offered fewer than three programs.[32] Things aren't much different in the United Kingdom, where a comprehensive survey found that most companies did the bare legal minimum to meet employee needs. Only 3 percent provided a daycare program, 5 percent "planned" to enhance maternity pay beyond legal minimum, 2 percent "intended" to contribute to the costs of childcare, and 2 percent "planned" to introduce new parental leave schemes.[33] The use of such programs remains limited despite evidence that family-friendly practices may produce positive outcomes, including higher productivity and more favorable employee attitudes.[34]

This weak response to the increasing percentage of female employees with children, plus greater time pressure on both men and women to be at work, may help explain the declining levels of civic and social engagement described by Robert Putnam in his book, *Bowling Alone*. "Pressures of time and money, including the special pressures on two-career families, contributed measurably to the diminution of our social and community involvement."[35] Legal concerns help reinforce the lack of organizational involvement and limited apparent concern about employees' nonwork roles. Employers that offer on-site daycare and other forms of assistance or encouragement for nonwork activities may become legally responsible for what happens in those settings. As a simple example, a Stanford Business School employee injured his knee while participating in a school-sponsored athletic event. He was eligible for worker's compensation for both lost time at work and for medical costs because it was a work-related activity. Given the risks, it is not surprising that employers often try to take a constrained approach to their employees and delimit their involvement in other roles and spheres of life.

Objective Decision Making

The essence of the modern organization is supposed to be rationality and its kin, impersonal objectivity. When the employment relationship first emerged, jobs and promotions went to friends and family. Sanford Jacoby describes how in the early days of industrialization, foremen literally sold jobs—if you wanted a job in a factory, you bribed the foreman. This practice of selling jobs has not disappeared. Rudy Crew, former chancellor of the New York City school system, discovered that a school principal's position in some of the city's districts could be purchased with a $40,000 bribe to the right official—a practice he quickly eliminated with the help of the FBI and the Justice Department. Such behavior is both illegal and inconsistent with building high-performance organizations. Discipline in the workplace in the early factories was both harsh and capricious. Workers not only had to bribe foremen to get their jobs, they had to keep bribing them to keep them. This arbitrary, personal, and crooked management system clearly would dampen performance and productivity.

Although the word *bureaucracy* now has negative connotations, when Max Weber originally described bureaucratic organizations, he meant it as a *desirable* archetype—because it was a system based on rules, due process, and objective decision making. Before the widespread advent of civil service hiring for government jobs, there were few attempts to specify job qualifications and patronage reigned. Similar hiring practices in private employers produced similar results. Jobs were filled with people whose only qualification was loyalty to and a personal relationship with the person who did the hiring. Little or no attention was given to qualifications and experience. Objective, merit-based rules for hiring and promotion decisions make sense for enhancing organizational performance, by ensuring that the best-qualified people get the jobs. Objective rules for firing and discipline ensure that employees are not subjected, for example, to bribing supervisors or providing sexual favors to keep their jobs. Both efficiency and fairness dictate that more objective hiring standards are better.

One of the most reliable ways to maintain fairness is to ensure that people do not make workplace decisions about family members or close friends. It is almost impossible to be an impartial judge of your relatives and friends. Antinepotism policies ensure, at a minimum, that a boss does not evaluate or make career decisions about family members. At the other extreme, such policies forbid hiring employees' relatives at all. Big companies install such policies to stop *horse-trading*, where I evaluate your family members favorably in return for your positive evaluation of mine. Many policies linked to the classic model of bureaucratic control—job descriptions and lists of skills, promotion processes that permit internal bidding for jobs, personnel files and formal appraisals, and career histories that incorporate job and educational experience—were designed to provide factual information and to ensure it was used in personnel decisions. Although many people rail against the silly rules imposed by human resource departments, those rules were initially meant to make organizational life more fair and objective. And this goal entailed separating work relationships from everything else and having evaluations and decisions at work, to the extent possible, based on competence and rationality instead of insidious self-interest.

Control and Maintenance of Organizational Boundaries

There are good reasons why organizations want control over their people. Leaders at ScottishPower in the United Kingdom probably had good reason to be concerned when they discovered that an administrator had exchanged 537 personal e-mails in just three days.[36] Organizations try to solve such control problems in numerous ways. They provide incentives, hire people prone to follow expectations, and directly oversee and guide people. They nag, warn, and punish people who don't conform as expected and sometimes fire them—as ScottishPower did with the administrator who sent all those e-mails. Organizations also need employees to treat organizational boundaries as real and to show more loyalty and commitment to people inside the boundaries instead of favoring outsiders like suppliers, customers, and regulators over the organization's interests.

The sanctity of organizational boundaries and management's ability to control employees can falter when outside social ties seep into the workplace. Organizations use subtle hints, guidelines, and written rules to segregate work from other roles like father, mother, husband, wife, lover, son, daughter, and citizen. The idea is to maintain social, mental, and physical boundaries to make sure that outside roles and responsibilities do not intrude on work performance and loyalty. So in 2001 Stanford instituted a policy forbidding faculty, staff, and students from bringing children to the workplace; exceptions were made for rare "emergency situations," where supervisors could allow parents to bring their children, provided steps were taken to avoid disrupting others. The not-so-subtle message at most organizations is that performance is bolstered when people keep their personal lives, relationships, and problems out of the workplace.

A second, less common approach takes the opposite tack, bringing other aspects of employees' lives into the workplace with the aim of using relationships with family, friends, private clubs, and school ties to further organizational goals. A small step in this direction is seen when companies persuade employees to use personal ties and alumni networks to find top talent. Google and Cisco pay cash rewards to employees who recruit candidates that are ultimately hired. Venture capital, law, and financial services firms sometimes make halting attempts to leverage nonwork relationships when they have off-sites at lovely resorts and invite spouses or significant others. The idea is to thank them for the sacrifices they, too, have made for the firm and to create a broader community with bonds to the firm. We say *halting* because a nice weekend is scant compensation for 51 other weeks of grueling hours and little time together, but such efforts are a small step toward inclusion. Some organizations take far more comprehensive steps to bring the rest of people's lives into the workplace. We explore the virtues of taking such steps next.

The Benefits of Integrating Work with the Rest of Life

Arile Hochschild studied a company that put on human resource workshops where trainers encouraged employees to use friends and family to solve work-related problems and help the company prosper. An HR executive explained, "You piggyback on ordinary friendships . . . We get them to call in some personal chips for work." Executives in this company realized there are costs to treating work as a separate domain and benefits to weaving the spheres together. We consider some powerful reasons why organizations benefit from creating porous boundaries between work and the rest of life. This approach is especially effective when organizations treat integration as a two-way street, with the aim of making employees' lives better, not just exploiting them for the company's benefit.[37]

Building Commitment Through Inclusion

Some organizations with strong cultures, including those ranked most highly on *Fortune*'s list of best places to work, not only make accommodations for family responsibilities, they embrace the whole person, including his or her family. When sincerely and effectively executed, this approach builds enduring bonds between companies and employees, including well-documented benefits such as lower turnover and greater employee effort, engagement, and cooperation aimed at helping the company get ahead. Southwest Airlines is famous for being the "love" airline (its stock ticker symbol is LUV), for embracing employees, and letting people like Libby Sartain be themselves—reasons why Southwest attracts 30 or more applicants for each open position. Colleen Barrett, chief operating officer at Southwest Airlines, described the company's family-oriented approach:

> We've talked to our employees from day one about being one big family. If you stop and think about it for even 20 seconds, the things we do are things you would do with your own family. We try to acknowledge and react to any significant event in our brothers' or sisters' lives, whether it's work related or personal. We do the traditional things, like sending birthday cards and cards on the anniversary of their date of hire. But if employees have a child who's sick or a death in the family, we do our best to acknowledge it. We celebrate with our employees when good things happen, and we grieve with them when they experience something devastating. You cannot publish the kind of mission statement we have . . . and talk about our core values, and then not do these types of things.[38]

Jody Hoffer Gittell's study of all major carriers in the U.S. airline industry found that this inclusion of the whole person created powerful attachments to Southwest. Gittell found that "employees . . . talked about the organization as though it were an extension of their own families."[39] And by including the families in its activities, Southwest avoided much divided loyalty and jealousy. Libby Sartain, former vice president of people, noted: "When we talk at company events, family members talk about Southwest as 'we.' If you get involved, you have to make sure family members become part of that or they get jealous. We encourage people to bring their kids to work to show them what work is."[40]

Southwest coordinates its interdependent operations through personal relationships as much as through formal structure and rules. Gittell concludes that it is such relationship-based coordination, rooted in the social capital Southwest has built with its people, that is most crucial to the company's extraordinary success. It is easier to achieve coordination through informal relationships because the company encourages relationships, including friendships and family interactions, in the workplace. Southwest is also relaxed about employees dating and marrying each other. About 2,000 of the airline's 35,000 employees are married to each other. "When Greg Crum, 56, vice president of flight operations . . . and Michelle Crum, 45,

Southwest's assistant manager for recruitment training for in-flight operations, were married in October, 2000," among the 127 guests were 110 Southwest employees including Herb Kelleher, then CEO.[41]

Employee loyalty, engagement, and commitment are important benefits, but not the whole story. In a typical organization, people charged with building and maintaining relationships with others—such as customers or employees—work in a place where many kinds of relationships are discouraged (or there is a don't ask, don't tell policy) and the only thing that matters is *business*. The analogy we make is this: just as it is difficult to have total quality management practices and high quality in one part of a factory and not in another, it is difficult to encourage some close and effective relationships, for instance with customers, while simultaneously discouraging, denying, or ignoring other relationships. The authentic emphasis on supporting employees' inside and outside relationships at Southwest and at places like CostCo, Genentech, Smuckers, Starbucks, and Wegmans means that employees have the desire and emotional energy and keep developing the interpersonal skills to build relationships that are in the company's best interest. These enduring relationships result in higher profits.

Recruiting Family and Friends

Some companies leverage blurred boundaries between work and the rest of life by using worker's friends and family members as customers, in some cases the company's main customers. Some organizations find ways to entice or pressure loyal family members to work on the organization's behalf for little or no pay. Direct sales organizations such as Amway, Tupperware, and Mary Kay Cosmetics all teach new salespeople (who aren't employees, but *distributors* or *sales consultants*) to focus initial sales efforts on family, friends, and anyone else they know, until that avenue is exhausted. One Mary Kay consultant, for example, approached friends at church, handed them lipstick samples, asked about their experiences with Mary Kay, and offered them a free facial. After all, when people already have a long-term relationship with you and like you, they have a hard time turning down such sales pitches, even if they really aren't interested in the product. The Girl Scouts of America uses the same tactic, as we can attest from the dozens of boxes of cookies that we really didn't want but bought from friends' daughters. [42]

When employees' families, lovers, and friends feel like part of the organization, it is easier to persuade them to work on the organization's behalf. One result is that they sometimes become, essentially, free labor. This advantage of blurring boundaries is rarely made explicit in traditional organizations, but it is routine in direct sales organizations like Amway and Mary Kay, especially with family members. Amway encourages distributors to "draw their spouses into business activities such as deliveries and bookkeeping, even if they are not selling and recruiting directly, so that distributors don't have to be 'married singles.'" When recruiting new sales consultants, Mary Kay often interviews husbands to see if they are willing to support their wives' efforts "by providing childcare and performing domestic chores while the consultant attends company functions."[43]

There is a history of family members providing free labor to the military. In the U.S. Army and Navy, for example, the wives of commanding officers (COs) have long been expected to lead and inspire the wives of other unit members and to support both their husband's careers and the military's mission. They welcome wives of new officers, organize social events, and provide emotional support to other spouses and their families—especially when spouses are gone on assignment for long stretches, in combat units or ships that are out at sea. Not all wives can support their husbands—one of our students was married to a CO, but couldn't be "Mrs. Major" because she was a major herself. But this tradition continues, as seen in the advice at Sarahsmiley.com, a Web site for U.S. Navy wives. Sarah, the daughter and wife of navy officers, advised a wife whose husband had just been made CO, "Certainly, a CO's wife is in a position to be a great support for the younger wives. With more age and experience under her belt, the CO's wife has a lot of expertise to share with her younger counterparts . . . Make sure you use this 'power' in good faith and for the benefit of everyone."[44]

Finally, in addition to the benefits of loyalty, employees who marry coworkers and have blood relatives in a company can call on their kin for advice and help, which can enable them to do their jobs better, and in turn can help the organization. Anne Mulcahy, the CEO of Xerox since 2001, provides an interesting example. Mulcahy has been credited with leading the company back from the brink of bankruptcy, in large part because she had such detailed knowledge about what made the company tick, what was killing it, and what needed to be changed most. Not only did Mulcahy know Xerox well because she started her career there as a sales representative in 1976, her husband is a retired Xerox sales manager and her brother is head of Xerox's Global Services Group. These relationships have helped her better understand what the company needs, and are, we suspect, one of the reasons that, as one major Xerox customer put it, "Anne brought a reality check to the leadership of Xerox."[45]

The Gains from Letting People Be Themselves

As authors ranging from Erving Goffman to Arlie Hochschild have observed, engaging in strategic self-presentation—trying to display emotions you don't really feel or presenting a self to the world that is not authentic—is distressing and depletes a person's cognitive and emotional resources.[46] Studies on occupations from call center employees, to flight attendants, white-collar workers, and managers show that when employees face constant pressure to display false emotions, they experience dissatisfaction, feel alienated from their authentic selves, have less organizational commitment, suffer more burnout, and feel a greater desire to quit their jobs.[47] In a competitive world in which success is difficult enough to achieve, it seems counterproductive to have people expend energy trying to be different than they really are just for the sake of appearances inside organizations.

We are not advocating that companies should let employees do whatever they want regardless of the consequences for others or company performance. We believe that rude service clerks, forgiving bill collectors, insulting professors, and nasty leaders need to change their behavior or find another job. What we are suggesting is that companies devote less effort to batting down who people really are and what matters to them, and more time to using their people's gifts, skills, and distinct charms to benefit both the company and their people. Research on creative organizations provides especially strong support for this conclusion. Creativity happens when people draw on what they know and who they are and say what they think, rather than pretend to be stifled clones of each other. The result is more ideas, more varied ideas, more combinations of ideas, and ultimately, more successful ideas.[48] A splendid example is Pixar, the imaginative company that brought us films including *Toy Story*, *Finding Nemo*, and *The Incredibles*. A case study by our students found that Pixar strives to hire people with strong and diverse skills, people who remain true to themselves, in part so they can show their bosses better ways of doing things. As Brad Bird, director of *The Incredibles* put it, "I've been fired for being disruptive several times . . . but this is the first time I've been hired for it."[49]

More Authentic Leadership

Can you think of any leadership books that contain the following advice: "Because leading is an important and demanding task, you should behave differently in leadership roles and situations than you do in other settings?"

We can't. Such advice clashes with every leadership book we know, whether it is based on research or testimonials from successful leaders. Bill George, longtime CEO of Medtronic, a medical device company, was named one of the top 20 managers in the country by *BusinessWeek* and one of the 11 "Good to Great" CEOs identified by Jim Collins. Under George's leadership, Medtronic's market capitalization grew from $1 billion to $60 billion. In his book *Authentic Leadership*, George urges leaders not to copy others. He tells you that if you want lead well, do what is true to your own values and nature, which requires, of course, reflection on who you are and what you believe in.[50] The message makes sense because people have pretty good ways of detecting when others, including leaders, are simply putting on a show and not being truthful. People are unlikely to respect or follow those who aren't honest with themselves and others.

But it is almost impossible to be authentic, honest, or compassionate when you try to be a different person in each role you play, one version of yourself outside of work and a drastically different version at work. That's why many, although certainly not all, of those recognized as truly effective leaders do not treat work and the rest of life as distinct domains. George Zimmer, the founder and CEO of the men's clothing retailer The Men's Wearhouse, sees his leadership role as completely integrated with the rest of his life. He is running The Men's Wearhouse and living his life, and the two happen to integrate quite well. Zimmer has carried his spirituality into the leadership style of the company, its philosophy, and its management practices. And he and other leaders we know do things such as relying on a circle of outside friends and advisers to ensure that they remain, even in their leadership roles, grounded in the values and beliefs that they hold in the rest of their lives. Of course, being yourself and being successful as a leader is more likely if you are a decent human being: a person that others respect, identify with, and want to be around. But we would argue that few people can hide their true colors very well for very long, so being authentic is worth considering in all circumstances.

Striking a Balance

When labor markets got temporarily tighter in the late 1990s, employers decided to become more employee-friendly, particularly for technology workers in the United States. They let employees dress casually and bring their dogs to work, provided free food and drinks and even concierges to run their personal errands. The underlying premise was sound: most workplaces aren't designed to accommodate people's needs, so to attract and keep people with many employment options, making work more congruent with who people are and want to be would be useful. Unfortunately, many of the changes were done more for show than out of real conviction—shallow things like allowing pets at work, loosening up dress codes, or buying a foosball table. The fundamental relationship of people to each other, their bosses, and the organization remained pretty much the same beneath the surface. And the impetus for pretending to have life-congruent workplaces evaporated in most organizations as soon as the labor market slackened.

The primary recommendation in this chapter is to incorporate more of the person and take human needs into account when designing work and organizations, and it is an old prescription. This advice goes back at least to research done at the Tavistock Institute in England over 50 years ago. Their research showed that organizations were not only technical and physical, but also social entities. So incorporating human needs and preferences into work design could bolster efficiency even as it enhanced employee satisfaction. This idea isn't new, but it is still true. And the fact that these evidence-based insights about managing the human side of companies are still largely ignored in most places remains troubling, at least if you care about making organizations more effective and humane.

Yes, work is serious business and most companies face massive competition. But that makes it even more crucial to harness everything that your people know, can do, and want to do, instead of checking most of who they are and hope to be at the door. As Joe Mello and Kent Thiry of DaVita say, it is because dialysis is such serious and demanding work that it is important to let people have fun and enjoy themselves and feel part of a larger community that accepts and supports them. Plus, emotions are contagious, and happy, fulfilled employees are more likely to create environments in which patients will feel better about being there, something that will produce better health outcomes. What follows, then, are two overarching management guidelines that emerge from the evidence in this chapter.

Don't Permit Behaviors in the Workplace That Would Not Be Tolerated Elsewhere

There has been an upsurge in writing and research on workplace bullying, which recognizes that bullying is not just something that happens in school or on the playground. This research shows that bullying damages those victimized by it, as well as the organizations where it is allowed to persist.[51] Bernard Tepper studied abusive supervision in a large random sample of working residents in a Midwestern city. A follow-up six months later found that employees with abusive supervisors were more likely to quit their jobs. And employees with abusive supervisors who still had their jobs reported less job and life satisfaction, lower commitment to their organizations, more conflict between work and family roles, and increased depression, anxiety, and burnout.[52]

In a *Harvard Business Review* essay, Sutton urged companies to implement *no asshole rules*: to refuse to hire people—even superstars—who are known jerks, and when insiders had episodes in which they belittled and bullied others—especially those with less power—they should be called on it immediately. Sutton pointed out that firms that applied such rules would likely enjoy less turnover and absenteeism, lower health care costs, and reduced litigation risks. He also pointed out that some companies already have such rules, usually worded in more polite language, and such rules do help them maintain more civilized workplaces. The Seattle-based law firm Perkins Coie, for example, has a "no jerks allowed" rule, which helped earn them a spot on *Fortune* magazine's "100 Best Companies to Work For" in 2003 and 2004. To show how this rule works, Perkins Coie partners Bob Giles and Mike Reynvaan were once tempted to hire a rainmaker from another firm but realized doing so would violate the rule. As they put it, "We looked at each other and said, 'What a jerk. Only we didn't use that word.'"[53]

Recognize and Accommodate the Needs of the Whole Person

As we've shown, it takes lots of effort and emotional energy to leave one's essential nature at the workplace door—be it a physical or electronic door. And it is simply impossible for many of the best people to stifle their true selves. Instead of trying to get people to be different from what and who they are, skilled leaders let people know what organizational objectives are, paths for achieving those objectives, and then to the extent possible, help people find, design, and perform roles that move the organization toward those objectives. One half-truth of modern human resource management is that jobs are filled because some need is recognized in advance, the position is advertised, and the vacancy is filled with exactly the kind of person that those rational planners had imagined in advance. It turns out that a surprisingly high percentage of jobs are *idiosyncratic*, created, designed, and customized to fit the preferences and skills of some unique person, not because some expert ever imagined in advance that the organization would need that job. A study of jobs filled at Stanford University over a three-year period showed that 202 out of the 1,675 jobs filled were idiosyncratic—roles that Stanford had created to capture one person's distinct skills and aspirations. Close to 20 percent of nonclerical jobs at Stanford are idiosyncratic. Start asking people how they got their jobs, even in large and seemingly rigid companies, and you might be surprised by how often they tell you how they carved out a niche for themselves.[54]

A classic example of how to create a place where people draw on their authentic selves comes from Joey Altman, a renowned chef. Altman was the owner and head chef of the Wild Hare, a restaurant near Stanford, and currently stars in a television cooking show called *Bay Cafe*. We were delighted with the cuisine and service at the Wild Hare and got to know Joey. We asked him how the restaurant produced such a marvelous dining experience. Joey had no formal management or leadership training, but developed an intriguing philosophy after working at 26 different restaurants. He hired primarily for attitude rather than experience, noting, "The right attitude for me is somebody who's passionate about what they're doing and they have a real desire to learn and they're doing this not because they think it's going to be some money but they really want to do it and they enjoy it." He tried to give people work they really enjoyed, defined roles broadly, blurred traditional roles, and gave people as much freedom as possible to be creative. And he let them be themselves:

> *What I decide is how the basic process should be handled. Not the means to get there, but what the end is. The end result is I want this to be beautiful, delicious, and hot. Whether you fry that first or you do that first and then do that, I don't care as long as it's beautiful and delicious. As far as service goes, I realize that I have ten waiters and ten different people. I don't want Darrell to be like Joanie, and Joanie, I don't want you to be like Susie. Paul, I want you to be the best Paul you can be. Susie, I want you to be the best Susie you can be. I just want you all to be knowledgeable and use your strengths of your personality to the best.*

With that philosophy, it was little wonder that turnover at Altman's restaurant was a fraction of that in the typical establishment; his employees enjoyed what they did, and this enjoyment, enthusiasm, and creativity carried over to the food and service, making the dining experience the best in the area at the time.

Accommodating the Rest of Life May Actually Be More Efficient

The students and executives we teach are often skeptical when we report that SAS Institute, a large privately owned software firm, is successful and really does have a 40-hour (or thereabouts) workweek. The joke in the software industry is that most companies have flexible hours—you can work any 18 hours a day you want. The key, as HR leaders at the company emphasize, is to remove distractions so that people can be truly productive on the job.

If you have a sick child, you are going to think about that child. If your childcare provider doesn't show up, or you can't afford one, you aren't going to leave your child at home and go to work without worrying. If you have responsibilities for elderly parents, those responsibilities are going to absorb part of your day and perhaps damage your focus and attention. Many studies have documented the lost time and absenteeism that occurs as people try to juggle their various responsibilities.[55] What those studies don't capture is how much productivity and creativity are lost because people can't concentrate fully even while they are at work if they are concerned about nonwork demands. David Russo, head of human resources at SAS for over 15 years and currently the head of HR at Peopleclick, told us the SAS philosophy is that the most important people to their employees are the people they are responsible for and to—their husbands and wives, domestic partners, children, and parents, not their bosses or coworkers. This means that SAS ensures that employees have the support and resources to attend to these important people and that these "outsiders" are incorporated into company life as much as possible and as much as they want to be—which results in increased performance and efficiency. Incorporation, rather than segmentation or exclusion, helps employees lead more integrated and coherent lives with less distraction, worry, and destructive spillover.

Leaders who act on the insight that it is not easy for people to play multiple, conflicting roles can help their companies and their employees. Although there are aspects of work and the rest of life that are best kept apart, the general idea of separate domains is a dangerous half-truth. And it is a half-truth that infects other management practices as well. The emphasis on incentives above all to motivate and direct behavior, for instance, stems directly from the idea that work behavior is and ought to be motivated differently than in other realms—where people supposedly have different motives like obligations to people they care about and the joys of feeling productive. Treating people as if they are playing a zero-sum game with a few winners and many losers, and focusing on hiring premade superstars rather than bringing out the best in people, are also beliefs that distinguish work from the rest of life—and are half-truths that cause as many problems as they solve.

There is bad news and good news about this first half-truth. The bad news is that the presumption that work is separate and operates under different rules than the rest of life is widely taken for granted. It is so ingrained in so many work practices that it does massive and widespread damage. The good news is that this half-truth can be toppled through evidence-based management. By challenging this half-truth with solid data and logic, and then borrowing, inventing, and experimenting with practices that weave together rather than segregate and tear apart our different roles, there are bright prospects for both progress and performance.

Do the Best
Organizations Have
the Best People?

EVERY COMPANY devotes enormous effort to choosing and judging its members. Such efforts make sense. There are huge differences between the best and worst performers. And renowned companies do have great people. Consider IDEO, one of the largest and arguably most successful innovation firms in the world. IDEO's products have won more than twice as many *BusinessWeek* Industrial Design Excellence Awards than the next best firm. IDEO's people have designed thousands of products and experiences, everything from the first Apple mouse, to full-size mechanical whales for the Free Willy films, to finding ways for DePaul Health Center's emergency room to make visits less bewildering. IDEO even designed and built a full-sized, working prototype of Dilbert's "dream cubicle" for Scott Adams, the cartoon character's creator.[1]

We spent a lot of time trying to figure out why IDEO is so creative. In the mid-1990s, we did an 18-month study that entailed spending a couple of days a week watching IDEO's designers and talking to them about their work. When we teach managers about IDEO, they often conclude that the firm is creative because it attracts and keeps talented people. David Kelley, the founder and chairman, reinforces this view when after being pressed to reveal IDEO's secrets, he grins and says, "I just hire some smart people and get out of the way." We repeat Kelley's quote to dissuade leaders bent on micro-managing creative work. It is true that IDEO hires smart people and does not monitor them closely. Yet this truth is also fundamentally misleading about the source of IDEO's success and about why other organizations succeed and fail, too.[2] The best evidence indicates that natural talent is overrated, especially for sustaining organizational performance.

Why Smart and Skilled People Fuel Performance

Not everyone agrees that talent and individual attributes are overrated. Psychologist Benjamin Schneider argues that "the people make the place," and that *those who compose* an organization—their abilities and personalities—"come to define how that place looks, feels, and behaves."[3] Schneider says "it only *looks* like organizations determine behavior." He argues that because people are so hard to change, *who* is in an organization is far more important than what happens to them, and that things like training, peer pressure, management action, and rewards have little or no effect.[4] He concludes that organizational culture and performance result mostly from who is hired and sticks around. Jim Collins, in *Good to Great*, echoes this sentiment when he emphasizes the importance of "getting the right people on the bus."[5]

These views are bolstered by research showing that better small groups usually contain better people. Experiments show that in groups doing everything from brainstorming to solving complex problems performance depends on members' individual skill (or lack of it). Psychologist Edwin Locke and his colleagues argue this is just common sense. They point out that in the 1960s, each of the five offensive linemen on the Dallas Cowboys weighed 300 pounds or more, and each was enormously strong and skilled before joining the team, so their teamwork was a trivial factor in their success compared to their individual traits. No matter how motivated, well-trained, or cooperative, a line made up of 200-pound "wimps" would be vastly inferior.[6]

The argument is that human skills, intelligence, physical attributes, and personalities are so enduring and hard to change that what organizations do, including their performance, mostly reflects an additive combination of the kinds of people who join and stay. This view pervades *The War for Talent*, a book by McKinsey consultants Ed Michaels, Helen Handfield-Jones, and Beth Axelrod.[7] They assert that talented people are scarce, better talent makes a huge difference in company performance, and the information revolution means that talent is among the most crucial competitive advantages for any company. They cite their surveys at 120 companies and 27 case studies to show this is the new reality. They advise firms to differentiate and affirm the best people: Aggressively remove "C players"; heap praise, mentoring, rewards, and promotions on "A players"; and offer far more modest kudos, compensation, and the like to the solid "B players," who form the majority of the workforce. This research has some deep flaws—especially, as we mentioned in chapter 2, that the claimed *cause* of performance (managing talent) was measured after its *effect*.[8] But some rigorous studies do imply that great people make great organizations. And there are numerous well-crafted studies that examine why some people are more talented and productive than others.

The Best *Are* Much Better Than the Rest

There are enormous and well-documented differences between the best and worst performers in numerous endeavors. Psychologist Dean Keith Simonton, who has spent his career studying greatness and genius, concludes: "No matter where you look, the same story can be told, with only minor adjustments. Identify the 10 percent who have contributed the most to some endeavor, whether it be songs, poems, paintings, patents, articles, legislation, battles, films, designs, or anything else. Count all the accomplishments that they have to their credit. Now tally the achievements of the remaining 90 percent who struggled in the same area of achievement. The first tally will equal or surpass the second tally. Period."[9] One study showed that a mere 16 composers produced about 50 percent of the classical music that is performed and recorded today, while 235 others produced the remaining half. Another study found that 10 percent of the authors had written about 50 percent of the books in the Library of Congress. Research on computer programmers showed that the most productive programmers were 10 times more productive than the least productive, and five times more productive than average programmers.[10] Such staggering variations suggest a strong argument for bringing aboard and keeping the best people, especially those in the top 10 percent.

Less dramatic but still large differences were uncovered by industrial psychologists Frank Schmidt and John Hunter, who analyzed *all* published studies (spanning 85 years!) "that measured or counted the amount of output for different employees." They found, in comparing superior workers (at the 84th percentile) with average workers (at the 50th percentile), that superior workers in jobs requiring low skill produced 19 percent more than average workers, superior workers in jobs requiring high skill were 32 percent more productive, and for professionals and managers, superior performers produced 48 percent more output than average performers. It is hard to quarrel with their conclusion that such differences can affect an organization's economic health.[11]

Organizations *Can* Spot the Best in Advance

Not only are there huge differences between the best and the worst performers, such differences in who is going to be the best or the worst can be predicted in advance, albeit not with perfect accuracy. Schmidt and Hunter's exhaustive study examined 19 methods that organizations used to select new employees. The best predictor of future job performance was general mental ability, like IQ and related measures of overall smartness. Other strong predictors were work sample tests (candidates do tasks associated with the job, like a typing test), job tryouts (candidates do the whole job for a few hours or days), structured job interviews (every candidate is asked the same questions in the same order), and conscientiousness (reliable and scrupulous people, with a strong sense of purpose and will). The worst predictors were age and graphology (using handwriting analysis to assess personality).[12]

Cognitive ability is not the only kind of intelligence that fuels job performance. Promising research on multiple intelligences, like practical, social, and emotional intelligence, has sparked interest and controversy.[13] The most heated arguments are about whether traditional IQ tests are fair, measure a sufficiently broad range of human abilities, and are strong or weak predictors of performance. We won't drag you through these arguments, many fueled by ideology rather than evidence, but virtually all researchers agree that traditional IQ tests predict job performance, although they disagree on how strongly. And practical intelligence does predict job performance over and above traditional IQ, especially practical problem-solving skills (e.g., focusing on what is important, not what is urgent) and interpersonal skills or social intelligence (e.g., showing respect and listening to others).

Other measures also can predict success in specific jobs. Salespeople face constant rejection and failure in their work, for example, so it seems reasonable that optimists would fare better than pessimists. Psychologists Martin Seligman and Peter Schulman predicted that optimistic salespeople who viewed setbacks as temporary and not their fault would be more successful than those with opposing pessimistic styles. Indeed, their study of 103 newly hired life insurance agents found that optimists sold more insurance and were about twice as likely to still be selling insurance a year later.[14]

In short, there is disagreement about exactly which factors best predict job performance, and no assessment is always accurate. But managers can make evidence-based decisions about who to hire and who to avoid.

Stars (Might) Attract More Stars

Advocates of the talent mind-set emphasize that, if you bring in great people, they will attract and bring in more great people. This argument is especially dear to consultants and executives who recommend that employees be sorted into star "As," ho-hum but acceptable "Bs," and "Cs" who need to shape up or ship out. Bradford Smart contends, based on over 100 consulting engagements, that "in practice, A players hire other A players. B players hire C players. C players hire F players. If you can woo a small critical mass of A players, you can start a favorable chain reaction and build a strong company."[15] Smart's book *Topgrading* emphasizes that the "fact" that "C players don't hire A players" is the biggest single hurdle to building a company filled with A players.[16] *The War for Talent* makes the same point. "We call it the Rule of Crappy People: Bad managers hire very, very bad employees, because they are threatened by anyone who is anywhere near as good as they are."[17]

Despite the vehemence of these claims, we can't find rigorous research on the Rule of Crappy People, or on related assertions that good people hire good people and bad people hire even worse people. The general conclusion that people want to be with others like themselves, and shun different people is, however, supported by research on similarity and attraction effects. In the battle of clashing clichés, study after study shows that birds of a feather flock together, not that opposites attract. Even when people try not to be swayed, they have warmer feelings and offer more positive evaluations of others who look like them, act like them, have the same birthday, or are similar on any dimension they notice. And they downgrade and shun different people.[18]

This similar-to-me effect helps explain why most organizations unwittingly "bring in the clones." Male interviewers prefer hiring males, white interviewers prefer white candidates to blacks and Hispanics, and so on.[19] So future studies may confirm the claims made in *Topgrading* and *The War for Talent* that a "virtuous cycle" starts when you hire A players. For now, the controlled study that comes closest was done with 40 Canadian college students who, based on a personality test, were classified as being in the top or bottom third in conscientiousness. Then they were shown videotapes of two candidates for a job overseeing students in a college dormitory. One candidate acted conscientious, describing himself as diligent, dedicated, and attentive to detail; the other was the opposite, describing himself as spontaneous, laid back, and not very systematic. A similar-to-me effect was observed: conscientious students rated the conscientious candidate as better suited to the job; less conscientiousness students didn't notice much difference between candidates. Conscientiousness was the second strongest predictor of job performance (after IQ) in Schmidt and Hunter's study, and certainly is part of the A player profile. So this research bolsters claims that good people want to hire other good people like themselves, but reveals nothing about the Rule of Crappy People.[20]

Why an Obsession with Individual "Talent" Can Be Hazardous to Organizational Health

Michael Schrage is right: "A collaboration of incompetents, no matter how diligent or well-meaning, cannot be successful."[21] But not being in the top 10 percent isn't the same as being incompetent—90 percent of the people in every organization simply fail to qualify. It is a mathematical fact that only 10 percent of the people are going to be in the top 10 percent. And despite claims in *The War for Talent, Topgrading,* and numerous other books on hiring the best people, the talent mind-set is rooted in a set of assumptions and empirical evidence that are incomplete, misleading, and downright wrong. A moment's consideration will reveal that the war for talent idea rests on three crucial assumptions:

- Individual ability is largely fixed and invariant—there are better and worse people.

- People can be reliably sorted based on their abilities and competence.

- Organizational performance is, in many instances, the simple aggregation of the individual performances; what matters is what individuals do, not the context or system in which they do it.

As we will soon see, each of these assumptions isn't so completely true that one would want to base organizational success on its validity.

Talent Isn't So Easy to Perfectly Identify

What do Steve Young, Kurt Warner, and Jake Delhomme have in common? All eventually became starting National Football League quarterbacks, but only after long stints sitting on the bench or playing in obscure football leagues because they weren't considered good enough for the NFL. All three played in Super Bowls, and Young and Warner won Most Valuable Player awards. Talent management "errors" like these "point out how . . . luck plays a much greater role than anyone would have you believe and sometimes, key players emerge from the most unlikely circumstances."[22] In fact, just about all professional sports teams—a domain where we might expect individual talent to be crucial and readily discerned—have numerous top players who were not deemed as such early in their careers.

Talent is not easy to identify for a number of reasons. First, even the best predictors don't do a very good job of selecting the best people. Take IQ. Intelligence is the most powerful predictor of job performance across studies, but IQ still seldom correlates more than 0.4 with performance. Since the amount of variation explained by a predictor is the correlation squared, intelligence accounts for no more than 16 percent of the variation in performance, leaving some 84 percent *unexplained*. Other alleged predictors have even lower correlations. This doesn't mean that companies should spurn valid indicators of ability when selecting people. But it does mean we all ought to be more circumspect about our ability to discern talent.

Second, performance naturally varies over time. Even the best athletes, the best musicians, and yes, the best professors, have off days. A study of output rates among foundry employees (machine molders, hand molders, and chippers and grinders) found week-to-week consistency in individual employee output that would leave about 50 percent of the variation unexplained. A review of other studies of variation in individual output in industrial settings where output could be precisely measured and both incentives and skills were constant reported that "individual output varied over a fairly large range from week to week"[23] This means that, depending on when you happened to look, A players would appear to be B players, or vice versa. An obvious implication is that you get better measures of performance or ability if you take more than one sample. Unfortunately, this simple insight is routinely ignored: hiring decisions are often based on a single test, work sample, or interview. Similarly, student achievement tests—used to measure whether schools are failing or succeeding—are administered once a year, at most.

Yet another problem with assessing ability or talent is that human judgments are clouded by invariable, potent, and largely inescapable psychological biases. A few years ago, one of us talked to an oil company executive who claimed he could identify top managerial talent at an early age. We asked how he could be so confident in his ability. He responded that the people he identified, who then were tapped for a fast track program, invariably turned out to be successful. This executive never considered that their success could stem mostly from being tapped, not from his ability to spot talent. Consider a more systematic study of managerial bias. Managers provided performance evaluations for two types of employees—subordinates they were involved in hiring versus subordinates they were not involved in hiring. As you might expect, managers gave higher performance evaluations to subordinates they had a voice in hiring, independently of other employee performance measures.[24] This is what happens when people expend effort and make a public commitment to a course of action—they think they have done a good job. If you help chose someone for a position, you will think more highly of that person's abilities compared to someone you didn't help select, in part to justify the decision you have made.

These uncertainties and human frailties mean that for most jobs in most organizations, assessing talent and ability is fraught with error and bias. Most dimensions of work performance are not as objective as how well someone can pitch, hit a ball, or throw a discus. In ambiguous, interdependent, subjective situations, all sorts of biases—including the commitment effect just described, as well as biases from similarity and liking—will intrude and affect how talent is assessed. These biases cloud how talent is judged even when objective performance indicators are present, such as how fast a person can type or how many points a basketball player has scored.[25]

Talent Isn't Fixed—Unless You Believe It Is

Yet another reason why talent is so difficult to assess is that it is a moving target. Despite all the myths, talent is not completely fixed or predetermined at birth or at a young age. Talent depends on a person's motivation and experience. Talent depends on how a person is managed or led. Assessments of talent depend on how it is defined by a given culture in a given era. Talent depends more on effort and having access to the right information and techniques than on natural ability. Talent, in other words, is far more malleable than many people want us to believe.

Consider the cultural and historical factors that shape whether a person is anointed as talented. Today Rembrandt is considered a great painter. Many people today consider Johann Sebastian Bach a great composer, and Mozart as one of the greatest composers. Yet these and many other geniuses were largely unrecognized and unrewarded during their lifetimes. Why? Because what is great art or what is great music depends so much on cultural conventions and reigning definitions of art and music. Judgments about talent depend on interests and tastes. For Bach's contributions to be fully recognized, ideas about music itself had to change so that his music fit the definition of greatness.[26]

Talent or ability also depends on what happens to people and how they are coached, not just their innate skill or motivation. Consider baseball. A study by Lawrence Kahn examined the effect of baseball managers on team and player performance. Kahn measured player ability by the average of their performance over their entire careers, a reliable indicator of player talent. He found that some managers inspired players to perform above their ability, and other managers stymied players, consistently driving players to perform below their ability. Ability or talent did not explain all of a player's performance in a given year. How the player was managed and coached mattered, too.[27]

There is no doubt that inherited abilities limit how well people can do in some pursuits. There aren't any horse racing jockeys who are 7'3" tall, nor any professional basketball players who are 4'10". But natural talent is overrated. Exceptional performance doesn't happen without exceptional effort, and even allegedly inherited abilities—like IQ and other "smartness" measures—improve markedly and continuously when people work hard, have good coaching, and *believe* they will keep getting better. The nature versus nurture debate persists in academia and society. But natural gifts are useless without lots of practice. People, teams, and organizations that are novices at something almost always do it badly at first; brilliant or at least competent performance is only achieved through raw persistence, coupled with the belief that improvement will happen. What people are able to do as beginners is far less important than whether they try hard and keep learning every day.

Decades of research by University of Florida's Anders Ericsson show that experts and superstars—at least in every endeavor where measurement is possible—act a lot like golf superstar Tiger Woods. By the time Tiger was 6 years old, he was playing golf almost every day and was coached by a skilled pro, Rudy Duran, from ages 4 to 12. Ericsson's research in dozens of domains reveals a similar story—exceptional performance doesn't happen without approximately 10 years of nearly daily, deliberate practice, for about four hours a day, by people who somehow (e.g., coaching, skilled peers or competitors, or books) have access to the best techniques. This 10-year rule holds in every domain he studied—chess, medicine, auditing, programming, bridge, physics, juggling, dance, and music.[28]

Once achieved, exceptional performance can't be maintained without relentless effort either. Dean Keith Simonton shows that in everything from science to the arts the most renowned geniuses—Mozart, da Vinci, Picasso, Einstein, and Darwin—don't have a higher success rate than their ordinary contemporaries. They simply *do more* than others. Everyone has heard of Charles Darwin's *Origin of Species*, but few know of his next book, a narrow and unheralded study of orchids. Simonton also shows that geniuses don't have hot streaks—the periods when they produce the most successes are those when they also produce the most failures.[29]

Practice and effort also counts for surgeons. Faculty in teaching hospitals notice a gifted resident now and then, someone, in surgeon Atul Gawande's words, "who picks up complex manual skills unusually quickly, sees the operative field as a whole, notices trouble before it happens." Yet medical school faculty believe that practice, not natural talent, is required to become a great surgeon, to "be boneheaded enough to stick at practicing this one difficult thing day and night for years on end." Gawande tells us that during his interviews for surgical residencies no one asked him to sew, tested his dexterity, or ever checked if he had steady hands.[30]

What is true for individuals is also true for organizations, groups, and teams. Exceptional performance depends heavily on experience and effort. No matter how gifted (or ordinary) team members are to start out, the more experience they have working together, the better their teams do. Think of the U.S. women's national soccer team, which has won numerous championships including two of the four women's World Cups and two of the three Olympic women's tournaments held to date. The team certainly has had enormously talented players, including Mia Hamm, Brandi Chastain, Julie Foudy, and Joy Fawcett. Yet every team member, including recently retired superstar Mia Hamm, will tell you that the most important factors in their success were the communication, mutual understanding, respect, and ability to work together that developed during the dozen or so years that the stable core group played together. Quantitative research on team effectiveness has demonstrated the power of such joint experience in every setting examined, including string quartets, surgical teams, student groups, top management teams, and airplane cockpit crews.[31] The sole exception is a study of R&D teams. These teams continued getting more and more productive during their first four years or so, but their output then slipped unless they brought in new members and had contact with outsiders—so old teams eventually go stale unless they bring in new ideas.[32]

Experienced teams perform better, because over time members come to trust each other more, communicate more effectively, and learn to blend each other's diverse skills, strengths, and weaknesses. Even a little experience together helps: a disproportionately high percentage of mistakes made during commercial airlines flights happen early in the typically 72-hour stint that a cockpit team spends together. The National Transportation Safety Board's study of incidents (serious mistakes and errors in flights, short of a crash) found that 73 percent happened the first day that crews were together, and fully 44 percent happened on crews' first flights.[33] And teams that have a lot of experience together gain a huge advantage. Professors Kathleen Eisenhardt and Claudia Schoonhoven conducted a study of 98 (of the 102) semiconductor firms founded in the United States between 1978 and 1985. They discovered that when a founding team's members had worked together before (plus had more industry experience and larger teams), firms enjoyed greater financial success in their first two years. This performance advantage became increasingly stronger during the third, fourth, fifth, and sixth years after a company was founded.[34]

These studies all suggest that the "talent mind-set" is dangerous because it treats talent as something fixed. This mind-set causes people to believe that it just isn't worth trying hard because they—or the people they lead—are naturally smart or not, and there is little if anything anyone can do about it. Yet raw cognitive ability—at least performance on tests that measure it—isn't nearly as difficult to enhance as many people think. When people believe they can get smarter, they do. *But*—and this is *very important*—when people believe that cognitive ability is difficult or impossible to change, they don't get smarter.

A series of studies by Columbia University's Carol Dweck shows that when people believe their IQ level is unchangeable, "they become too focused on being smart and looking smart rather than on challenging themselves, stretching and expanding their skills, becoming smarter."[35] Dweck finds that most people believe either that intelligence is fixed *or* that it can be improved through effort and practice. People who see intelligence as fixed believe statements like "if you are really smart at something, you shouldn't have to work hard at it," don't take remedial classes to repair glaring deficiencies, avoid doing things they are not already skilled at because it makes them look dumb, and derive less pleasure from sustained effort and commitment.[36] After all, they believe, if you have to work hard at things, it means you aren't that smart.

Dweck concludes that when people believe they are born with natural and unchangeable smarts, it causes them to learn less over time. They don't bother to keep learning new things and improving old skills, and even when they do try, they don't enjoy it. But people who believe that intelligence is malleable keep getting smarter and more skilled at what they already can do, and are willing to learn new things that they do badly at first.

This research means that your theories of performance and ability become self-fulfilling. If you believe that ability is fixed and communicate this to the people you lead, they will see their performance as an opportunity to judge their competence in terms of where they fall in the distribution of immutable intelligence. If by contrast, you—and they—believe that performance and ability are malleable, they will see tasks as learning opportunities, not tests that determine if they are preordained to be good or bad at something. These findings also mean if you believe that only 10 percent or 20 percent of your people can ever be top performers, and use forced rankings to communicate such expectations in your company, then only those anointed few will probably achieve superior performance.

This research explains why Southwest Airlines tells new employees that they are the "cream, cream, cream of the crop." Southwest is selective about who it hires, but by believing that everyone is capable of the highest performance levels, and having a system that makes it possible, it turns that belief into reality over and over again.

Great Systems Are Often More Important Than Great People

People need to share what they know, coordinate with others, and understand where their jobs fit in because organizations, or networks of organizations, are often complex systems that only can perform well when the pieces mesh together well. People's performance depends on the resources they have to work with, including the help they get from colleagues, and the infrastructure that supports their work. Wide-ranging research on software development, airlines, the air traffic control system, oil refineries, nuclear power plants, aircraft carriers, NASA, and the automobile industry show it is impossible for even the most talented people to do competent, let alone brilliant, work in a flawed system. Yet a well-designed system filled with ordinary—but well-trained—people can consistently achieve stunning performance levels.

NASA's space shuttle program provides a painful illustration. It is a classic case of smart, hardworking, and well-meaning people trapped in a system with such ingrained flaws that even a horrible accident, the *Challenger* shuttle explosion in 1986, didn't change it much. That is the conclusion reached by the Columbia Accident Investigation Board, a blue-ribbon panel charged with determining why the shuttle *Columbia* disintegrated upon reentry on February 1, 2003.[37] One chapter compares the *Columbia* accident with the *Challenger* explosion 17 years earlier. It begins with a comment by board member Sally Ride, the first American woman in space and a member of the Rogers Commission, the earlier task force that examined the *Challenger* accident. Ride concluded that there were remarkable echoes of the *Challenger* accident in the one that befell the *Columbia*.

The report lists one haunting parallel after another. Although nearly all of the personnel involved in the two accidents were different, the system and organizational culture were largely unchanged. The shuttle program was treated as a routine operation governed by budgets and schedules rather than an experimental operation, where it was unrealistic to adhere to predictable budgets and schedules—even though the Rogers Commission had demanded exactly that change. The focus on budget and schedule meant that *Challenger* and *Columbia* engineering teams were held to a dangerous decision rule when making "go, no-go" launch decisions. "[I]nstead of having to prove it was safe to fly, they were asked to prove it was unsafe to fly." NASA remained a dysfunctional bureaucracy where, rather than deferring to people with the greatest technical expertise, leaders believed that "an allegiance to hierarchy, procedure, and following the chain of command" decreased the odds of failure. People with greater prestige and power routinely ignored and stifled those with more expertise but less power and overturned their recommendations. In both tragedies, pressures to cut costs and meet schedules meant that NASA administrators outsourced so much of the shuttle design, manufacturing, and repair that they didn't know enough about its components to make informed decisions—they were managing a system they didn't understand.

The Columbia Accident Investigation Board concluded that the organizational system that caused *Columbia*'s failure must finally be fixed or "the scene is set for another accident." They add that, although people must always take responsibilities for their actions, "NASA's problems cannot be solved simply by retirements, resignations, or transferring personnel." In other words, the problem is the system, not the people.

Over 15 years of research in the auto industry also provides compelling evidence for the power of systems over individual talent in a business context. Wharton Business School's John Paul MacDuffie has combined quantitative studies of every automobile plant in the world with in-depth case studies to understand why some plants are more effective than others. MacDuffie has found that lean or flexible production systems, with their emphasis on teams, training, and job rotation, and their de-emphasis of status differences between employees, build higher quality cars at a lower cost.[38]

Toyota developed and still uses such practices, consistently achieving lower cost and higher quality than other companies—although some Honda plants give them a run for the money, and there are signs that General Motors is finally catching up. Toyota's success stems from its great system, not stunning individual talent. This starts at the top of the organization. One study showed that Toyota was the only major automobile company where a change in CEO had no effect on performance.[39] The system is so robust that changing CEOs at Toyota is a lot like changing lightbulbs; there is little noticeable effect between the old one and the new one.

Or consider the NUMMI (New United Motor Manufacturing) plant in Fremont, California, a Toyota–General Motors joint venture. When GM closed its Fremont plant in 1982, it was one of the worst plants in the country, producing cars with more defects and at a higher cost than nearly any other U.S. plant. Daily absenteeism was nearly 20 percent. Wildcat strikes and drug and alcohol abuse were rampant. Following an agreement between GM and Toyota, the plant was reopened by Toyota in 1985; 85 percent of the initial workforce was rehired from a pool of employees who worked at the old, awful plant, and who still belonged to the United Auto Workers union. Before the plant was reopened, workers were given extensive training in the Toyota Production System. Over 400 trainers were sent to NUMMI from Japan and over 600 workers were sent to Japan for training. The year the plant reopened, the 6,500 Novas it produced were among the lowest cost and highest quality cars made in the United States. Absenteeism was less than 3 percent. Toyota took a bunch of F players, retrained them, put them into a great system, and magically they became superstars. A better place made them much better people.[40]

Some will say that automobile manufacturing is not really a setting consistent with the current emphasis on knowledge work, and that NASA and the space shuttle represent a complex, interdependent system in which it would be difficult for a single individual to make a profound difference. So perhaps the best, most compelling, and most interesting study of the relationship between systems and the stars that are imported into them is by Boris Groysberg and his colleagues on the ultimate star system in business: investment analysts. Analysts are treated like stars, hired away at enormous salaries, and many achieve great media notoriety. Because analyst star quality can be measured by their listing in *Institutional Investor* magazine, and because their mobility is traceable, as is their performance, this is a revealing setting to study what happens when stars move. Groysberg found that after a company hires a star, bad things happen all around: "The star's performance plunges, there is a sharp decline in the functioning of the group or team the person works with, and the company's market value falls." In particular, "46% of the research analysts did poorly in the year after they left one company for another . . . their performance plummeted by an average of about 20% and had not climbed back to the old levels even five years later." Groysberg reports that even when stars do maintain or return to their prior status as top performers, they are unlikely to help their new employer over the long haul "because stars don't stay with organizations for long, despite the astronomical salaries firms pay to lure them away from rivals."[41]

Given all the evidence on the importance of systems, something that W. Edwards Deming and the quality movement emphasized for years, why do so many companies still place so much emphasis on getting and keeping great people and so little on building and sustaining great systems? A big part of the answer is that Western countries, like the United States, glorify rugged individualism so much that we make a cognitive error. We forget that history, organizational goals, rewards, and structure are potent causes of what people and organizations do. We give too much credit to individual heroes when organizations do things right and place too much blame on individual scapegoats when things go wrong. This perceptual blindness pervades the talent mind-set, and you see it in story after story in the business press, in corporate histories, and in advice given by gurus and management consultants.

This tendency to overattribute success and failure to individuals can be overcome, but to do so requires focusing on locating and dealing with systemic causes of performance issues. MIT Professors Nelson Repenning and John Sternman contrasted a successful and a failed process improvement effort in a manufacturing firm.[42] In the unsuccessful effort, undertaken to speed product development, managers attributed performance to individual skills and effort, not the system. Heroes and scapegoats were constantly held up as examples, but little learning and change occurred. Managers who missed targets were, in their words, "beat up" by executives. So they pressured workers to try ever harder, resulting in immediate productivity increases, which reinforced the misperception that problems were due to lazy people. But setbacks kept happening. The effort ended in failure despite more monitoring (one project manager was required to give hourly updates to his boss), more precise measures for pinpointing who was to blame, and tougher penalties for poor individual performance. Repenning and Sternman found that this effort failed largely because, rather than improving the system, managers focused on monitoring, motivating, and punishing people.

A different approach was used in the successful effort, which focused on improving cycle time. Managers consciously fought their natural tendency to focus on who deserved credit and blame, and instead worked on strengthening the system. A supervisor explained, "There are two theories. One says 'there is a problem, let's fix it.' The other says 'we've got a problem, someone is screwing up, let's go beat them up.' To make improvement, we could no longer embrace the second theory, we had to use the first."[43]

The Right Kind of Talent

This chapter provides numerous lessons about managing talent, but four main guidelines stand out. The content, and especially the spirit, of these guidelines clash with the talent mind-set advocated in many books and by many consultants, but are supported by more and better evidence.

1. Treat Talent as Something Almost Everyone Can Earn, Not That Just a Few People Own

John Wooden was the most successful college basketball coach ever. Over a 12-year period, his teams at the University of California at Los Angeles won the national championship 10 times—no other coach has ever come close to that record. Yet Wooden didn't define success in terms of winning or losing games or championships. To him, it was "knowing you gave your best effort to become the best of what you are capable."[44] This sounds corny, but the best evidence shows that superior performers believe in themselves, try hard, and learn constantly. Wooden believed that some players were more talented than others, and worked to recruit the best, but he believed that all those championships came from effort and teamwork, not just because his people had natural talent. Wooden asserts his definition is also superior to one based on wins and losses because it focuses on things people can control, not things they are powerless over.

The virtues of Wooden's philosophy become crystal clear when it comes to overcoming negative stereotypes. There is strong evidence that many African-Americans are subtly brainwashed to believe that intelligence is fixed and they have inherently lower ability than members of other races. The myth that African-Americans are hardwired to have lower IQs and they can't do anything about it has been perpetuated by everyone from Nobel Prize winner William Shockley to the academic psychologists who wrote the controversial *The Bell Curve*.[45] These stereotypes undermine academic performance even among African-American students who earn the best grades and test scores. Some fascinating research shows, however, that if you can convince people that smarts come from what people do, rather than what they were born with, performance improves markedly. In a study with Stanford undergraduates, randomly selected students were persuaded to believe that intelligence was malleable rather than fixed. Over two months later, they reported being more engaged in and enjoying the academic process more than students in control conditions. Most impressively, students persuaded to believe that smartness was malleable got better grades the next term, especially African-American students.[46]

Managers are not omnipotent. Performance is also driven by advice and support from peers and conscientiousness, and may be marred by personal problems like poor health and family problems. Unfortunately, managers may continue to lavish money, attention, and opportunities on anointed stars, while failing to notice (or admit) that others are performing better and learning faster. Entrenched beliefs can cause them to notice and remember the good things that their favorites do, and ignore and forget the bad. And if they notice their darlings aren't up to snuff, they might be too proud to confess they are wrong. A study of the National Basketball Association (NBA) by Barry Staw and Ha Hoang found, for example, that teams displayed irrational commitment to players they picked early in the college draft.[47] NBA teams pick the most widely heralded players first, followed by players thought to be increasingly less talented. Staw and Hoang's analysis of the 1980–1986 NBA drafts found that players picked earlier were given more playing time, were less likely to be traded to other teams, and had longer careers than lower-paid and less-hyped peers *regardless* of their actual performance. The NBA's head of public relations claimed "coaches play their best players and don't care what the person costs. Wins and losses are all that matters."[48] But Staw and Hoang showed that simply proclaiming and paying a player as a superstar can lead to biased judgments about his actual performance. So if you decide that one of your people is better than the rest, it can cause you to ignore and forget evidence that clashes with your beliefs—and that can be bad for your team or company.

2. The Law of Crappy Systems Trumps the Law of Crappy People

We've emphasized that managers, consultants, gurus, the press, and just about everyone else gives individuals too much credit and blame for organizational performance. This misguided faith in the omnipotence of saviors and villains is due largely to a cognitive error made by most people in Western countries. This fundamental attribution error was uncovered decades ago by psychologist Lee Ross.[49] It means that people place excessive weight on individual personality, preferences, and efforts when trying to explain what people (and groups and organizations) do and why they do it, and underplay the setting, culture, or system. This occurs partly because of how human perception operates. When we look at a situation, like a company, we *see* individuals—individuals acting, making decisions, doing great or awful things. The *context* in which this happens, the industry and general economic environment, the actions of all of those people we don't see, are less obvious and vivid. So it is not surprising that we overattribute actions and consequences to individuals rather than to the constraints under which they operate.

An insidious consequence of this fundamental error is something we have come to call the brain vacuum syndrome. This is where an organization hires one apparently brilliant person after another, and then places them in the same badly designed jobs in the same badly designed system. Each new incumbent seems smart and savvy until they start the job, and in a flash they start acting stupid. We first noticed this syndrome by watching friends who took jobs as deans and associate deans in business schools. These jobs come with much responsibility but little authority and few resources. Demands from students, faculty, staff, university administrators, companies, and alumni are intense, unrealistic, and in conflict. These jobs are hard, perhaps impossible, to do well. But that doesn't stop virtually every major constituency from focusing attention on the incumbent's personality and skills rather than the impossibility of doing the job. To most observers, it seems like every ounce of intelligence, common sense, and skill is sucked out of people the minute they become academic administrators. Much the same thing happened at NASA, where the Columbia Accident Investigation Board was dismayed to see that, although most of the people had been changed, the same system produced the same mistakes seen 17 years earlier—it was a system that made it difficult for smart people to do smart things.

Don't get us wrong. There are people who can't or won't do the jobs they are given. Incompetent people damage organizations and there will always be rotten apples who need to be retrained or moved to different jobs, and if all else fails, fired. But the law (or "rule") of Crappy People is a dangerous half-truth. We propose the "law of Crappy Systems" instead: bad systems do far more damage than bad people, and a bad system can make a genius look like an idiot. Try redesigning systems and jobs before you conclude that a person is "crappy." And if you keep hiring people who seem good, but turn crappy, stop blaming them and fix the system, at least if you want to turn off the brain vacuum.

3. Wisdom: The Most Crucial Talent?

Wisdom, not intelligence, is probably the most important talent for sustaining organizational performance. Organizations need people who think quickly and well when they work alone on problems with known correct answers—that is what IQ tests measure. But having people who know the limits of their knowledge, who ask for help when they need it, and are tenacious about teaching and helping colleagues is probably more important for making constant improvements in an organization, technical system, or body of knowledge. Also, as research on intelligence suggests, such wise actions help people become smarter and smarter.

Our first big clue about the wisdom-performance link came when we studied IDEO. We opened this chapter with founder and chairman David Kelley attributing IDEO's success to "hiring some smart people and getting out of the way." But that is only part of the story. The rest of the story is that Kelley can get out of the way because IDEO has intertwined cultural values, work practices, and rewards—a system—that requires little intervention from senior management. Kelley deserves much credit for designing and tinkering with this system during the 20-plus years that he served as CEO. Gwen Books, who was Kelley's assistant for over a decade, once told us, "David never stops thinking about IDEO, it is like a prototype he is constantly redesigning in his head." The genius of the design is that IDEO was, and still is under current CEO Tim Brown, largely run and policed by peers.

One of the main reasons that IDEO's system works so well is the attitude its people have toward knowledge. We mentioned this attitude of wisdom in chapter 2 as essential for practicing evidence-based management. Recall that wisdom is about "knowing what you know and knowing what you don't know." This attitude enables people to act on their (present) knowledge while doubting what they know, so they can do things *now*, but can keep learning along the way.[50] Wise people realize that all knowledge is flawed, that the only way to keep getting better at anything is to act on what you know now, and to keep updating.

Table 4-1 displays key elements of how wise (and unwise) people think and act in organizations. These elements stem from theory and research, but an episode at IDEO provides perhaps the best summary and explanation. Robert Sutton was sitting with two engineers, Larry Schubert and Roby

Stancel, who were talking about designing a device for Supercuts, a chain of hair salons that specializes in inexpensive, fast haircuts. They were talking about a device that could be attached to an electric razor to vacuum away cut hair. We were in front of Rickson Sun's workstation. Rickson looked mildly disturbed as he shut his sliding door to muffle the noise of our meeting—a futile gesture because his stylish cubicle had no roof and low walls. Rickson still looked a bit annoyed when he emerged minutes later to tell us that he had once worked on a product with key similarities to the device Larry and Roby were designing—a vacuum system that carried away the fumes from a hot scalpel that cauterized skin during surgery. He also brought out a report describing different kinds of plastic tubing sold by vendors. Larry Schubert commented, "Once Rickson realized he could help us, he had to do it, or he wouldn't be a good IDEO designer."

This simple episode illustrates the attitude of wisdom and why it enables people to keep learning and systems to keep getting better. Larry and Roby are smart people but knew that if they acted like know-it-alls, the design would suffer. They deferred to Rickson's knowledge. They reacted with a

TABLE 4-1

The attitude of wisdom: elements and antithesis in organizations

Wisdom *Acting with knowledge (while doubting what you know)*	Antithesis *Acting without knowledge or without doubting your knowledge; also inaction combined with endless analysis or, worse yet, no effort to learn what to do*
• Understanding and acknowledging the limits of your knowledge	• Acting like a know-it-all, not seeming to understand, accept, or acknowledge the limits of your knowledge
• Having humility about your knowledge	• Being arrogant or insecure about your knowledge
• Asking for and accepting help from others	• Not asking for, or refusing, help from others
• Giving help	• Not giving help, even when people clearly need your knowledge and skill
• Being curious—asking questions, listening, constantly striving to learn new things from the events, information, and people around you	• Lacking curiosity about people, things, and ideas; answering questions and talking only to show people how smart you are, without learning anything from them

kind of confident humility we saw many times at IDEO. When Rickson offered to help, they knew and he knew that to improve the design they had to listen to him, and follow up on his offer to help in the future.

IDEO may sound like a warm and fuzzy organization, but no matter how smart designers are, if they refuse to work cooperatively and act unwise, the consequences are swift and unpleasant. Every now and then, IDEO hires designers who act as if taking time to help others—and asking for help—aren't parts of their job. These selfish designers are the subjects of nasty gossip. They are teased, shunned, and given boring work. Some learn to be wise. Those who don't are treated as if they are invisible; there is no need to fire them, they realize that they better leave.

IDEO is just one organization that fosters and displays an attitude of wisdom. Others include Southwest Airlines, the Toyota Production System, and U.S. Navy aircraft carriers with remarkable safety records. Once you start studying organizations where people keep learning and moving forward, and where systems keep getting better instead of inducing the same errors again and again, you see the attitude of wisdom.

4. Encourage People to Be Noisy and Nosy—It Promotes Wisdom

Here is a trick question. Imagine that you just had a major operation and are given the choice: do you want to stay in a nursing unit that administers the wrong drug or the wrong amount, or forgets to give the right drug, about once every 500 patient days, or would you rather be in a unit that blunders 10 times as often? In the mid-1990s, Harvard Business School's Amy Edmondson was doing what she *thought* was a straightforward study of how leader and coworker relationships influence errors in eight nursing units. Edmondson, and the Harvard physicians funding her research, were flabbergasted when nurse questionnaires showed that the units with *best* leadership and *best* coworker relationships reported making *10 times more errors than the worst!*

Puzzled but determined to understand this finding, Edmondson brought in another researcher to observe these nursing units. Edmondson didn't tell this second researcher about her findings, so he wasn't biased. When Edmondson pieced together what this researcher observed with her findings, she realized that better units reported more errors because people felt psychologically safe to do so. In these units, nurses said "mistakes are natural and normal to document" and "mistakes are serious because of the toxicity of the drugs, so you are never afraid to tell the nurse manager." In the units where errors were rarely reported, nurses said things like "The environment is unforgiving, heads will roll." The physicians who helped sponsor her research changed their view of medical errors 180 degrees. They no longer saw errors as purely objective evidence, but partly as a reflection of whether people are learning from and admitting mistakes or trying to avoid blame and, in the process, possibly covering things up.

Edmondson and her colleagues have since done multiple studies on how hospitals, surgical teams, doctors, and nurses learn from problems and errors, which reveal much about talents and behaviors that promote wisdom. Especially pertinent is a study of nurses that examined 194 patient care failures, everything from problems caused by broken equipment to drug treatment errors. Edmondson and colleague Anita Tucker concluded that those nurses whom doctors and administrators saw as *most talented* unwittingly caused the same mistakes to happen over and over. These "ideal" nurses quietly adjust to inadequate materials without complaint, silently correct others' mistakes without confronting error-makers, create the impression that they never fail, and find ways to quietly do the job without questioning flawed practices. These nurses get sterling evaluations, but their silence and ability to disguise and work around problems undermine organizational learning. Rather than these smart silent types, hospitals would serve patients better if they brought in wise and noisy types instead.

Table 4-2 lists these talents of wisdom. All of these characteristics help people act on what they know, and keep improving their own skills, peers'

TABLE 4-2

The talents of wisdom: people who sustain organizational learning

Noisy complainers	Repair problems right away and then let every relevant person know that the system failed
Noisy troublemakers	Always point out others' mistakes, but do so to help them and the system learn, not to point fingers
Mindful error-makers	Tell managers and peers about their own mistakes, so that others can avoid making them too. When others spot their errors, they communicate that learning—not making the best impression—is their goal
Disruptive questioners	Won't leave well enough alone. They constantly ask why things are done the way they are done. Is there a better way of doing things?

Source: Based on research by Anita L. Tucker and Amy C. Edmondson.

skills, and organizational practices and procedures. The crux is, if you want better performance instead of the illusion of it, you and your people must tell everyone about problems you've fixed, point out others' errors so all can learn, admit your own errors, and never stop questioning what is done and how to do it better. These actions can annoy doctors and administrators—or any other authority figure—who prefer quiet and compliant underlings, but if we want organizations that do as much good and as little harm as possible, these talents are essential.[51]

Similar advice came from the Columbia Investigation Board, who emphasized that the risk of future accidents would be reduced if people felt safer to complain, point out mistakes and risks, and ask questions. They concluded:

> For both accidents there were moments when management's definition of risk might have been reversed were it not for the many missing signals—an absence of trend analysis, imagery data not obtained, concerns not voiced, information overlooked or dropped from meetings . . . [P]eople who are marginal and powerless in organizations may have useful information or opinions that they don't express. Even when these people are encouraged to speak, they find it intimidating to contradict a leader's strategy or a group consensus. Extra effort must be made to contribute all relevant information to discussions of risk.[52]

Prestige, Pride, and Performance

A couple years ago, one of us give a speech at a renowned (but declining) high-technology firm that used a forced-ranking system. They called it a stacking system. Managers were required to rank 20 percent of employees as A players, 70 percent as Bs, and 10 percent as Cs. Just as the *War for Talent* advises, they gave the lion's share of rewards to As, modest rewards to Bs, and fired the Cs. But in an anonymous poll, the firm's top 100 or so executives were asked which company practices made it difficult to turn knowledge into action. The stacking system was voted the worst culprit. This is not just one company's experience. A survey of more than 200 human resource professionals from companies employing more than 2,500 people by the Novations Group found that even though more than half of the companies used forced ranking, the respondents reported that forced ranking resulted in lower productivity, inequity and skepticism, negative effects on employee engagement, reduced collaboration, and damage to morale and mistrust in leadership.[53]

Research on the link between talent and organizational performance reveals why these findings aren't surprising. It is not that all employees deserve equal treatment. All human organizations, or for that matter, all mammal groups, have status hierarchies. Some members are valued, respected, and have great influence. Others are held in low esteem, shunned, and made powerless. Those at the top of the heap feel pride; those at the bottom feel shame. It would be impossible, and probably undesirable, for any leader to eliminate status differences. People who help the organization succeed deserve prestige, and those who help it fail deserve to be shunned. Figuring out who deserves a place at the top—and the bottom—of the pecking order, and how to get them where they deserve to be, is part of a manager's job.

But we can't find a shred of evidence that it is better to have just a few alpha dogs at the top and to treat everyone else as inferior. Rather, the best performance comes in organizations where as many people as possible are treated as top dogs. If you want people to keep working together and learning together, it is better to grant prestige to many rather than few, and to avoid big gaps between who gets the most and least rewards and kudos. A related, and equally crucial, lesson is that smart people are typically granted more prestige than they deserve, and wise people are granted less. Smartness is important, but wisdom is more crucial for fueling organizational (and individual) performance over the long haul.

We also can't find any evidence that organizations benefit from routinely firing people in the bottom 10 percent or 20 percent. If an organization selects and trains people right, and places them in an effective system, there is no reason why 10 percent or 20 percent would automatically become incompetent every year. On the other hand, research on maintaining group and organizational culture shows that stigmatizing and removing destructive misfits is crucial to organizational health. There are sound reasons for reserving the bottom rungs for people who never bother to learn new things, don't help others learn, or don't try to improve how the organization works. If reeducating them, or even ignoring and shaming them, doesn't change their ways, it is probably best to expel them. Getting rid of such people signals that their behavior is destructive and unnecessary.

5

Do Financial Incentives Drive Company Performance?

THERE'S A LOT OF MONEY in financial incentives. Type the word *compensation* into Amazon.com and you get more than 47,000 book entries, with some 43,000 entries associated with the word *incentive*. Hordes of people are clearly interested in reading—and writing—about compensation and incentives. There are large compensation consulting companies such as Towers Perrin, Hewitt Associates, Mercer, and Watson Wyatt, plus scores of small ones, that make good money selling advice about how to design incentive systems that attract, retain, and motivate employees. Human resource executives devote huge chunks of time to designing pay systems and dealing with unusual cases and complaints from employees, contract workers, and consultants about compensation issues. Compensation committees of boards of directors devote vast energy to installing the right incentives for senior executives. These efforts typically involve "aligning the interests of executive officers with the long-term interests of the company's stockholders."[1]

These tremendous efforts to "get the pay system right" are guided by several deeply held, widely shared, and intertwined beliefs and assumptions about what motivates people in the workplace. Incentives are seen as the primary tool for aligning individual behavior with organizational objectives, because without effective incentives people would do nothing—the technical term from the economics literature is *shirking*, and the assumption is that work is aversive so people must be bribed to expend any effort. Or if they did expend effort, people are presumed to be almost certain to do things that undermine organizational or management goals. Underlying all this is the belief that people work primarily for money, and that because motivation is the most important factor affecting individual task performance, financial incentives are the most important of all motivators. It follows that getting the incentive scheme right is critical for organizational success, for both motivating and aligning behavior. There are hundreds of books on pay in organizations that make exactly these points and emphasize the critical role of pay in determining organizational performance. The unremarkable and seemingly obvious assumption is that "basic to the effective functioning of any organization is its pay and reward system."[2]

This emphasis on the importance of financial incentives is scarcely new. It goes back at least to the time of Frederick Taylor, the founder of scientific management at the turn of the 20th century. Taylor wrote in 1911, "What workers want most from their employers beyond anything else is high wages."[3] In his classic pig iron shoveling experiments, financial inducements based on productivity were used to persuade workers to accept scientific management's prescribed methods. Pretty much the same view of financial incentives is also seen in many well-regarded economics theories, as well as influential psychological theories. In economics, "a cornerstone of the theory in personnel economics is that workers respond to incentives . . . it is a given that paying on the basis of output will induce workers to supply more output."[4] In psychology, Skinnerian learning theory argues that behavior is a function of its consequences, so if you want more of some behavior, like hard work, that behavior needs to be reinforced. And most operant conditioning theorists who study and intervene in organizational settings treat financial rewards as the most potent form of reinforcement.[5] Decision-making theory makes somewhat more complex assumptions about human behavior than reinforcement theory. But that theory also presumes that people choose actions—or at least want to choose actions—on the basis of the expected probability of obtaining valued outcomes.[6] People generally desire more money, so if they believe that working harder will result in getting more money, they will expend the effort. In short, the belief that financial incentives are the most powerful drivers of organizational performance is seen in a host of enormously influential and widely held theories about human behavior in work settings.

The problem is that these basic assumptions about financial incentives and how they work are just that—assumptions. They are usually taken on faith rather than tested or even subjected to critical thought. The result is that companies build complicated and expensive incentive schemes that routinely fail to produce the behavior that leaders want or ever intended. But since companies don't base their designs on sound evidence or logic, when they try to "fix" the system with "new" solutions that seem different on the surface, they often end up with solutions (and problems) that are nearly identical to the old ones. Or they change from one misguided plan to another with remarkably little learning along the way. This chapter provides ideas, data, and perspectives to help you think constructively about ways to stop, or at least reduce, the problems that so many financial incentive systems inflict. We do so by examining the evidence and underlying logic that form the foundation of financial incentive systems.

What Incentives Can Do

There are three primary avenues through which incentives can enhance organizational performance, or if badly designed or misapplied, damage performance. First, financial incentives could motivate more effort—a *motivational effect*. This is the effect usually sought and assumed when companies and consultants recommend instituting pay-for-performance schemes—people will work harder to achieve a greater financial reward. Increasing people's motivation can't affect their ability (at least in the short run), only their effort. So interventions that focus on increasing effort presume, by definition, that if people would only try harder, they'd get better results. Yet interventions aimed at increasing motivation through incentives can be effective only if people have enough information to perform their work effectively and if other organizational systems and technologies are not the primary roadblocks to poor performance. Compensation consultants rarely acknowledge these limits of motivation, perhaps even to themselves. But most of the interventions they recommend presume that greater effort alone will bolster performance—without system redesign, information sharing, or upgrading people's skills.

Interventions that use money to drive motivation also presume that job performance is under the control of the people who are given the incentives, and that individuals' actions then drive organizational performance. But swings in performance aren't always under an executive's or an employee's control. Take the case of a senior executive from Florida Power and Light, who told us, while attending a Stanford executive program, that his compensation was based on the profitability of the utility. The utility's profitability, since in the short run most of its costs and rates were fixed, depended mostly on the amount of electricity sold, and the amount of electricity sold depended mostly on the temperature. The hotter the summer in Florida, the more power was sold, and the more profitable was the utility. That summer was a particularly hot one in Florida, so the executive got a big boost in pay during the month that he spent at the Stanford Executive Program in California. This executive noted that this incentive system made no sense—unless you believed he could control the weather in Florida.

Incentives are effective motivators only when certain assumptions hold—including the idea that differences in employee ability and knowledge do produce performance differences—and when performance outcomes are under the control of people who receive the incentives. If these assumptions don't hold—performance outcomes aren't controllable and employee efforts don't make a difference—then the motivation that comes from greater financial incentives can't and won't positively affect performance. Instead, financial incentives can undermine motivation and performance as a result of the frustration, unhappiness, and dismay that people experience when working harder in a system that makes it impossible for them to effect performances—even when they are getting rich at the moment, like that executive from Florida. This point about the futility of expecting better performance just by trying to bolster individual motivation has been made repeatedly by W. Edwards Deming and other writers in the quality movement, but is still forgotten by many executives and their advisers.[7]

Second, financial incentives can provide people with information about what the organization values and what its priorities are, an *informational effect*. In a world where people can't possibly give equal attention to every dimension of their jobs, and where companies often send conflicting messages about priorities—for example, pay attention to quality or customer service but also cut costs and increase efficiency—people tend look to the pay system to figure out what really matters to senior leadership. When Continental Airlines undertook a cultural and service transformation in the 1990s, going from worst to first in on-time performance in a year, the company paid each employee $65 for every month that Continental ranked in the top half of the Department of Transportation rankings for on-time performance. Not only did this financial reward motivate people to try harder, it signaled to employees that on-time performance was something Continental actually cared about, as did posting monitors that displayed the proportion of flights arriving on time each day. Research on customer service shows that sending clear signals can have powerful effects. One analysis of airline on-time performance reported that whether or not airline executives seemed to care about flying on time was among the most critical differentiating factors in whether airlines actually flew on time.[8]

The third way that differential financial rewards may drive performance is that they presumably attract the right kind of people and repel the wrong kind, a *selection effect*. Think of recruits who face the choice between working for one company that offers performance-based pay and another one that offers pay based more on seniority. The idea is that motivated people who are driven to outdo their peers will choose workplaces where their superior performance will translate into more money in their pockets. And people who are less able or motivated will seek out less competitive workplaces where their lower performance will be penalized less. One argument that you hear about government or other quasi-civil service systems that don't reward performance is that they can't attract the best and most ambitious people; their failure to offer differential financial incentives undermines the ability to attract and retain the best—presumably the most financially ambitious—people. Stanford economist Edward Lazear believes that this selection effect is as important to organizational performance as any effect on motivation. "Pay that is only mildly related to output can be very powerful in sorting workers and providing information."[9]

As you will see in this chapter, each of these three mechanisms operates in every organization, but each also has unanticipated effects on the people it is meant to motivate, inform, and attract—effects that dampen performance with alarming frequency. Even when executives have the best of intentions, take great effort to study best practices, and bring in top compensation consultants, many still end up with pay systems that undermine performance—which makes the idea that financial incentives drive company performance a particularly dangerous half-truth. Bad compensation systems are so damaging, in large part, because people use pay as a signal of whether the organization values them—their status and importance—and to figure out whether or not they are being treated fairly. Status and fairness both matter *a lot* to people. So making mistakes in pay can cause people to withhold discretionary effort, ideas, and information—and can fuel unwanted turnover. Financial incentives have a potent impact on performance, but not necessarily in the positive ways that executives and their advisers anticipate.

The Growth in Incentive Pay

There is no question that incentive pay is now ubiquitous and that the use of incentive-based pay systems has grown in recent decades, spreading from the United States to companies around the world. Even as early as the 1980s, surveys showed that over 80 percent of employees worked in organizations with merit pay plans, in which at least some employees received raises based on their rated performance.[10] The prevalence of incentive or contingent pay has increased at all organizational levels during the last 15 years, with incentive schemes such as bonuses becoming particularly pervasive at more senior executive levels.[11] Hewitt Associates, a compensation consulting firm, reported that in 1991, 51 percent of the companies participating in its salary survey offered at least one pay-for-performance plan. By 2003, that number had increased to 77 percent, after peaking at 81 percent in 2001. And 50 percent of the companies in 2003 had variable compensation plans that covered virtually every employee.[12] Nor is this trend confined to the United States. A 2003 Hewitt survey of 115 Canadian organizations found that 81 percent offered pay-for-performance plans, up from 43 percent in 1994.[13]

There is also growing interest in using merit pay in noncorporate settings such as schools and government, places that have traditionally not used contingent pay. In Albuquerque, New Mexico, garbage truck drivers were put on an incentive pay plan, and more than $4 million was paid out to the 180 unionized drivers over a six-year period.[14] Denver schoolteachers are subject to a pay-for-performance system that rewards them for their students' progress, while in Houston, every school employee receives a bonus based on students' test scores. In Florida, school districts are now required to create salary systems that reward teachers for student performance.[15] In the U.S. government in 2003, the administration proposed having the Office of Personnel Management administer a $500 million human capital performance fund to allow federal agencies to institute pay-for-performance practices. And the General Accounting Office issued a report praising governmental efforts to rely more heavily on financial incentives.[16] In this spirit, the Office of Homeland Security unveiled a new incentive system that did away with traditional seniority-based pay in January 2005. Office of Personnel Management Director Kay Coles James boasted to reporters, "We really have created a system that rewards performance, not longevity . . . It can truly serve as a model for the rest of the federal government."[17] The presumption is that merit pay fixes performance problems, so incentive pay becomes a cure for any organization that might have them, including schools or government agencies.

Why Money Is Used So Much: We Think Others Are
Motivated by Money, Even If We Are Not

The growing use of variable pay and other financial incentives and the belief in their effectiveness stems in part from something that researcher Chip Heath calls an "extrinsic incentives bias." This is the tendency to overestimate how much employees care about extrinsic job features such as pay and to underestimate how much employees are motivated by intrinsic job features like being able to make decisions or having meaningful work.[18] Heath's research shows that individuals believe that *others are motivated by money, even as they know that they are much less so.*

- A survey by Kaplan Educational Centers of almost 500 prospective lawyers preparing to take the Law School Admissions Test revealed that 64 percent of the respondents said they were pursuing a legal career because it was intellectually appealing or because they were interested in the law, but only 12 percent thought their peers were similarly motivated. Instead, 62 percent thought that others were pursuing a legal career for the financial rewards.

- In data collected from surveys over a 25-year period, respondents to the General Social Survey (a representative sample of people in the United States) rated "important work" that "gives a feeling of accomplishment" as the most important aspect of their jobs, with pay typically ranking third. But when people were asked about others, 73 percent thought that large differences in pay were necessary to get people to work hard and 67 percent agreed with the statement that people would not be willing to take on extra responsibility at work unless they were paid extra.[19]

Heath conducted an experiment demonstrating that people consistently overestimated how much other people were motivated by pay. Heath found that "participants listed an extrinsic incentive in the top position for themselves only 22% of the time, but they predicted that the [customer service representatives] would list an extrinsic incentive in the top slot 85% of the time."[20] Participants in the experiment would have done a much better job predicting the motivation of others—and thereby earning a reward for their accuracy—had they simply extrapolated their own feelings about the importance of financial incentives to others.

Other evidence bolsters Heath's findings that management places excessive faith in the motivational magic of extrinsic rewards. A Watson Wyatt

2003–2004 survey of 1,700 high-performing employees—as identified by their employers—from 16 organizations found that these top performers rated a desire to maintain a positive reputation as the most important factor in their motivation. These top performers ranked being appreciated second, belief that the work is important third, interesting assignments fourth, and expecting a significant financial reward *ninth* out of 10 items.[21] A survey of 205 executives from diverse industries found that 68 percent reported their companies had executive bonus plans because senior management believed that such rewards would motivate executives.[22] These same executives reported, however, that they did not make daily business decisions based on how such decisions would affect either their bonus or those of their people.

Organizations ought to offer members sufficient—and correct—inducements to motivate and direct their efforts, and to attract the right people. Heath's experiments and other survey data "suggest that lay theories of motivation may hinder this process" by overemphasizing financial incentives and underemphasizing the importance of work and its intrinsic interest.[23] Heath's findings and the other evidence we've presented help explain why managers continue to rely too much on extrinsic rewards—they have flawed assumptions about how others are motivated. Moreover, even when incentive systems do work more or less as intended, we may not like the consequences.

Incentives Signal What Is Important, but the Signals May Be Blunt

Incentives and measurements provide information, not just motivation, and the effects of the information alone on motivation can be pronounced. A classic demonstration of the power of external reinforcements was a study in the early 1970s at Emery Air Freight, a freight forwarder. Before the development of large package companies with their own airplanes, freight forwarders picked up packages and shipped them on airlines. They got a better rate to the extent the packages were placed in larger containers that were easier to handle. So Emery management wanted employees to put as many packages as possible into larger containers to cut freight costs. The company conducted a performance audit and found that, although managers thought they were using larger containers 90 percent of the time it was feasible, only 45 percent of the eligible packages were actually being put into larger containers.[24] So the company announced a new program that provided rewards such as praise—not financial rewards—for improvement. On the *first day*, the proportion of packages placed in the larger containers increased to 95 percent in about 70 percent of the company's offices.[25] The speed of this overwhelming improvement suggests that the change in performance derived not just from the rewards that were offered, but also from the information provided that the current performance level was poor and this action—consolidating shipments—was important to the company. The intervention showed people how well they were doing, whereas before they didn't have such information. It also helped people realize the importance of this specific dimension of their job. The Emery Air Freight experience demonstrates that letting people know how they are doing and what is important can have substantial effects on their behavior, even in the absence of financial incentives.

Unfortunately, signals from financial incentive systems about what behaviors the organization values are not always what the company may desire or need. One day in August 2003, Jeffrey Pfeffer and his wife Kathleen went to look for a new car. They were inclined to buy a Toyota, but had heard good things about the Mazda 6 and the Nissan Altima, so they wanted to test drive all three on the same afternoon. They first went to Putnam Toyota in Burlingame, California, where they were greeted by a typical, commission-based car salesman. When they explained what they were doing—test driving three vehicles to decide which they would choose—the salesman immediately concluded, correctly, that they were unlikely to purchase a car that afternoon. He didn't want to waste his time with Jeffrey and Kathleen because he was paid on commission—a signal that the company believed his primary responsibility was to move metal. So the salesman sent them to the garage where the company's new cars were housed, about a block away. When Jeffrey and Kathleen arrived, they learned that they needed a salesperson if they were going to test drive a car. This salesman achieved his goal—to get rid of two customers who were not ready to buy immediately. When Jeffrey and Kathleen finally decided to purchase a Toyota Camry, needless to say they did not return to Putnam. They bought it from Toyota 101 in Redwood City, California—a dealership where the salespeople are not paid on commission and the emphasis is on customer service.

Putnam Toyota and many other organizations use pay systems to signal what is important, and the signals are not completely misguided. Car dealers want salespeople to generate revenue and not stand around and waste time. So the Putnam salesman did *precisely* what the pay system signaled him to do—he didn't waste time with people who had a low probability of generating revenue *immediately*.

There is just one problem. The many companies that use similarly crude or blunt incentive systems *aren't* interested *solely* in maximizing revenues during a single customer encounter. Having invested in advertising and other promotions to get people into the stores in the first place, their leaders are interested in maximizing sales over long periods and, even better, building customer loyalty so that less marketing and advertising expenses are required to get people to return to their establishments. But using the wrong incentive systems sends employees signals that clash with the companies' overall objectives.

Consider another example. Marshall Industries was a $500 million electronics distributor before a major transformation and cultural overhaul turned it into a $2 billion competitive powerhouse in a few years. Prior to the transformation, which entailed eliminating sales commissions and other individual bonuses, people looked to the incentive system to learn what was important and behaved accordingly. Here are some of the bad results listed by then-CEO Robert Rodin:

- Our salespeople would ship ahead of schedule to make a number or win a prize. Our customers, on the other hand, were insisting on delivery in a window of one day early to zero days late.

- We held customer returns. We had to make sure that the returns coming in did not get counted against sales in the period for which we were trying to hit the numbers. So, if a customer returned items, sometimes our salespeople would put them in the trunks of their cars.

- We opened bad credit accounts. Any order was a good order as far as a salesperson paid on gross profit was concerned.[26]

Financial incentives do signal what is important and do focus people's attention on those dimensions. But this is both good and bad news. It is good news in that incentives can be powerful in shaping behavior, but it is bad news if management doesn't fully understand the implications and subtleties of the behavior shaped. The problem is that the typical financial incentive system is too blunt and narrow a way of communicating what is important, unless the company has a very simple business model—where one or just a few behaviors matter. Incentive systems do have to be simple to be effective; people can only keep a relatively small number of things in their heads at any one time, so incentive schemes with multiple criteria are too complex to send straightforward signals that guide behavior. But simple signals cause damage when there are multiple, interrelated dimensions of individual performance—

when judgment and wisdom are required to figure out the best ways to enhance overall organizational performance.

Incentives Motivate—Sometimes the Wrong Behavior

There is no question that financial incentives motivate people and, under the right conditions, can drive big increases in performance and productivity. Take, for example, Safelite Glass headquartered in Columbus, Ohio, one of the largest installers of automobile glass in the United States. Stanford economist Ed Lazear did a statistically sophisticated, detailed study of Safelite over 19 months when, under a new CEO and president, the company gradually moved from using hourly wages to paying employees based on how many windshields they installed.[27] Because the company carefully tracked output per employee with a sophisticated computer system, and because some employees worked under both payment systems, Lazear obtained precise estimates of the effects of the new variable pay system on individual productivity and on turnover.

Lazear estimated that there was a 44 percent gain in productivity—the number of windshields installed per day per worker—under the new incentive system. He further estimated that approximately half of the gain in productivity resulted from the same employees doing more work under the new system.[28] Lazear also found that the effects of increased productivity persisted, actually increasing over time, which rules out the explanation that the effect was simply due to a shift in payment scheme from one system to another, a novelty or *Hawthorne effect*, which would diminish over time. Instead, "after workers are switched to piece rates, they seem to learn ways to work faster or harder as time progresses."[29] Part of the productivity effects came from retaining and attracting better employees. Turnover at Safelite was high—close to 4 percent per month. After the new incentive system was installed, the average employee hired had higher productivity than those already in the plant and turnover was higher among the least productive people. The average wage went up about 7 percent, much less than the increase in productivity, so the cost per unit declined from an average of $44.43 under the hourly wage system to $35.24 under the piece rate system.[30]

Several characteristics of Safelite make it especially suitable for a successful variable pay or incentive system. First, the task was readily learned and, more important, involved little or no interdependence with other employees. It is possible that people learned from each other and shared tips on how to do the job more efficiently, but the task itself was done by one person working alone. Individual incentives did not undermine teamwork because there wasn't any need for teamwork. Second, it was easy to both measure and monitor quality, so employees could not simply work faster at the expense of doing a decent job. If a windshield broke, it was easy to identify the culprit. The company required the installer "to reinstall the windshield on his own time" and to "pay the company for the replacement glass before any paying jobs are assigned to him."[31] Third, the company already had a sophisticated computerized work monitoring system, so the incentive system did not require new innovations for measuring employee productivity. And finally, employee goals were unambiguous and one-dimensional—to install windshields as quickly as possible, while doing a job of sufficient quality to keep the windshield from falling out or breaking.

Lazear is careful to explain why this setting was so ideal for using individual incentives: "output is easily measured, quality problems are readily detected, and blame is assignable."[32] Unfortunately, few of the numerous other organizations that have implemented incentive systems have been as thoughtful about the scope conditions that make such systems effective. The literature is littered with tales of disastrous implementations, which often occur not because incentives *don't* work, but instead because they work *too well*. Given an incentive to achieve some outcome, people do take that incentive seriously and work hard to obtain the goal that will earn them the financial reward. The problem is that most organizations have more complex, multidimensional objectives and optimizing on just one thing creates other difficulties.

Consider a few of many possible examples. In Albuquerque, New Mexico, the city decided to put garbage truck drivers on an incentive system: if drivers finished their routes early, they could go home and still receive pay for their full eight-hour shift. The program was instituted to cut down on overtime by encouraging drivers to finish their prescribed routes on time or even early. This meant that "a driver who completes a route in five hours would get five hours of regular pay plus three hours of incentive pay."[33] But an audit discovered numerous problems. "Fifteen of the twenty-four drivers who received the most incentive pay in 2002 consistently went to the landfill in trucks over the legal weight limit." Plus there was evidence that the incentive to complete the routes early resulted in more preventable traffic accidents. Some drivers missed picking up all of the garbage on their routes and many were reluctant to stop using a truck that might need repairing. The audit of the program concluded, "the unintended results of the incentive program could be an increase in safety risks, cost of operations, legal liabilities, and customer dissatisfaction."[34]

In New Orleans, once the murder capital of the United States, the police felt pressure to make the city safer. The city instituted a program under which "districts that showed improvement in crime statistics got awards that could lead to bonuses and promotions, while districts that didn't faced cutbacks and firings."[35] To further encourage improvement, districts were put in competition with each other to see which one could cut crime the most. It turns out there are at least two ways to cut serious crime—by reducing the incidence of serious crime *or* by reclassifying crimes that do occur as less serious. Faced with pressure and incentives to cut serious crime, you can imagine what happened. In the First District, the top cops cut serious crime by simply reclassifying crimes. An "investigation found that in the last year and a half in that one district, 42 percent, nearly half of all serious crimes, were classified as minor offenses and never fully investigated."[36] The result: when the reclassifications came to light, the police chief fired five senior officers, including the district commander, for falsifying crime statistics.

These fudging problems aren't confined to the public sector. An analysis of the overbooking of oil reserves by Royal Dutch/Shell that resulted in the resignation of the chairman of the company and its head of exploration, followed shortly by the departure of the chief financial officer, pointed the blame at incentives. Shell compensated its executives with stock options, so there were incentives to keep the stock price up. One way of maintaining the stock price was to overstate reserves. "In a 2001 report, Houston consultants Rose & Associates noted the pressure on managers at publicly traded energy companies 'to push the envelope of credibility in an effort to buoy investor confidence and thus increase stock value.' Among other things, the consultants pegged the overbooking to incentive programs that offered bonuses for big reserve estimates."[37]

The lesson here is a variant on an old adage: be careful what you pay for, you may actually get it. When the tasks that people do are even modestly complex, it is often impossible to think up every possible way that they might achieve those goals. And even if it were feasible to imagine every contingency, the long and convoluted list of rules and conditions would render the system incomprehensible and ineffective. Financial incentives are best applied when there are simple, clear, agreed-upon measures that make cheating almost impossible, or perhaps, when the powers that be care only about optimizing performance on those measures, regardless of what it takes for people to hit the numbers.

Incentive Systems Do Attract Talent—Often the Wrong Kind

There is little doubt that the level of financial incentives offered and the system used—for instance, individual pay for performance—attracts different people to different organizations. Incentive systems are a big part of an organization's culture. Some organizations explicitly select for cultural fit, so they recruit people who fit their values, including those reflected in the incentive system. Even for those organizations that are less systematic about selecting for fit, prospective employees will try to determine if they are likely to succeed in the company—after all, who wants to work at a place where they will fail? So candidates use the incentive system as an important way of diagnosing the organization's or occupation's culture and values. There are occupations—investment banking among others—where most people are in it mostly for the money. A few years back, Pfeffer listened to videotapes of focus groups conducted anonymously for a large San Francisco law firm in which 2-Ls, law students between their second and third year of law school, discussed the advantages of working for a particular firm that paid well. But the firm also required long hours and provided poor feedback and supervision for associates, as is typical of many large law firms. The students discussed working at the firm mostly in terms of the high salaries that would make paying back their student loans easier and faster. So Lazear's findings about which existing employees left Safelite Glass and which new employees took jobs are not anomalous; incentive systems and the amount of financial incentives offered do attract different people to different companies.

This finding does not, however, answer the question of whether you should *want* people who come to your organization because of the financial incentives you offer. Years ago, when James Treybig was CEO of Tandem Computers (a company since merged into Ungermann-Bass), the company would not tell people their salaries before they were hired, even at the most senior executive levels. After extensive recruiting and many meetings, people would be told (if it were true) that there was a good fit between them and the company and that there was every expectation that they would be successful at Tandem and that the company wanted them to join. If they asked about their salary, they would be told that Tandem paid a competitive salary and offered a competitive financial package. If people insisted on knowing their precise salary, they would *not* be offered the job. To paraphrase Treybig, "if people come for money, they will leave for money." He recognized that financial incentives are the most fungible resource, available to almost any organization. People who came only for the pay package could be lured away by the next company that offered a little bit more, and since turnover was disruptive, Tandem wanted people who would have a greater likelihood of staying with the organization. Treybig and Tandem believed that if people joined because they liked the work, the business, the management, the culture, and their coworkers, they would be more likely to stay than if they came just for the money.

This lesson about joining an organization for the right reasons is also relevant for the law firm just described. The students in the focus groups were quite clear that they would stay with the firm until their student loans were paid off or greatly reduced, and then leave. And, indeed, this particular law firm lost more than 50 percent of its associates by the end of their third year of employment, which was precisely the point at which they had enough experience to become profitable for the firm.

Contrary to some popular lore, the hardest-working people are often those working in the government. Because they are doing their jobs out of a sense of service and to make a difference, you often see more, not less, commitment and effort among public service employees.[38] Our colleague James Baron makes a similar point about not necessarily wanting to rely on financial incentives when teaching his MBA course on human resource management. He poses the following hypothetical question to the students (and you can answer it for yourself). If you had a choice, when confronting a serious, possibly life-threatening illness, of going to see one of two doctors, which would you choose: (a) a doctor who had entered medicine primarily to make a lot of money, or (b) a doctor who had entered medicine because he or she was interested in the subject matter and had a desire to serve people? Think about which doctor you would choose and why. Not surprisingly, the majority of the MBA students, who are more oriented toward financial incentives than most people, choose the second doctor. The reasons the MBAs provide are often consistent with the sociological concept of *professionalization*—that is, a professional is an individual who puts the clients' interests first, who has an obligation to do right and do well by that client, regardless of that professional's own self-interest. We expect doctors and other professionals to take our interests and needs into account, and not to think only or even mostly about what will enrich them. We want professionals serving us to choose treatments or courses of action based on the best available evidence for efficacy, not what will make them the most money in the short term.

Even in nonprofessional contexts, there may be good reasons why you should be cautious about hiring people who join your organization only or mostly for the money—especially when employees are in high demand. Let's return to the example of Safelite Glass for a moment. As Lazear points out, the average pay per employee went up 7 percent, while firm productivity went up 44 percent.[39] How can this gap between pay and firm productivity be explained—with firm productivity increasing much more than pay? Safelite is in Columbus, Ohio, where there is an oversupply of workers clamoring for decent-paying jobs. So workers lacked the leverage to get more than a fraction of the value produced by their greater efforts—Safelite could exploit an imperfect, somewhat "sticky" labor market. But such is not always the case. When employees hold the upper hand, and companies battle for top talent with money alone, then their best people will keep leaving for more money, as they are working for nothing else. Consider major league baseball. The advent of free agency and de-emphasis on team loyalty has produced rapidly increasing salaries for players and a system in which most teams lose money on an operating basis.

These examples demonstrate part of James Treybig's "if they come for money, they'll leave for money" concern. Playing a financial incentive strategy in a labor market where people can and do search for all available opportunities and move for higher compensation will do precisely what economic theory predicts: ensure that employees will receive their marginal revenue product and further ensure that companies will be forced to pay wages that are fully at market, thereby reducing the company's profits from what they might have been had they offered employees a less wage-centric employment bargain. If you believe that people work *only* for the money, such departures would be impossible to stop. But it would also be impossible to explain why people ever join the Peace Corps, enlist in the military when they have better-paying jobs (as professional football player Pat Tillman, who later died in Afghanistan, did), and why even in professional baseball, players still accept lower salaries to stay with teammates and managements they enjoy working with—as San Francisco Giants player J. T. Snow did in 2003.

And there is one other reason not to select those people who want to be in your organization only or mostly for the money they can make. There is evidence, at least from student populations, that people who choose a place for more instrumental reasons are much more likely to engage in dishonest behavior. Don McCabe and his colleagues have conducted numerous studies of college student cheating over the years.[40] They have found that students who are in school or have chosen a major for instrumental reasons—in order to get a better job or to make more money—are much more likely to cheat than students who have chosen a course of study because of their interest in the subject matter. This result makes perfect sense if you think about it. If I am trying to master a subject because of my intrinsic interest, cheating makes no logical sense—it defeats my desire to learn the material. If I am, on the other stand, studying just to get a credential, than what matters is the credential—getting out with the piece of paper—not necessarily what I learn. The implications for companies are clear. If people are there for the money— at Enron, for instance, or anywhere else—then they will do what it takes to get the money, regardless of what that is. Much better, it would seem, to have people who actually have some interest in the company, its customers, its products and services, and its values.

Variable Pay = Pay Dispersion = Lower Performance

The use of individual financial incentives nearly always increases the dispersion or inequality in rewards. At Safelite Glass, the variation in monthly salary earned by employees doing glass installation was approximately 43 percent higher under the piece rate plan than under the hourly pay system. This result is scarcely surprising, as variable financial incentives are meant to create wider gaps between what the best and worst people are paid. The intention is to get away from the *mayonnaise theory* of salary administration, in which raises are spread rather equally and thinly across the entire employee base, and instead, give bigger rewards to employees that contribute most to organizational performance. The empirical question is what does the evidence say about the consequences of creating more unequal financial rewards?

There are two basic assumptions behind the idea that more dispersed financial incentives are desirable and will enhance organizational performance:

- Employees who make outstanding contributions want to be recognized.

- Employees believe it is unfair that they get the same raises as colleagues who do not expend the same level of effort or accomplish as much as they do, so most employees prefer more dispersed pay.

These assumptions sound perfectly reasonable on the surface, but each becomes problematic when organizations actually try to implement differential rewards. As to the first assumption, although people may want to be recognized for their outstanding contributions, this causes a big problem because the world of work is lot like the Garrison Keillor's mythical Lake Wobegon, "where all the children are above average." A vast literature demonstrates that in virtually every sphere of life—from driving ability to a CEO's power to extract value out of mergers and acquisitions—most people believe they are far above average. These are called *self-enhancement effects*, or the desire of people to think more positively about themselves. Most people are more likely to perceive themselves as superior to others along numerous positive dimensions, see themselves more positively than others see them, believe they are above average and not recognize their lack of competence, and take credit for their success but see their failures as outside of their control.[41]

The consequences of such overestimates of ability and performance are painfully obvious to any manager who has ever administered differential raises or given a performance review. The employee almost always has an opinion of his or her performance that is higher than that held by the manager. When performance can be reliably and unambiguously measured—which means that the performance can be quantitatively and objectively assessed, measured along one or just a few dimensions (so trade-offs between dimensions are not required), and performance does not result from joint efforts with others (which raises questions of relative credit)—differential financial incentives can be justified by recourse to these objective measures. In all other cases, there can be and usually is debate about relative merit, and people who receive a smaller reward than they expect routinely resent the organization and the manager who, in their judgment, has made a biased and flawed assessment that denigrates their excellent work.

These battling performance perceptions are one reason why compensation consulting companies find that most pay-for-performance programs fail to achieve their objectives, and dissatisfaction with such programs is usually so high. A 2004 survey by Hewitt of 350 companies showed that "83 percent of organizations believe their pay-for-performance programs are only somewhat successful or not successful at accomplishing their goals."[42] To add insult to injury, after first forcing managers to "stack" their employees from best to worst—which has profound implications for employees' feelings of self-worth and status and is done through a process often fraught with disagreements among managers about who deserves what rating and ranking—most organizations then seriously underfund their pay-for-performance programs. As Watson Wyatt noted, "merit budgets are so constrained that they do not sufficiently reward exceptional performance or differentiate top employees from others."[43]

There is also mixed evidence about whether people really want to be differentiated from their fellow employees. Executives in some companies we've encountered report that their managers resist pressures to strongly differentiate among the financial rewards given to their subordinates, and such resistance appears to be wise at times. One Cisco manager complained to us that he couldn't understand why HR insisted that he give big bonuses to his top few people and fire a couple people at the bottom each year, as he had assembled an excellent and cooperative team—by carefully hiring the right people and easing out the wrong people, his team was composed of *all* excellent people. Controlled experiments with temporary teams composed of strangers show that participants usually choose to avoid handing out big differences in rewards that mirror the big differences in individual performance seen in groups—and this is in a context where there are far weaker social connections among people than in ongoing work settings.[44] The reason seems clear. People derive satisfaction from their social relationships in the workplace. Differential rewards people drive people apart, sorting them into categories as "winners," "nothing special," and "losers." The result is jealousy and resentment, which damages social ties and diminishes trust and sociability in the workplace. Few organizations adequately fund their financial incentive programs well enough to provide economically meaningful and substantial differences in rewards anyway.[45] So why should organizations pay the price of damaged social relations, people suffer through arguments about relative merit for insignificant financial benefits, and managers devote so many hours ranking and rating their people? Despite what so many compensation consultants and HR executives advise, most people prefer to avoid these nasty side effects and, given a choice, choose to work for more equal rewards.

Individual incentives and highly differentiated reward and recognition distributions make more sense when performance can be objectively assessed *and* when performance is mostly the result of individual effort rather than the product of interdependent activity. So there is evidence that jockeys perform better when pay is contingent on performance, that tree planters in British Columbia are more productive when paid on a piece rate, and that loggers produced more when their piece rates were set at higher levels.[46] Similarly, the evidence suggests that more dispersed financial rewards increase the performance (particularly of the highest performers) when tasks entail little or no interdependence and outcomes are clear. A study of 379 trucking companies found that larger differences in financial rewards between the best and worst paid drivers was associated with better company performance. A controlled experiment in picking oranges also found that greater dispersion in rewards produced higher level of performance.[47] Studies of golf tournaments and race car drivers—both activities where winning was clearly measurable and there was little interdependence—demonstrated that a greater difference in rewards (or a larger first prize) produced better performance.[48] In the case of the golf tournament study, this happened even when the quality of the participants was statistically controlled, although larger prizes in automobile racing produced faster times but also more accidents.

Yet when work settings require even modest interdependence and cooperation, as most do, dispersed rewards have consistently negative consequences on organizations. A study of college and university faculty showed that the greater the dispersion of pay within academic departments, the lower the job satisfaction, the less collaboration, and the lower the level of research productivity.[49] A study of 67 publicly traded companies found that firms with greater differences between the best- and worst-paid executives in the top management team had subsequently weaker financial performance (measured by total shareholder returns).[50] The study also found that the negative effect of pay disparity was especially pronounced for high-technology firms, because these firms had the greatest need for collaboration and teamwork to cope with complex and rapidly changing competitive conditions. A sample of 102 business units found that the greater the gap between top management and employee pay, the lower the product quality.[51]

The same negative effects of dispersed pay are seen in professional sports. Studies of baseball teams are interesting because, among major professional sports, baseball requires the least coordination and cooperation among team members. But baseball still requires some cooperation; for example, between pitchers and catchers, and among infielders. And although individuals go to bat, teammates can help each other improve their skills and break out of slumps. Matt Bloom's study of over 1,500 professional baseball players on 29 teams over an eight-year period showed that—controlling for the effects of base pay, past performance, age, and experience—players on teams with dispersed pay performed consistently worse, especially the lower-paid players. Not only that, teams with more dispersed pay had lower winning percentages, gate receipts, and media income.[52]

Guidelines for Using Incentives

It isn't easy to build pay systems that inspire, guide, and energize people without, at the same time, damaging your organization and people. If you look at the best evidence, instead of listening to the best-paid consulting firms and gurus, you will see that simple palliatives like pay for performance aren't likely to fix all—or even any—of your performance problems and may instead drive up costs, hamper cooperation, and stifle new ideas. But you do have to pay people. What is a manager to do? You might begin by using the ideas and data outlined in this chapter to develop a more complete view of human psychology and its implications for using financial incentives. This research about pay and people leads us to four overarching guidelines for managers to use as they think about and implement financial incentives.

Don't Try to Solve Every Problem with Financial Incentives

The biggest problem with financial incentives is that they are tremendously overused. *Incentives* has emerged as the first answer to almost every problem. Are your schools failing? Bribe teachers with incentive pay. Is the medical system inefficient, with vast differences in treatment protocols for the same disease in different regions? Set up a managed care system that provides financial incentives to doctors, insurers, patients, and hospitals. Bad customer service? Provide financial incentives for better customer service. Airplanes not flying on time? Pay employees if the planes fly on time. Too much overtime in garbage collection? Give truck drivers a financial incentive to finish early. Stock price not high enough? Give senior management financial incentives to get the stock price up. And on and on it goes, often with disastrous results.

But incentives often aren't that effective. Beyond all the problems we have enumerated, consider one more: people adapt, fairly rapidly actually, to the rewards. The result is that bonuses for performance become part of people's total compensation and come to be expected. As David Russo, formerly the head of human resources at SAS Institute, once commented, "a raise is only a raise for 30 days. After that, it's just somebody's salary."

To obtain the benefits of the informational effects of financial incentives, here's an idea: instead of using subtle, often misunderstood financial rewards that people may try to game, try talking to people about the company, its strategy, and its priorities. What a novel idea. SAS Institute, the largest privately owned software company in the world with sales of over $1.3 billion and a 98 percent customer renewal rate, has largely eschewed an emphasis on financial incentives in its management approach. As Barrett Joyner, former head of North American sales and marketing, commented, "We have sales targets, but mostly as a way of keeping score. I want to make the numbers, but I want to make the numbers the right way . . . I'm not smart enough to incent on a formula. People are constantly finding holes in incentive plans . . . Here, we just tell people what we want them to do and what we expect."[53]

To obtain great employee motivation, instead of signaling people through lavish and contingent financial rewards that they are working mostly for the money, let them see and experience other benefits from their work, such as being part of a supportive community and doing work that helps benefit others. So, for instance, Southwest Airlines talks about bringing people together. Low fares, which are possible only because of the low costs that come from a productive workforce, become not just some competitive strategy but something that enables customers to see their family and friends more often. The Men's Wearhouse, the large retailer of tailored men's clothing, encourages its employees to help each other become better people than they ever thought they could be, even as they describe their job as helping men look better, feel more confident, and be more successful in their lives. DaVita, which runs kidney dialysis centers, shows pictures of its patients and has a video segment in which dialysis patients and their families, students (in the case of a teacher), and work colleagues say, "thank you DaVita," for keeping the person alive. SonoSite, a developer and manufacturer of high-quality, small, lightweight ultrasound equipment, encourages its employees to consider how lives are saved by bringing diagnostic ultrasound to previously unreachable places. At one annual meeting, a captain from the U.S. Army described the use of SonoSite equipment to provide care to the wounded during the war in Iraq, while the company's Web site has a section entitled "SonoSite Moments" that displays unsolicited stories from doctors and other medical professionals about how the company's machines helped save lives.

Instead of using financial incentive plans to sort people, consider trying to attract people for other reasons—such as believing in the company, liking its culture, and enjoying the work. Justin Kitch, the founding CEO of Homestead.com, talked to us about recruiting at Harvard Business School at the height of the Internet boom. He recounted how students mostly asked questions that indicated they were primarily interested in figuring out how rich they could get how quickly. He didn't hire anyone and stopped recruiting at business schools. Kitch thought that the company would be better served, and better able to survive the inevitable reversals of fortune and business difficulties, if its people wanted to be there for its mission, technology, and culture. Perhaps that is why, while so many dot-coms failed and so many executives come and go in Silicon Valley, Homestead—although it has had its ups and down—survived the dot-com bust and kept its top management team largely intact as well. Homestead finally had its first profitable year in 2004 and currently has over 60,000 paying customers.

The point is that there are other ways of accomplishing the motivational, selection, and informational effects of financial incentives. And in many instances, these alternatives are not only less expensive, but they are actually better methods for accomplishing these important organization-building objectives.

Sometimes Less Is More Effective

In the late 1990s, The Men's Wearhouse faced a challenge. On the one hand, its commission structure for wardrobe consultants rewarded salespeople on an individual basis for the clothes they sold, with a higher commission for larger orders to signal the importance of cross-selling merchandise. On the other hand, the company emphasized the concept of teamwork and team selling—helping others when they were waiting on customers. For instance, a participant at one of our executive programs described how she, her husband, and her children went to a Men's Wearhouse store to buy a blazer. When they arrived, one wardrobe consultant began to wait on them while another took the kids in the back for juice, cookies, and video games. When the couple had purchased what they came in for, the mother and father went to get the kids—who were having so much fun they didn't want to leave. With the children being cared for, the woman and her husband stayed in the store longer and bought more clothes. This is one example of team selling— the person with the kids in the back was going to get no commission for the sales made by his colleague. Other examples included helping fellow wardrobe consultants answer questions, providing peer coaching to teach others about clothes and selling, and helping everyone maintain the appearance of the store and the merchandise displays.

To help build a team atmosphere, in addition to encouraging sports activities and socializing among the staff, the company gave either no award, a $20 award, or a $40 award, paid in cash, to employees at a store at the end of the month depending on the store's *shrink*—levels of lost and stolen inventory. In commenting on the modest size of these awards, CEO and founder George Zimmer demonstrated a remarkable insight into the psychology of incentives and how they could be both too big and too small. He asserted that the award was just the right amount, because it engendered some excitement but was not so big that it distorted behavior or became the focus of attention. Rather, the focus remained on the celebration of the store's achievement and the spirit of camaraderie, rather than the money. By the same token, Zimmer noted the amount had to be large enough to be meaningful, and in this instance, the company went to the trouble to pay the award in cash. Zimmer's insight is particularly prescient in the context of executive financial incentives that do distort behavior and that distract attention from the business, employees, and customers.

Be Careful What You Wish For, You Might Just Get It

If you are going to pay people for doing something, you need to be very, very thoughtful about the possible consequences of the behavior you have just signaled them to do. You need to think hard about what will happen if people take the financial incentives seriously, and really do seek to maximize their performance along those dimensions, and only those dimensions, that you reward. Much as in medicine or engineering, where people think about what could or might go wrong in recommending a treatment or designing a building, this is precisely how managers need to think about financial incentives. By first anticipating what might go wrong, you can then balance the risks and costs against the potential benefits, and you might even be able to redesign the financial incentives to minimize the risks while retaining the benefits. It is impossible for any human being to anticipate every behavioral eventuality that financial incentives will produce, so it is crucial to consider incentive systems as works in progress, or as experiments being run, not as things to be put in place and left alone indefinitely, regardless of the outcomes.

This recommendation flies in the face of the immense difficulty companies have in changing their pay systems and how, once implemented, incentive systems become institutionalized. But it is only by learning by doing and being open to such learning that serious problems can be avoided. The belief that your pay system is best viewed as a prototype, something that you will change when better information is discovered, reflects the mind-set we introduced in our opening chapters that best sets the stage for evidence-based management: the attitude of wisdom, that managers need to act on the best knowledge that they have right now, while doubting what they know. And managers can also better practice evidence-based management if they teach their people—and yes, provide incentives—so that they will accept and help support experimentation with the pay system.

Worry About Comparisons and Distributions, Not Only Individuals or Levels

Organizations are social entities, and people are social creatures. What this means for leaders is that social relations are important. People compare themselves to others and derive feelings of worth and status from that comparison. Consequently, pay differences have not only substantive but symbolic meaning. If a colleague makes $1,000 more, that $1,000 permits the person to buy more goods and services—the substantive difference in wages. But once people are beyond the point where they need every cent to buy basic necessities, small differences in pay can still have huge effects on motivation, attitudes toward the company and its management, and turnover. What may seem like trivial differences to a manager—say if a person gets $74,000 a year and his or her colleague gets $75,000—may be interpreted by the lower-paid employee as a sign that the organization values that other person more, so tiny differences can have great consequences for a person's ego and feelings of self-worth. Social comparisons are part of the human condition—and are magnified in individualistic and competitive cultures like we have in the United States. Lots of companies get into trouble by forgetting this simple fact and not considering what the distribution of rewards looks like and what messages that distribution sends to everyone.

Take the most notorious example, CEO pay. CEOs who make several hundred times more than what the average employee in their companies makes send the signal that what they do is hundreds of times more important. Is that really the right signal to send? If frontline people think that what they do doesn't matter very much for the organization's success or in the opinion of senior management, why bother to worry about how well they are doing their job? It is not by accident or coincidence that many of the most successful, consistently best-performing companies have CEOs who are not outrageously overpaid—Amazon.com, CostCo, and Southwest Airlines are a few current examples. By sending a signal that performance is a collective, not just an individual, endeavor, those companies are more likely to induce thought, creativity, and effort on the part of their people.

We have seen in this chapter that the use of financial incentives is a subject filled with ideology and belief—and where many of those beliefs have little or no evidence to support them. Pay is also an important topic, consuming time and resources and doing a lot of harm when it is mismanaged. As a consequence, you might think that using financial incentives to improve performance would be a domain where there would be heavy reliance on the best evidence. As we have seen, however, consultants, gurus, and executives charge ahead with assumptions and practices that reflect a reckless disregard for the evidence. But this gap between evidence and action provides opportunities for those organizations wise enough to examine their assumptions about pay systems, and to find and use the best evidence.

6

Strategy
Is Destiny?

S TRATEGY may or may not be destiny, but it certainly seems to be cool. Type the word *strategy* into Amazon.com books and some 29,209 entries appear, including 9,496 for business strategy. The word *implementation* produces about half as many entries—5,031—with many of those entries focused on computer systems implementation, such as enterprise resource planning (ERP) software. Google reports 120 *million* entries for the word *strategy*, and less than half that number, 58.6 million, for the term *implementation*. Google has 4.5 million entries for *business strategy*, but just 34,000 for *business implementation*. Judging by mentions in book titles and search engines, *figuring out what to do* seems to be far more important, or at least far more interesting, than *the ability to actually do something*—such as operate the business effectively.

Strategy is big business. Strategy consulting companies such as Monitor, Bain, Booz Allen Hamilton, McKinsey, and Boston Consulting Group charge higher fees, typically have larger total revenues, and enjoy higher status among business school graduates seeking jobs than consulting firms such as A. T. Kearney, Proudfoot, and Celerant that focus on operations and implementation. Higher status and higher margin work should attract more competitors, or at least wannabes, and that is exactly what happens. The lure of lucrative work has enticed firms that specialize in the technical work of computer systems implementation, like Accenture, and firms that focus on human resources, such as Watson Wyatt, Hewitt, and Towers Perrin, to add practices that link strategy more closely to their other businesses.

This emphasis on strategy has infiltrated the world of corporate governance. The National Association of Corporate Directors issued a report on the board of director's role in corporate strategy, which noted that "a recent survey of CEOs showed that strategic planning ranked number two in importance to their companies."[1] The role of strategy was seen as important in governance because "disagreement over strategy . . . led to shorter CEO tenure in general and abrupt departures at many highly visible companies."[2]

The justification for the prestige, high prices, and attention lavished on strategy seems straightforward: doing the right thing, even if it isn't done perfectly, is more important than doing the wrong thing exceptionally well. This means that it is paramount for companies and organizations of all types to understand what they should be doing to achieve success—to devise a strategy that helps them survive in an increasingly competitive world. Many strategy consultants and researchers also assert that instituting a disciplined process of decision making—considering threats and opportunities, for instance, communicating assumptions more widely throughout the organization, and using budgets and plans to set goals and monitor performance—helps to enhance organizational performance.[3]

We have no quarrel with the conclusion that leaders and their people need to know what to do and how to compete. Being the world's most efficient and effective electric typewriter company won't produce success when the product in question is disappearing because of changes in technology and markets—a story that holds true for companies making the proverbial buggy whips or, more recently, those making electromechanical calculators, slide rules, or record players. But like many of the half-truths we consider in this book, a fixation on strategy can obscure as much as it illuminates. The corporate obsession with strategy can cause leaders to overlook other, even more crucial and more sustainable avenues for success. Even corporate successes attributed to great strategy often turn out, on closer examination, not to stem from strategy at all, and the empirical evidence shows a surprisingly weak link between the activity of strategic planning and company performance. There are also many ways of figuring out the right thing to do, and emphasizing strategy is only one method and possibly not the best. So, this chapter considers whether strategy really is destiny. We offer guidelines on how managers can best think about strategy and the means they can use to get their organizations to head in the right direction and do the right things.

Strategy as a Source of Success

A history of the field of business strategy is well beyond our scope, and in any event, has been done admirably by others.[4] It is useful, however, to understand how the emphasis on strategy as a source of success originated. Strategy is a central theme in business schools, the capstone course where the curricula from all other courses are woven together, typically one of the most popular courses, and a core subject in both undergraduate and graduate curricula. A strategy course is mandated by the Association to Advance Collegiate Schools of Business (AACSB) as a required part of the MBA curriculum. Virtually every business school has a strategy area or department. The rise in the interest in strategy is almost certainly linked to the rise in the prominence of business education and business schools over the past several decades, with the MBA degree now constituting more than 20 percent of all master's degrees awarded in the United States. Strategy, with its emphasis on quantitative analysis, fits well with the quantitative, analytical orientation of most business education and gives students a sense of personal efficacy in making big, important decisions based on the information contained in the cases they analyze.[5]

Evidence demonstrating the connection between strategy and business education is seen in an analysis of best-selling Harvard Business School cases and best-selling Chinese cases. That study concluded that "the rational perspective is the dominant framework adopted by both Chinese and American case writers" (more than 95 percent of the cases) and that there is a "tendency in many cases to focus on strategic decisions at the top of the organization" because a "strategy focus . . . is now considered by many to be 'ideal.'"[6] A full 60 percent of the cases examined had strategy formulation as their primary focus.

This emphasis on analysis runs through most descriptions of strategic management. "The strategic management paradigm was introduced as a rational analytical approach to provide strategic direction to organizational actions in an increasingly dynamic business environment . . . This approach, often considered synonymous with strategic planning, has become a dominant framework."[7]

The field of strategy, as taught in business schools, rests on two crucial assumptions: that a company will be better suited to doing some things than others, and that financial resources—as well as resources of time and attention—are limited. These assumptions mean that the most fundamental questions every organization must answer are "first, what business (or businesses) are we going to be in, and second, how are we going to compete in those businesses?" The two generic strategies are competing on the basis of cost or price versus competing on the basis of offering a differentiated, presumably superior product or service.

In answering the question of what business it is in, a company decides what it will focus on and, by extension, what it will ignore and what it won't do. Strategy provides focus for a business and its people, helping them set priorities and allocate resources. In the original conception of strategy, this question of purpose and focus and, therefore, resource allocation, was answered by top management, with the details of implementation and execution to be left to people farther down the organizational hierarchy.[8] Strategy is still viewed in many quarters as within the purview of top management and the board of directors, indeed, as their most important task. Much research shows, however, that strategy is often produced and altered by people farther down in the hierarchy. Managers and engineers often pursue products and technologies not necessarily blessed by top management, as happened in Intel's transition from the memory chip to the microprocessor market, Atari's persistence as a computer game developer after it was acquired by Warner Brothers, as well as the development of successful technologies and products at 3M, Hewlett-Packard, Sony, and Microsoft.[9] An alternate view is that top management's most important role is to be an architect of the corporate culture and the management systems in which strategy and implementation get produced. Yet the view that strategy setting is top management's central activity remains dominant. Because of the obvious importance of focus and the need to optimize the allocation of scarce resources, it became almost axiomatic that strategy was the most important single cause of a firm's success.

Evidence on the Effects of Strategy and Strategic Planning

The rise of strategy and strategic planning in both business school curricula and corporate management in the 1960s and 1970s led to research on whether or not these management activities actually affect company performance. This strand of research largely disappeared after the 1980s, as the importance of strategy assumed a taken-for-granted quality. Yet the empirical evidence on whether strategy and strategic planning actually matter for companies' financial performance is quite mixed, in part because this is a question inherently difficult to study and in part because many of the studies designed to examine it have not been well done. Gordon Greenley's review of empirical studies of the strategic planning–performance relationship concluded that most studies made highly subjective assessments of planning processes, as well as of whether any planning was done at all, and scant attention was devoted to untangling the effects of strategy setting from other causes of performance.[10] One review of the effects of planning noted that "two decades of empirical research have not produced consistent support" and that there have been "inconsistent planning-performance findings," a conclusion echoed by others as well.[11]

Another line of research demonstrates the apparent importance of strategy. It came out of industrial organization economics, with important scholars in this tradition including Richard Caves and possibly his most famous student, Michael Porter. A study of the intellectual structure and foundation of the field of strategic management concluded that Porter had more influence on the development of this discipline than any academic.[12] Industrial organization economists focused on the existence and persistence of differences in profit margins across industries. So, for instance, margins in the pharmaceutical industry greatly exceed margins in the grocery store industry. In competitive markets, over time high margins are expected to erode through increased competition, including competition created by new entrants to attractive markets. So this observation of persistent profit margin differences led to research on what accounted for the ability to achieve higher profit margins over a long stretches of time, which resulted in Porter's famous *five forces* model.[13] Porter and his colleagues in industrial organization economics found that the ability to earn exceptional returns over long stretches was related to factors of industry structure—specifically, whether or not the industry had market power with respect to customers and suppliers, whether or not there were barriers to entry that kept the high profit margins from being competed away, and whether or not there was limited rivalry, again a constraint on the competition that would erode margins.

This view of strategy emphasizes *location* or positioning—being in the right industry or industry sector. Presumably there are things management can do to shape its existing location. A company can erect barriers to entry through, for instance, developing proprietary, patented technology. Or a company might reduce competition within an industry via mergers that eliminate competitors, something that has occurred with increasing frequency as antitrust enforcement has waned. Another way of affecting industry structure and increasing market power over suppliers or customers could be accomplished by merging or otherwise growing so that the company achieved a dominant position in its industry, something that is often said to contribute to the success of Wal-Mart, a company that is able to squeeze its suppliers on price. This conception of strategy as selecting the right business to be in is reflected in the famous Boston Consulting Group matrix, categorizing businesses as *stars*, *dogs*, *cash cows*, and *question marks*, with its implicit assumption that depending on the nature of the business and the industry environment, management is constrained in its ability to turn dogs into stars and should use the cash generated from businesses in less desirable segments to invest in more favorable industry sectors.

Industry structure does predict much about outcomes achieved by companies operating in various industries, including their conduct and behavior and also their performance, as measured by realized profit margins.[14] More recent research has tried to decompose measures of profitability and examine to what extent performance is preordained by the particular industry that firms are in and the characteristics of those industries. This research has produced conflicting answers about the importance of firms and industries.[15] But there is clear evidence that company performance varies widely among firms in the same industry, suggesting that competitive advantage may reside at least partly at the level of the company and its management, not only at the level of industry structure.

The Problem with the Industry Structure–Performance Paradigm

In 2002 on the occasion of its 30th anniversary, *Money* magazine asked Ned Davis Research to compile a list of the best-performing stocks since *Money* debuted in 1972. The top 10 (and their compounded annual returns) are listed in table 6-1.

The industries represented by these companies for the most part did not fit what the five-forces model would predict were the conditions under which companies would flourish. The airline industry, home to the top-performing company Southwest, has been beset by waves of bankruptcies, both in the early 1990s and then again following the tragedy of September 11, 2001. Moreover, following industry deregulation in the 1970s, new entrants came into the industry on a regular basis. Walgreens, Wal-Mart, Circuit City, and Krogers, four other top-rated performers, operated in the highly competitive retail sector, which also has witnessed numerous bankruptcies, including some of the major players. Although one might argue that by 2000 these companies were large enough to enjoy some market power with respect to their suppliers, this was not the case through much of their histories. Moreover, there are few barriers to entry into retailing; fierce interfirm rivalry; and limited power with respect to customers, who, in the case of drugs, appliances and cars, groceries, and general merchandise, have many choices where

TABLE 6-1

The 10 best-performing stocks, 1972–2002

Company	Compounded annual return
Southwest Airlines	25.99%
Wal-Mart Stores	25.97%
Kansas City Southern Industries	25.61%
Walgreen Company	23.72%
Intel Corporation	23.49%
Comcast Corporation	21.99%
Circuit City–CarMax Group	21.71%
Forest Laboratories	21.69%
State Street Corporation	21.45%
The Kroger Company	21.16%

to shop. Although Forest Laboratories is a drug company, it is certainly not large or well known, in part because in addition to making some branded and patented products, it makes generics using controlled-release technology. State Street offers investment management services to institutions, another reasonably competitive sector, and although one could argue that Comcast has local monopolies in its cable television business, many of its competitors have fared poorly nonetheless. As *Money* noted, the idea that Walgreens would be a better investment choice than Pfizer and that Kroger would outperform IBM in terms of stock market returns challenges most conventional ideas that emphasize finding great industry sectors in order to do well. The article concludes that, when it comes to picking great stocks, industry sector matters less—a lot less—than the quality of a company's management.[16]

What accounts for this great performance by companies operating in undesirable industries? The answer is to be found by considering the dependent variable. Coming out of the economics tradition, the industrial organization approach to strategy sought to understand the development of market power, and one good measure of market power is the ability to charge a high price compared to costs—the price-cost or profit margin. But there are other measures of company performance, such as total shareholder return (the measure chosen by *Money* and one that is increasingly in vogue) or even growth in things such as sales or market share—potential indicators of increasing market acceptance—or profits. It turns out that there is evidence that these alternative measures yield very different results with respect to what affects company performance. In a study of more than 1,800 companies traded on U.S. stock exchanges with a market capitalization of more than $500 million in 1994, researchers at Booz Allen Hamilton found that "companies in slow-growing, more mature industries are somewhat more likely to create superior returns for shareholders than companies in fast-growing industries.[17] A study of growth rates of companies in different industries found that industry growth rate did not predict the growth of individual companies within each industry.[18] In other words, there was as much variation in companies' ability to grow within as across industries, reinforcing the concerns of academic scholars as to how much industry really matters.

The Intel Story: Does Strategy Matter?

For our colleague Robert Burgelman, there is no question mark after the phrase, "strategy is destiny." His extensive field research in the Intel Corporation, which he describes as one of the most successful companies in history, led him to conclude that "since its founding in 1968, Intel's corporation strategy has driven, or in other cases, adapted to a rapidly changing technology and industry context."[19] Intel's strategy has remained constant over time, being "centered on technological innovation and leadership."[20] Burgelman sees Intel's history divided into three periods: from its initial founding until the early 1980s when it was a broad-based semiconductor supplier focused primarily on the memory chip market (dynamic random access memory, or DRAM), from the mid-1980s until the late 1990s, during which Intel enjoyed a dominant market share in the microprocessor market, and from the late 1990s on, when Intel, facing more competition in the microprocessor market as well as some market saturation in the personal computer industry, began casting about for new products related to the Internet and wireless networking products. Each transition, or strategic inflection point, required "the change of one winning strategy into another; the replacement of an existing technological regime with a new one."[21] The role of top management as strategy maker in all of this is crucial: "managing strategic dissonance requires . . . the capacity of top managers to appreciate the strategic importance of managerial initiatives *after* they have come about but *before* unequivocal environmental feedback is available."[22] Top management must know when to exit an existing business—in this case, Intel's DRAM business—and be able to decide on the right strategic intent in highly dynamic environments.[23]

There is no question that Intel has impressive strengths in research and development and manufacturing, and that it has come to be a dominant force in the microprocessor industry with over a 70 percent market share and enormous sales and profits. Burgelman's story of how Intel evolved its product line from an emphasis on memory chips to placing a large bet on the nascent microprocessor market is a model of detailed analysis of the organization's transition and the processes that facilitated that transition. Attributing Intel's success to its own strategic decisions is, however, at least partly incorrect. According to Craig Barrett, the company's former CEO and current chairman, Intel was given the chance to move into microprocessors largely as a result of a strategic decision by IBM to outsource the manufacture of microprocessors for the IBM PC, a lucky break that Intel was smart enough to capitalize on but that had little to do with any planning, rational analysis, or strategy formation by Intel's senior team.

As Barrett noted at a meeting that Pfeffer attended a few years ago, IBM was competing with Apple Computer at the time and launched its own personal computer in 1981. IBM could have chosen to manufacture its own semiconductors for its PC. IBM was then, and still is, a large manufacturer of electronic components, including semiconductors and disk drives for its own use. IBM chose instead to use Intel as an outside supplier. Barrett remarked that Intel, having been given a monopoly in the PC microprocessor chip marketplace by IBM, was clever enough to hold onto its early market-leading position. Burgelman himself seems to acknowledge the role of luck, writing that "Grove's [Andy Grove, the CEO at the time] role in driving Intel's strategy making relied more on strategic recognition than on foresight. Intel had been lucky to invent the microprocessor and even luckier to obtain the design win for the IBM PC."[24]

So if Intel did achieve its dominant and profitable position in the microprocessor business as a result of a strategic decision, it was a strategic decision made by IBM to outsource both the manufacture of its key components and the design of its operating system (in the process creating an even more successful company called Microsoft). Intel's executives did have the wisdom to get out of the less profitable DRAM business and to focus on microprocessors, but recognizing and capitalizing on their good luck likely explains more about the company's success than the brilliance of Intel's strategy formulation process.

Why Strategy May Not Be That Important: The Logic and the Evidence

Doing the right thing is important. It is better to be a monopoly than to be forced to compete with other companies. And having a clear strategy is essential for producing focus and facilitating communication and coordinated action inside companies. Yet there is good reason to be skeptical that merely making the right strategic choices is the key to business success. The first reason to question whether or not strategy is destiny is simple logic. For something to provide sustained and sustainable competitive advantage, that something must, by definition, be difficult to imitate or copy. So, according to perhaps the most popular theory in organizational strategy right now, called "the resource based view of the firm," competitive advantage comes from a company possessing resources that are both valuable and rare. But for some resource to provide sustainable competitive advantage, that resource also must be difficult to imitate or substitute to prevent rivals from copying what the company does and quickly competing away its advantage.[25] So the question becomes: is the strategy that may make a company successful difficult to uncover and imitate?

Difficulty in imitation could potentially arise from problems in figuring out what an organization's strategy is—you can't imitate something if you don't understand it. But difficulty in understanding a particular company's strategy is unlikely to be a big problem. Almost every corporate annual report and 10-K *announces* what the organization's strategy is, and sometimes even describes the steps the company plans to take or is taking to execute that strategy. If that were not enough, there are many strategy consulting companies that would be happy to both determine what others are doing and provide advice as to what your company should do. So uncovering strategy—what to do—turns out not to be that difficult. A few years ago, Robert Sutton was invited to give a speech at a retreat for a large law firm. The chairman of the firm—who had just finished working with a name-brand consulting firm—made much ado about unveiling the firm's "secret" strategy. Sutton, who had worked with and talked with partners from several other large law firms, asked if he could guess the major elements of their strategic plan before seeing it. A small set of consulting firms work with large law firms, most give similar advice, and the strategies used by the most profitable firms are spelled out in numerous published sources including the *American Lawyer*. Sutton guessed that the firm's strategy focused on growing high-margin areas and getting out of low-margin areas; easing out historically unprofitable partners and (through both individual hires and mergers) bringing in more profitable partners; moving from a "location-based" to a "practice-based" structure; and increasing the firm's presence in New York, as much of the highest-margin work happens in that market. The chairman laughed and said that Sutton had got it pretty much right, and then noted that everyone in the business knew what to do, the problem was actually figuring out how to do it!

As this leader suggested, what actually provides competitive success and what is difficult to copy is not so much knowing what to do—deciding on the right strategy—but instead having the ability to *do* it. That is why Richard Kovacevich, CEO of the large and tremendously successful Wells Fargo Bank, has repeatedly argued that organizational culture and the ability to operate effectively—successful implementation—is much more important to organizational success than having the right strategy. A number of years ago he commented, "I could leave our strategic plan on a plane, and it wouldn't make any difference. No one could execute it. Our success has nothing to do with planning. It has to do with execution."[26] This is also why, in explaining how she led her company back from the edge of bankruptcy, Xerox CEO Anne Mulcahy emphasizes that the company's turnaround didn't really stem from a brilliant strategy. Rather, she asserts, it happened because Xerox's people worked toward common objectives, especially pleasing customers, selling products, and cutting costs.[27]

Or take the case of Dell Computer. Again, the company's strategy is not too difficult to discern: operate extremely cost-driven and incredibly effective assembly plants, sell direct to consumers and companies, use as much just-in-time manufacturing as possible to minimize inventories and the associated carrying costs and costs of obsolescence, try to gain market share and the associated economies of scale (including economies in purchasing from suppliers) by offering low prices, and provide good customer service as a way of achieving some degree of differentiation in a commodity-like business.[28] Others have tried to compete with Dell, but none have yet been nearly as successful. Dell continues to gain market share not only in the personal computer business but also in related businesses such as printers and monitors, and lately in plasma televisions. Yet Dell's enormous success is not based on some secret way of competing that its competitors don't know, nor on some proprietary technological knowledge or other resource that cannot be imitated because of patent or other intellectual property protection. Rather, a case can be made that Dell's amazing financial performance comes from its ability to implement its strategy of low-cost manufacturing and distribution coupled with decent customer service—from its ability to execute its strategic intent in a superior fashion. At least that is how CEO Kevin Rollins explains Dell's competitive advantage, as well as that of other industry leaders: "What Wal-Mart does isn't rocket science—it's retailing. Why can't everybody be Wal-Mart or JetBlue or Samsung or whatever the best company in their industry is? Because it takes more than strategy . . . the key to our success is years and years of DNA development within our teams that is not replicable outside the company. Other companies just can't execute as well as we do."[29]

In U.S. football, virtually every play is designed to go for a touchdown. Why doesn't it? Failures in execution. Linemen miss blocks, running backs stumble, receivers run the wrong routes or drop the ball, the quarterback doesn't throw the ball where it was supposed to go, and so forth. There is no question that there is, on occasion, brilliant play calling—the sports equivalent to strategy—that can make a difference in the outcome. But most of success in football and in other sports is based on being able to effectively execute the plays that are designed or accomplish the task of hitting the ball (in baseball or golf) or throwing it where you want it to go (baseball pitchers). Competence and capability are important for corporate success. Too much attention to getting the strategy right can divert attention away from building the capability to operate effectively. We have seen that many organizations use planning and talking about implementation as substitutes for action—a syndrome we called "the smart-talk trap" in *The Knowing-Doing Gap*. To help his players avoid this trap, former San Francisco 49ers head coach Steve Mariucci told them, "I never wear a watch because I always know what time it is. It is always NOW. And now is when you should do it."[30]

Some Costs of Strategic Planning

It is not just that strategic planning or worrying about corporate strategy may fail to positively affect performance or provide sustainable competitive advantage. There are two costs that companies and other organizations ought to take into account in thinking about the role of strategy in their management process. The first cost is the resources consumed in planning and the second is that leadership attention is diverted to strategy and, as a result, away from fixing operational problems.

For many companies, planning is conflated with and inextricably linked to the budgeting process—the nearly ubiquitous process of setting financial goals and objectives that frequently form the basis of management compensation as well as guiding investment and expenditure decisions during the period covered by the budget, typically a year.[31] This planning and budgeting process is enormously time consuming and expensive in many organizations, and whether or not budgeting helps or hinders effective management is very much open to question. The typical budget process "starts with a mission statement that sets out some of the aims of the business," which is then followed by a "group strategic plan that sets the direction and high-level goals of the firm. These form the framework for a budgeting process" as resources are agreed upon.[32] Jeremy Hope and Robin Fraser's book *Beyond Budgeting* shows that the resources consumed by this activity are enormous. "The average time consumed is between four and five months. It also involves many people and absorbs up to 20 to 30 percent of senior executives' and financial managers' time. Some organizations have attempted to place a cost on the whole planning and budgeting process. Ford Motor Company figured out this amounted to $1.2 billion per annum. A 1998 benchmarking study showed that the average company invested more than 25,000 person-days per billion dollars of revenue in the planning and performance management process."[33]

The second cost of this obsession with strategy and planning is that managerial attention is diverted away from solving fundamental problems and instead focuses on the intellectually more engaging and analytically tractable issues of strategy. Consider the case of a company Pfeffer worked with that was at one-time a market-leading producer of tamper-evident plastic bottle caps, bottles, and fitments for the dairy, water, and juice industries. As the dairy and water industries consolidated significantly over time, the proportion of the company's business derived from its largest 10 customers increased dramatically and, as is to be expected in a situation of growing buyer power, the customer concentration resulted in the shrinking of profit margins as customers demanded price concessions. Although the company was the largest producer in most of its markets, it was *not* the lowest-cost manufacturer, in part because it gave short shrift to plant operations and the people in the plants. Facing declining margins and profits, the company had a choice: to devote time, attention, and resources to becoming ever more efficient and effective in its manufacturing and product design efforts for its existing markets, or to devote time, attention, and resources to finding different market segments in which it could hope to earn higher margins even as existing sales to its base business and markets eroded.

One only has to read descriptions of how people at Dell spend time figuring out how to remove one screw from the finished product (which saves four seconds of assembly time) to see that such an exercise in enhancing manufacturing efficiency is boring and was not of interest to the smart MBA who ran the company and who had hired others like himself to help him deal with the company's difficulties.[34] Moreover, the senior leadership believed their best hope was to redeploy resources to more promising parts of the packaging industry, something that could have come straight out of any typical analysis that emphasizes the importance of industry structure for company success. So, off they went, commissioning an extensive (and expensive) consulting study of packaging markets, hiring even more MBAs (which, by the way, drove their cost structure up) to scout for potential acquisitions in the most promising markets, and engaging in long and protracted board-level discussions of strategic options. In the end, the company borrowed money to complete a merger into a different segment of the packaging industry even as it lost its most talented manufacturing executives—who could see their relative lack of status in the organization. As of this writing, the merger has to be judged an abject failure; it has not produced any incremental profits at all, and the firm's equity is almost worthless. Meanwhile, the manufacturing issues and potential for wringing more profits from the existing business that it once dominated went unexplored and unrealized, until the board finally removed the founder-CEO and brought in a packaging industry veteran to return the company to the basics of effective execution.

This is an all too common story. As the strategy literature suggests, time and attention are indeed scarce resources. Time spent pursuing strategic options may be time and attention—and resources—diverted from solving operational problems that could potentially provide more certain and quicker returns. This is not to say that it is never appropriate to reexamine strategy and redeploy assets and enter new markets. But it is important to recognize the temptation to avoid fixing what needs to be fixed as, with the help of consultants, firms try to find ways of avoiding doing the hard work that in many instances needs to be done to fix operations and improve elements of strategy execution.

The Downside of Strategic Focus

One of the basic purposes of setting strategic direction is deciding what not to do, to concentrate resources on a smaller number of projects, products, and markets, and by so doing, to have a better chance of being successful than if efforts are more diffused. This approach seems sensible enough, but like many things, there is also a downside to strategic focus.

The best way to see this downside is to ask the question: how are many (maybe even most) new companies formed, and why? Although some are developed by people coming directly from universities or research institutes, some are founded by people who were laid off and couldn't readily find new work, and some entrepreneurs are motivated by money or a great idea, many companies are founded by people who were not able to pursue their ideas with their previous employer and therefore started a new company to do what they could not do in their previous job.

Think about it—companies are employing people and giving them lots of training and experience as well as tacit knowledge of technology and markets acquired through their work, and then not only letting them walk out the door with all that intellectual and human capital, but in many instances, actually encouraging them to leave because what they know and what they want to do with what they know doesn't fit the organization's current strategy. Sometimes the projects, products, or markets don't seem large enough for the company to worry about. Sometimes, however, there is also an issue of strategic fit with the company's business focus.

This is a variant of the story told by Clayton Christensen in *The Innovator's Dilemma*. Christensen found that entrenched incumbents seldom lost out to new entrants because the incumbents did not have the internal skills or know-how to build the latest and greatest products; in fact, in many instances the incumbents had developed the new technologies and ideas *first*.[35] Instead, bound by commitments to existing customers and, we might add, by commitments to existing technologies and strategies, incumbents were unable to use their skills and knowledge to bring the new products to market. Kodak and Polaroid are perfect examples. Both had impressive R&D efforts and people who were deeply knowledgeable about digital photography, but Kodak's slowness to act on that knowledge has deeply wounded the company, and Polaroid's more pronounced inability to capitalize on its deep knowledge of digital photography ultimately led to its demise.[36]

Focus is great. But it can create blinders. In a world of uncertainty and change, and in an organizational world in which everyone, including senior management, is inevitably fallible, too much focus and too little peripheral vision leaves organizations susceptible to being replaced in the marketplace by new entrants or more nimble competitors. Take a look at *Winning Through Innovation* by Michael Tushman and Charles O'Reilly, which lists industry after industry—everything from watches, to cement, to tires, to airlines— where strong incumbents were displaced by newcomers and upstarts. The rise and fall of leading companies is a well-known story. But the role of too much strategic focus in this inability to maintain competitive advantage is a part of the tale that is all too infrequently told.[37]

What to Do About Strategy

Based on the logic and the evidence, there are some general guidelines that can help leaders navigate the extremes: on the one hand, believing that strategy is truly destiny and spending all of their time and attention on this or, on the other, forgetting to think about strategy and what a company's way of competing and focus should be at all. Here are a few.

An Alternative Way of Figuring Out What to Do

One reason that strategy may not be destiny and that strategy setting is an overrated determinant of performance is the finding, already discussed in this chapter, that strategy reduces peripheral vision and flexibility in adapting to uncertain and changing environments. Henry Mintzberg forcefully articulates that position, arguing that explicit strategies are "blinders designed to focus direction and block out peripheral vision" and that "setting oneself on a predetermined course in unknown waters is the perfect way to sail straight into an iceberg."[38] But the fundamental requirement remains: to focus efforts and allocate scarce resources, including time and attention. What is an organization to do?

One answer was provided by John Sall, a cofounder of SAS Institute, the largest privately owned software firm in the world, in the course of an interview for a case on his organization. After the interview, he asked a series of questions. "Stanford is very selective and takes in only the best and the smartest students?" Of course. "The MBA program is a two-year program, correct?" Yes, that's also true. "Why should it take two years to teach such smart people the secret to success: listen to your customers, listen to your employees, do what they tell you?" That, in a phrase, is the "strategy" that has permitted SAS Institute to achieve sales of over $1.5 billion, employee turnover that has never been over 5 percent even in the height of the technology frenzy of the late 1990s, a customer retention rate of 98 percent, and incredible customer loyalty. The idea: listen to what the environment is telling you—your customers and employees—and act on what you hear. So, once again, the notion that being wise is more important than being smart pops up; Sall is saying that hearing true things is more important than saying smart things, and that people need to ask good questions before they can come up with smart answers.

This responsiveness to customers and employees is a variant of the "strategy" pursued by IDEO, among the most successful and honored innovation firms, and in fact, one that has gone far beyond product design and now designs customer service experiences and work settings, helps companies develop work practices that make people more creative, and works with the senior management teams of large companies to foster innovation. How did IDEO go from designing things like the Apple mouse and high-technology medical and telecommunications equipment to emergency room "experiences" for hospitals and products for Procter & Gamble? Not by sticking to a narrow niche of design for high technology, or even to a niche of designing only physical products, or to a stable and unchanging view of its customer base and markets. IDEO values creativity and innovation—not just in what it designs, but also in its business and business model. It is constantly experimenting with different organizational designs, work practices, and people with intriguing skills that it can't quite figure out how to use—for now. It is a company that wants to try different things so that it can learn in the process of experimentation, see what works, and continually develop its competencies and skills even as it evolves its business.

But doesn't this produce a lack of focus? Maybe not. For example, both IDEO and SAS are intently focused on the customers and their expectations. As Peter Drucker once observed, "there is no business without a customer." What is interesting is that many strategies often neglect the customer and what that customer wants and needs. Maintaining a focus on customers and the quality of the work environment, something IDEO also does, provides focus on building core strengths while permitting the organization to react to changes in the business climate and market context. It provides an emphasis on what matters—customers and the intellectual talent and organizational culture to serve them well—even as it permits adaptation to new challenges and opportunities.

Don't Confuse Operational or Implementation Problems with the Need for Changing Strategy

In the human resources class at Stanford and in our executive programs, colleagues often teach a case about a luxury hotel in San Francisco. Competing in the luxury segment, the Portman Hotel, which already had many physical amenities (e.g., marble bathrooms and great views from its upper floors), decided to differentiate itself from other luxury hotels through a high-service strategy implemented by personal valets working on each floor—a service delivery concept that one can see in some Asian hotels like the Regent in Hong Kong. The plan was, however, poorly executed. Portman's managers hired the wrong kind of people, didn't have adequate staffing levels, kept moving people across floors (which disrupted teamwork), and had a poorly designed compensation system. The result was they did the right thing in the wrong way, and as a consequence, suffered excessive turnover and provided mediocre to poor service—in short, a great case for an HR class.

What is interesting is that, invariably, when MBA students analyze and discuss this case, they start out by arguing that Portman had the wrong strategy, that a service strategy wouldn't work, and that the hotel never should have sought to differentiate itself on that basis. The facts speak otherwise: one of the most successful hotels in San Francisco is the Mandarin Oriental, which has both the highest prices and the highest occupancy because of a successfully executed high-service strategy. In other words, class members are quick to both criticize the company's strategy and recommend changing its basic approach to its business, *even though they acknowledge that the organization never actually implemented the strategy that they now claim doesn't work and recommend changing!*

Our MBA students (and executive program students too) do the same thing that many companies do: reject a strategy that isn't working because it is poorly implemented, not necessarily because it is the wrong strategy. This problem of confusing strategy problems with implementation problems seems particularly common in service industries such as retail, hospitality, dining, and transportation where aspirations to provide outstanding service run into implementation and execution difficulties and the companies then conclude that the only thing that works is to change the strategy to one of cost cutting. But competing on the basis of cost, price, product quality, or innovation requires effective implementation to be successful as well.

Pfeffer worked with a manufacturer of leading-edge medical imaging equipment that was experiencing virtually no growth in units sold in the U.S. market. The executive team wondered: Was it a problem with the product strategy—did the product have the wrong features? Was it a problem of the pricing strategy—was the product priced too high for the market, even though it was a leading-edge, innovative technology that offered numerous price-performance benefits, as well as portability, over existing solutions? Did the company need to sell expendables along with capital equipment in order to grow its revenues faster? Pfeffer suggested to company executives that, before engaging in a big strategy exercise and questioning their business model, they might first examine the effectiveness of the U.S. sales organization and its leadership, which was performing far below the foreign sales organization. Sure enough, replacing the head of U.S. sales with someone more competent and hiring better salespeople resulted in sales growing from

2 percent to more than 20 percent in less than a year. The problem wasn't the product or pricing strategy, it was sales-force execution.

Our simple recommendation is to avoid unnecessary or counterproductive strategic change based on faulty inference, with a failure in implementation being interpreted as doing the wrong thing or having a business model or strategy that won't work. Before you blame your strategic approach make sure that it is the approach that is to blame and not how well that business model has been executed.

Keep It Simple

Can you and your colleagues describe your company's strategy in a sentence or two? Do you and your colleagues even agree on what the strategy is? There is one powerful lesson from the strategy literature and that is the importance of having people understand what they are supposed to be doing and develop some consensus about where, in their view, business success comes from. In simple terms, you aren't likely to get anywhere if you don't know where you are going.

One of the barriers to communication and coordination, and to actually implementing strategy, is complexity. Apparently some companies seem to think that complicated is better. Maybe they believe that complicated strategies will be more difficult to imitate or discern. Maybe they believe in a complex, complicated, and uncertain world, the only way to succeed is to do complex things. Complicated, difficult-to-explain strategies may or may not confuse your competitors, but they will almost certainly confuse your organization. Consider what Steve Jobs encountered when he returned as acting CEO of Apple in July of 1997. The company was losing money and rumors were swirling that suitors, including Sun and Oracle, were poised to buy the company. Apple was selling so many different kinds of computer hardware at that time that, as Jobs put it, "we couldn't even tell our friends which ones to buy." These included the 1400, 2400, 3400, 4400, 5400, 5500, 6500, 7300, 7600, 8600, 9600, the 20th Anniversary Mac, e-Mate, Newton, and Pippin. As you might expect, this long list not only confused Apple customers, it confused Apple developers who wanted to know which products to work on and which to ignore, and it confused outsider software developers as well.[39] By the end of 1998, Apple was selling none of these products; its product line had only four computer platforms—a laptop and desktop for home and educational markets, and a laptop and desktop for business markets. This simplification was crucial to Apple's return to profitability in 1999.

The transformation at Apple demonstrates why many of the most successful organizations have simple, easy-to-remember strategies that are repeated over and over again. Consider another example. Under the leadership of Richard Kovacevich, Norwest Bank achieved extraordinary results and eventually merged with Wells Fargo, with Kovacevich going on to lead the combined bank. In 1992, Kovacevich printed the first version of a Vision and Values booklet that continues to be used (with revisions) to this day. The company's strategy was described then: "Our strategy to achieve our goals is simple. I hope you can say it in your sleep. First, we want to 'out local' the nationals and 'out national' the locals. We must offer better products and a broader product line than our local competitors so we can be the financial institution of choice for all transactions. We also must outperform our national competitors by staying close to our customers in each of our communities, understanding their needs, and providing professional, personalized, timely service. Second, we want to earn 100 percent of every creditworthy customer's business."[40]

The second part of the strategy leads directly to a measurement that has become a cornerstone of Wells Fargo's reward system: the number of Wells Fargo products a given customer uses, which is a measure of cross-selling. The first part of the strategy, also easy to understand and communicate, directs attention to both offering a broad, comprehensive range of products while simultaneously remaining close to customers and their communities. It is not only a simple strategy; it is also actionable.

Learn As You Go

Southwest Airlines is famous for its quick airplane turnarounds at the gate, something that permits the company to fly more segments and earn more revenue with the same number of planes because the planes are flying more and sitting on the ground less. What people don't often know is how this strategy began. When Southwest started in the early 1970s, its competitors waged a fierce legal battle to keep it out of the air, something possible in those days of airline regulation. In fact, a law was passed—the so-called Wright Amendment, named after Congressman James Wright—that prohibited airlines operating out of Love Field in Dallas, Southwest's base, from flying to any place (or even connecting to any place) beyond eight contiguous states. When Southwest finally got permission to fly, it had almost no money left and its fleet of aircraft had shrunk from four to three. The small company and its employees decided to try and fly its original schedule with just the three planes it had left. So Southwest's strategy of rapid turnarounds was born. The lack of emphasis on strategy formulation has persisted at Southwest over the years. As former CEO Herb Kelleher puts it, "We don't do strategic planning. It's a waste of time. You can spend three months coming up with something, and then you have to get buy-in from the other leadership. By the time you sell it to the board, things could have changed. Then you need to un-sell it to everyone before you can react. We don't do navel gazing. You miss opportunities while you're off thinking."[41]

A small company called Audible Magic, which designs, programs, and sells technology to preclude the transfer of copyrighted material such as records or movies over networks, also has a technology and service that permits automated, low-cost monitoring of advertisements and broadcasts—something that is necessary for accurate royalty payment and to assure advertisers that their ads are being played as purchased. At one point, the company was going to close down the broadcast monitoring business and product line because no deals had been closed and the sales cycle seemed to take forever. Less than six months later, this service was the largest, most rapidly growing, and highest-margin part of the business. The lesson according to the firm's CEO was that "in the digital media business, markets are changing all the time and we just can't predict what segment of our product offerings are going to take off. We have to keep building a great portfolio of products and services, take care of the customers, and see where the opportunities develop."

Similarly, CEO Meg Whitman attributes much of eBay's success to the fact that the company spends less time on strategic analysis and more time trying and tweaking things that seem like they might work, and learning along the way. She said in 2005, "This is a completely new business, so there's only so much analysis you can do." Whitman suggests instead, "It's better to put something out there and see the reaction and fix it on the fly. You could spend six months getting it perfect in the lab or six days in the lab, and we're better off spending six days, putting it out there, getting feedback and then evolving it." Whitman bolsters her arguments about the limits of planning by adding, "You can't predict what's going to happen. It's another way of saying 'perfect' is the enemy of 'good enough.'"[42]

The idea is a simple one, but one that is not often implemented and is belied by the focus on planning and strategic focus: learn as you go. As Andy Grove, former CEO of Intel, said in an interview with Clayton Christensen of the Harvard Business School, "None of us has a real understanding of where we are heading. I don't. I have sense about it . . . but decisions don't wait. Investment decisions or personnel decisions and prioritization don't wait for the picture to be clarified. You have to make them when you have to make them. So you take your shots and clean up the bad ones later."[43]

Balance Attention to Strategy with Attention to the Details of Implementation

One of the most dangerous management practices that we've seen throughout *Hard Facts* is the tendency for mangers and their advisers to latch onto some idea—the "war for talent," keeping personal lives out of the workplace, getting incentives right, seeing more leaders and more leadership as the answer—and drive it to extreme lengths and lose perspective and balance. The same misguided obsession happens with the "strategy is destiny" idea. Certainly, a company can benefit from good decisions about what business to be in and how to compete against other firms, and from using a data-driven, analytical process to guide such decisions. Unfortunately, too many leaders fall prey to a consulting industry that exaggerates the magical powers of strategic analysis and to a business press enamored of the grand idea that will cure all their problems once and for all. The result is that too many companies overemphasize strategy, which detracts time, resources, and focus from the less glamorous and gritty details of implementation and undermines adaptation to shifting conditions.

There may be no better examples of this malady than the source of so much writing and teaching about strategy, business schools themselves. In the 1950s, spurred on by reports by the Carnegie and Ford Foundations and by the example of Carnegie-Mellon University's Graduate School of Industrial Administration, business schools decided to pursue a strategy of emphasizing scholarly research oriented toward the basic disciplines such as economics, sociology, and social psychology. The idea was to teach *foundational concepts* to students rather than the traditional practice of providing them with institutional knowledge and guidelines for action. The strategy has been variously described as *balanced excellence* or *relevance with rigor*.

Two things happened. First, almost every business school soon attempted to implement the same strategy in pretty much the same way, trying to hire the same people and publish in the same journals. This led to a remarkable lack of differentiation in business schools—and also in the research they produced, the courses they taught, and the students they graduated—something commented on by people from the strategy consulting firm Booz Allen Hamilton.[44]

Second, once every major business school decided that this was the right strategy for achieving success, this decision was used to justify why it was best to continue down this path. After all, a clear strategic direction was valued and one wouldn't want to respond too quickly to changing subject matter interests, pressures from the environment, or even encroaching competition. Many observers have noted the amazing stability of business school curricula and research approaches in the face of all kinds of other changes in how companies operate and the kinds of skills that managers need, as well as evidence suggesting that this strategy produces irrelevant faculty research and suspect MBA student outcomes. Indeed, Henry Mintzberg's recent book *Managers Not MBAs* argues that MBA education has the effect of producing managers who are less rather than more effective than those who have never been to business school.[45]

Because of a lack of concern as to whether or not the strategy could be implemented, business schools have done little about the chronic shortage of faculty that meet their standards of relevance and rigor. And because of a commitment to strategic persistence, complaints by students, alumni, and recruiters—unless captured by the now-proliferating rankings done by magazines and newspapers—have engendered very little response. As a consequence, the business school industry is very much in question and facing challenges, including the inability to fill the classes of some surprisingly elite MBA and executive MBA programs.

It ought to be possible to be concerned with strategy and implementation at the same time. It ought to be possible—and indeed desirable—to not overemphasize doing the right thing at the expense of being able to do things effectively. It is in balancing investments of time, attention, and other resources in both strategy and operational implementation that better performance is to be found. Once again, Andy Grove of Intel provides a nice perspective on this issue.

> *I don't think we should forget that there is more to running an enterprise, small or large, than strategy. The revolution in quality control, and the revolution in manufacturing techniques that has taken place in the last 15 years were all data driven . . . And the U.S. economy has benefited incredibly over the last 15 years without a change in strategy, just by seriously embracing the science of manufacturing and quality control. So strategy is important. Figuring out what to do is important. Doing them and doing them well is equally important.*[46]

7

Change or Die?

NO ONE in the business world ever says that you, your people, or your company are good enough and you can rest on your laurels. The not-so-subtle message is that if you aren't constantly getting better by generating new products, services, and business models, or aren't borrowing and installing best practices, then you deserve to be mocked and fired, and your company deserves its inevitable, swift, and certain death. If you resist new ways of thinking or acting, if you aren't ready to start *Winning Through Innovation*, if you are always worried about *Who Moved My Cheese?*, if you chafe at advice like *If It Ain't Broke, Break It*, and are frozen in your tracks by *The Change Monster*, it is better for you and everyone else if you "get off the bus" and make room for those who are ready and willing to embrace change and innovation.[1] We glorify firms that make successful changes, deify their leaders, and demonize those that cling to the past. After all, isn't the choice "change or die"? Or as one creativity guru put it, "Innovate or die? Which of the two appeals to you most?"[2]

These slogans and beliefs aren't exactly wrong, but they are half-truths. Change and innovation are nasty double-edged swords. When companies try something new, it usually fails. And avoiding the wrong move isn't easy—in part, because many people have perverse incentives for downplaying the odds that things will turn ugly and for overestimating the benefits of new technologies, business models, and products. Consider enterprise software, those ubiquitous enterprise resource planning (ERP) systems. There are a lot of people who try to sell you the stuff (and help with implementing it) because it makes them richer, not because it will help your company. The Oracle Web site lists hundreds of success stories about customers who use their software to save money and speed transactions.[3] Of course Oracle doesn't mention that the typical enterprise software implementation takes about twice as long and costs twice as much as projected.[4] And the company certainly doesn't list any failure stories. But implementation of an Oracle financial system at Stanford University was such a nightmare that the administration apologized to the staff for putting them through it, and the State of Ohio, on behalf of Cleveland State University, sued PeopleSoft over a botched ERP implementation.[5]

ERP implementations are only one case of how something that sounds so good can turn out so bad. Too many executives either don't admit or don't know the chances that an ERP implementation will fail, or if it does succeed, how much it will really cost, how much fear will reverberate throughout the organization, or the hours of sheer frustration users will endure before they get these notoriously clumsy and complex systems to work. Knowing the facts about ERP or any other large-scale change *before* taking the leap can avert miseries of all stripes. So, too, can thinking diagnostically about who is going to gain, and who is going to lose, if your organization embraces some particular change.

Fact-based decision making about proposed changes sounds obvious until you see what organizations actually do. Hewlett-Packard (HP) insiders told us they were flabbergasted to discover that HP had done no research on how consumers viewed Compaq products until months *after* HP CEO Carly Fiorina announced that the two firms intended to merge. Fiorina was unhappy to hear that consumers viewed many Compaq products as among the worst in the marketplace and saw most HP products as far superior to Compaq's products. But this information was only considered long *after* HP's top management and board were committed to the merger and after Fiorina had told her top management team that she didn't want to hear any dissent over the merger plans.

These aren't isolated cases. Consider the evidence about the effects and effectiveness of common organizational changes that we've summarized in table 7-1. Although start-ups born with high-commitment HR practices fail less often and perform better than other start-ups, those that later try to switch to such "better" practices perform worse and die at higher rates compared with those that don't make such changes, apparently because of the disruption caused by trying to switch. Quality improvement programs can help companies, as General Motors' and Hyundai's long, hard, expensive, and ultimately successful efforts demonstrate. But many quality programs are just costly window dressing that fails to reduce defects or enhance service. Business process reengineering (BPR) was ballyhooed as a cure for every organizational problem in the late 1980s, but even BPR guru Michael Hammer—who got rich off the movement—now admits that most BPR efforts failed to achieve their goals and that the failure rate of such programs was almost 70 percent. Layoffs are an increasingly common and widely accepted way to cut costs, and research by Darrell Rigby at Bain shows that 26 percent of S&P 500 firms used layoffs just between August 16, 2000, and August 15, 2001. But there is no solid evidence that using layoffs rather than less draconian methods to cut costs increases performance, and there is plenty of evidence that involuntary reductions in force damage both displaced employees and "survivors."

The same problems plague changes in products and services. New products fail at a high rate. Despite all the marketing research and testing that companies now do, there is no sign these failure rates are falling. And if you start a new company, chances are it will fail. We encourage our Stanford students to start companies. It teaches them how to manage, and they often look back on it as one of the great experiences of their lives. But we warn them: "There is a tiny chance you will get rich like the Stanford students who started Google, Yahoo!, or Sun; a big chance your company will be sold for a little bit of money; and a bigger chance that your company will die—leaving you a few years older, with no more money, and an interesting story to tell." Table 7-1 presents evidence about the risks of some of the most common changes that organizations undertake.

Yet, despite all these costs, risks, and horror stories, refusing to change isn't the answer either. Even the riskiest changes can succeed when and if they are done right. Hewlett-Packard completed a series of successful enterprise software implementations in the 1990s, which were completed faster and for less money than originally forecasted.[6] The 1998 merger between Wells Fargo and Norwest was a big financial success, with persistent increases in revenue, profits, and earnings per share in the following five years. Yes, as table 7-1 shows, naysayers who oppose every new change and innovation will be right much of the time. But companies that *never* try anything new or introduce new products or explore new strategies are almost *certain* to die in the long run because customer tastes will change, better technologies will come along, and competitors will find faster and better ways to please their customers. That's the trouble with organizational change: the only thing more dangerous than doing one is never doing any!

TABLE 7-1

Dangerous organizational changes: look before you leap

Type of organizational change	Risk involved	Representative evidence*
Mergers and acquisitions	Despite case studies of successful mergers like Exxon-Mobil and Wells Fargo–Norwest, the typical public company merger has negative effects on the acquiring firm's long-term financial performance. There is also no evidence that health care mergers cut costs.	A study of 947 acquisitions between 1970 and 1989 shows that bigger firms that buy smaller firms (with stock) suffer substantially (25%) inferior returns over a five-year period compared with otherwise similar firms that do not attempt to grow through acquisition. Shareholders of acquired firms do benefit if they sell their stock quickly (especially in the first few months), but not if they hold on to their stock for five years. A subsequent study shows that losses were especially pronounced between 1998 and 2001, when acquiring firms lost an average of 12 cents for every dollar spent (a total of loss $240 billion). A 2004 analysis of 93 published studies showed that, on average, the negative effects on an acquiring firm's performance emerge less than a month (22 days) after an acquisition is announced and persist thereafter. A study of all health maintenance organization mergers in the United States between 1985 and 1997 shows no evidence that mergers decrease costs, despite claims that bigger is better due to economies of scale.[a]
Implementing new enterprise software	Implementation is usually far more expensive and time-consuming than expected. Botched implementations are linked to serious setbacks and failed organizations.	A survey of 232 IT executives by consulting firm Robbins-Gioia found that 51% viewed their ERP (enterprise resource planning) implementations as unsuccessful. A survey of 365 IT executives by the Standish Group showed the typical enterprise software project took about twice as long and cost about twice as much as originally planned, and over 30% were cancelled before completion. Botched implementations happened at Boeing, Dell, Hershey's, Nike, and Stanford. FoxMeyer claimed that a poor implementation drove them into bankruptcy.[b]

Switching to better HR practices	Changing to the "best" HR practices may be so disruptive that it isn't worth it.	The Stanford Project on Emerging Companies study of 181 Silicon Valley start-ups between 1995 and 2001 found that changing people-management systems (even to "better" practices) after the firm had been founded was linked to increased turnover, reduced performance, and double the failure rate.[c]
Quality improvement efforts	Six Sigma and Total Quality Management (TQM) efforts can increase quality and incremental innovation. But focusing on tiny improvements in old systems can distract management attention and resources from the big picture. And many quality efforts are all talk and no action.	Harvard studies of the paint and photography industries show that a focus on process improvement is linked to less radical innovation. Studies of TQM implementations show that, especially after TQM became a fad, companies would often talk about their TQM programs, perhaps do some TQM training, but not take steps to improve the quality of their products or services.[d]
Business process reengineering (BPR)	Although this management fad promised to cut waste and make organizations more efficient, by the mid-1990s, it was clear that most BPR projects were falling far short of their goals and many projects entailed layoffs of people who were actually needed.	A 1994 CSC Index "State of Reengineering Report" of 99 completed reengineering initiatives found that 67% were seen as producing mediocre, marginal, or failed results. Co-architect of BPR Tom Davenport argues that it was never meant to be about just cost cutting, laments that it is "the fad that forgot" people, and asserts that top consulting firms and information technology vendors are the main winners. Even Michael Hammer, the management guru who was made rich and famous by the fad, now admits that only about 30% of BPR projects achieve their goals.[e]
Layoffs	Layoffs alone can't help companies improve profits or long-term performance, and they reduce administrative costs less than believed. They have hidden costs like lawsuits and lost skills, and damage surviving employees' morale, commitment, and physical and mental health.	A University of Colorado study of S&P 500 firms between 1982 and 2000 showed no link between downsizing and subsequent return on assets. A Bain study of S&P 500 companies found that the 158 firms that used layoffs primarily for cost cutting suffered modest drops in stock price. Bain warned it can take 18 months to realize the cost savings from a layoff, and by then the person might be needed again. Other studies suggest that layoffs are focused on workers rather than managers—a process called *featherbedding*—so the proportion of dollars spent on administration increases during "cost-cutting" phases. A Right Associates study found that 70% of managers who remained in downsized firms reported that layoffs were followed by lower employee morale and trust in management. A five-year study of 300 firms by Cigna and the American Management Association showed that "surviving" workers in downsized companies had 100% to 900% increases in medical claims, especially for mental health, substance abuse, and cardiovascular problems.[f]

(continued)

TABLE 7-1 *(continued)*

Dangerous organizational changes: look before you leap

Type of organizational change	Risk involved	Responsive Evidence*
Launching a new product	Developing new products and improving old products are crucial to long-term survival. But most R&D efforts don't result in products, many new products fail, and product failure is often a root cause of firm failure.	Less than 1% of the chemical compounds developed in the R&D process by pharmaceutical firms are ever sold, and only 30% of compounds tested on people are ever sold. The claims that "90% of new products fail" often made in the business press are likely exaggerated. Nevertheless, research using large samples suggests that 30% to 60% of new products that are introduced fail to generate profits. For example, a study of 151 companies showed that the new product failure rate was 40% in food processing firms and 30% in medical instrument firms. A Booz Allen Hamilton study of 700 firms found that nearly all the money spent on new product development was devoted to failed products.[g]
Starting a new organization	The death rates of new and young organizations are substantially higher than for established organizations.	Dun & Bradstreet report that only a third of retail and service businesses live longer than five years. Large-scale studies of semiconductor firms, newspapers, and labor unions suggest that failure rates are substantially higher during the first years of life. A study of 171,000 West German firms shows that new firms have a *honeymoon period*: failure rates are lower at first and then jump to highest levels *during adolescence.*[h]

*The sources for this information appear in "Table 7-1" in the notes section.

Companies in the automobile, computer hardware, computer software, pharmaceutical, and biotechnology industries typically depend on products that are less than five years old for over 50 percent of their sales. And although a Booz Allen Hamilton study of 700 firms found that 46 percent of the money spent on product development led to failed products, it also found that new products accounted for 28 percent of these companies' growth over a five-year period. There are great firms where innovation seems to be continuous, like 3M and Johnson & Johnson. Case studies abound of companies that have thrived through relentless devotion to innovation and change and, in some cases, have reinvented themselves. Nokia started as a lumber company in 1865; sold tires, rubber boots, and computers along the way; and eventually became the leading producer of mobile phones. Hasbro started out selling carpet remnants in 1923 before becoming a toy company. Marriott started out selling root beer in 1927 before evolving into one of the largest hotel chains in the world. IBM is evolving from a computer company to, increasingly, a services company—it still sells servers, but just sold its personal computer business. There is also evidence from large-scale studies that keeping pace with technological innovation is crucial to long-term survival. Glenn Carroll and Albert Teo studied every American automobile company that operated between 1885 and 1981, almost 2,200 companies. Nearly all are gone today, but some lived longer than others, and General Motors and Ford survive. Carroll and Teo examined the introduction of 631 product and process innovations over these 100-plus years and found that firms that introduced a steady flow of new innovations were more likely to live longer than those that didn't.

We wish we had magic answers about which changes are certain to help your organization and how to implement them so that you and your people will never suffer a moment of doubt, fear, or confusion. Business books like *Seeing What's Next* and *Change Without Pain* have noble aspirations, but such titles aren't promises that any leader can actually keep.[7] An evidence-based approach to change does, however, suggest steps that you can take to diminish the risk and the pain.

Is the Change Worth Doing?

Executives, employees, analysts, academics, and business reporters may have vehement opinions about whether a merger, new product, layoff, reorganization, or software implementation will save, bolster, maim, or kill an organization. Yet, at the time a company decides to make a major change, no one really knows if it will succeed or fail. Even though no one can predict the future, there are steps that leaders and their teams can take to increase the odds that they are making the right change, set expectations so that they can learn along the way, and make it easier to pull the plug if the initial decision was probably wrong. We've woven together research by economists, psychologists, sociologists, and business researchers to identify eight questions that, if considered honestly at the outset, will lead to better decisions about which changes to make, delay, and avoid. We summarize these in Table 7-2.

1. Is the Practice Better Than What You Are Doing Right Now?

Some changes may not be improvements because your organization is actually already doing them—you just don't know it! Every few years, we hear the same story about a different company. Someone comes up with a "new" product or business practice and starts implementing it, and then—often quite late in the game—discovers that someone else in the company is already working on it, or worse yet, it has been in place for years. We once supervised a team of Stanford students who were developing a workforce planning model for a large technology company. The team was asked to use historical data to predict how many temporary workers a large division would need as demand for the firm's products waxed and waned. About six weeks into this 10-week project, the division's management discovered that such a model already existed and that the CFO had used it for *years* to determine staffing levels for the division. The project was ended abruptly.

Assuming that what you are considering is something truly new to your organization, not something you are already doing but don't know about, you might want to consider learning from the experience of others. This is hard to do, as the usual human confidence drives leaders to believe that, regardless of the problems that others may have encountered, they will do better. We hear this all the time when we talk about, for instance, mergers or ERP implementations—that the other companies weren't as clever, didn't do as much or as good planning, didn't have the same level of talent—a lot of stories about why "this time, it will be different." Our general advice is to view such stories with a proper amount of skepticism—not that they are never true, but the temptation to believe that you will do better is almost overwhelming regardless of the reality.

There are, however, times when the evidence about how a particular change has worked elsewhere may be weak or inconsistent. For example, one organizational change not evaluated here is whether there is a *first-mover*

TABLE 7-2

What to ask before launching a major organizational change

The big question	Probing for the right answer
Is the practice better than what you are doing right now?	• Are you already doing it under another banner? • How often does it succeed elsewhere? • Can you test it in your organization first?
Is the change really worth the time, disruption, and money?	• Are your time line and budget realistic given what actually happens to other companies? • Do the people who are selling you the solution have incentives for underestimating the costs?
Is it best to make only symbolic changes instead of core changes?	• Is this a core change that will actually hurt the organization's performance? • Are powerful groups inside or outside the organization clamoring for this change anyway? • If you fail to make any changes, will it damage your organization's reputation and key relationships?
Is doing the change good for you, but bad for the company?	• Will doing it increase your fame, prestige, or pay? • Will doing it mean that someone powerful owes you a favor? • Will it make your job easier and everyone else's harder?
Do you have enough power to make the change happen?	• Do you have enough internal support and resources? • Are your current allies powerful enough? • Do you have a strategy for strengthening supporters and weakening opponents?
Are people already overwhelmed by too many changes?	• Do people believe that this change will actually stick, or is it just a flavor of the month? • Are people still trying to recover from the last major change? Are they still implementing it, or still so exhausted that they are not ready for the new change? • Are so many other things being changed at once that people couldn't possibly do everything well?
Will people be able to learn and update as the change unfolds?	• Do they view the change as a beautiful and perfect thing, or prototype—work in progress—that will need to be tweaked, or even drastically changed, as new information emerges? • Is the team showing that they can learn and improve the planned change in response to resistance, criticisms, and suggestions—or do they simply dismiss all concerns as stupid ideas from stupid people?
Will you be able to pull the plug?	• How will you know it is failing? • How will you know when it is time to quit? • Who will judge it a failure and pull the plug?

advantage for companies that introduce the first product in a category or are first to enter a new market—the evidence is so inconsistent that developing simple guidelines for management action isn't possible yet, at least in our judgment.[8] And even when there is strong evidence about certain changes, as with mergers or ERP implementations, you can't predict exactly how they will play out in your organization.

There are ways to look before you leap. In addition to collecting evidence about the wisdom of some change, companies can limit risk by first running experiments or pilot programs: if the idea still seems promising, they can refine it before rolling it out to everyone. General Electric, for example, didn't design its renowned "Work-Out" process in finished form, and then roll out the perfect solution in one division after another. There was constant trial-and-error learning in each business, different consultants tried competing variations in different businesses, and CEO Jack Welch pressed his people to spread the best features of the best variations around the company.[9]

Experiments or pilot program aren't always possible—you probably can't do a trial merger, for example. But if and when you can use small experiments, you have a leg up on competitors. And it is sometimes possible even to do major, systemwide changes in a gradual process that permits learning and experimentation along the way. In the mid-1990s, Hewlett-Packard (HP) did several successful SAP software implementations by taking an approach that they called *fresh engineering*. Managers Mei-Lin Cheng and Julie Anderson assembled a 35-person team that implemented a new order-fulfillment system from the ground up. This system was crucial to HP because one-third of its revenue flowed through the system. To learn how the system worked, team members started by "stapling ourselves to an order." Mei-Lin Cheng told us, "We went to the Port of Oakland, went back to corporate headquarters in Palo Alto with our toothbrushes to signify that the darn order sat overnight in the mainframe system, went to the customer, and so on," which showed the team the pain points and taught them how the new system should work. Next, they began using the software to simulate the ordering process. The first time they put an order into the system, they couldn't even get it to the HP warehouse. After they finally worked out the bugs, the team began by replacing the process used for just *one* product line that was shipped to *one* HP customer. When that worked (after getting the bugs out), they spread the system to a second product line for that customer, and then another, as they slowly turned off the faucet on the old system. No customer ever had to choose which system to use. Once the team turned on the new system for a given product line, the old was shut off for good—but only when they were sure the new one would work.

Mei-Lin Cheng emphasized it was unrealistic to expect anything so complex could work right the first time. Getting the system to work through trial and error and rolling it out one product line at a time enabled them to learn without forcing the HP North American distribution system to grind to a halt. After just eight months, they were able to deliver products to one of their biggest customers in eight days (versus 26 days before) while cutting inventories by nearly 20 percent.

2. Is the Change Really Worth the Time, Money, and Disruption?

Even when another practice is better than what you are doing right now, the pain might not be worth the gain. Getting good estimates of costs may not be easy; senior executives and their advisers consistently underestimate the cost of changes, as the rather appalling evidence about everything from layoffs to business process reengineering to product development shows.

People not only underestimate the costs, they also frequently overestimate the gains from implementing business practices, technologies, and strategies, particularly things that others are doing. This is partly because of the *grass is greener* phenomenon. When we are outsiders watching another company doing something, what we mostly see are the great results—not the hard work, the problems, the pitfalls, and the failures. So, we rush to copy what others are doing and often ignore our own homegrown expertise and ideas. We saw this process unfold a few years ago during our research at Fresh Choice, a buffet-style restaurant featuring salads, pasta, and breads. Fresh Choice was constantly chasing the next idea to help solve its business and operational problems by looking outside—for instance, purchasing a small, competitive concept called Zoopa that was, ironically enough, itself a copy of Fresh Choice, but with better execution. During the evaluation process, Fresh Choice executives concluded that Zoopa was a great company that could provide great new ideas for Fresh Choice to use. Once the deal was consummated, however, Fresh Choice executives found that Zoopa people were not endowed with magical powers and practices, they just did what Fresh Choice knew should be done, but they did it more consistently and better. The Zoopa people were soon driven out of the company and the acquired restaurants came to resemble, in all aspects including performance, the Fresh Choice units. The lesson: beware of overestimating what you will get by copying what you see at other companies. They may not know anything more than you, and indeed, they may have many of the same problems that you have. Once Fresh Choice acquired Zoopa stores, and began trying to run them, they realized that the Zoopa system had most of the same challenges as the Fresh Choice system, Zoopa store managers were just more skilled at finding ways to minimize the damage. So things often look better from a distance where the various problems and blemishes are less visible.[10]

3. Is It Best to Make Only Symbolic Changes Instead of Core Changes?

Every organization is besieged by multiple and conflicting demands. There are times when groups—employees, the press, a public interest group, analysts, or shareholders—demand changes that are simply too expensive or disruptive to install throughout the organization. There are other times when companies want to send the message that they've adopted the latest business practice but really don't want to change how the organization operates. Simply ignoring such demands can get a company in trouble. Most executives won't admit it, but almost every company makes visible changes in how the company appears to the outside world but that don't actually change how the company actually does things. Two examples include announcing stock buy-backs as a signal of confidence in the future success of the company but not buying back all the shares authorized, and instituting executive pay-for-performance schemes that the outside world—especially stock analysts—love, even though research has shown that these schemes have little if any affect on how much pay is ultimately handed out to executives, and even though many companies that announce programs for linking executive pay to long-term performance (and enjoy a short-term increase in share prices as a result) never actually implement those programs.[11] Companies sometimes put up such camouflage for the wrong reasons: so they can keep cheating, treating employees badly, or spewing out pollution. But the fact is that to maintain a favorable reputation while protecting core business from excessive and well-meaning but flawed intrusion, every effective company makes symbolic changes in its structures, training, management practices, and language that change more of how it looks than what it does.

4. Is Doing the Change Good for You, but Bad for the Company?

When it comes to adopting management fads like employee empowerment, Barry Staw and Lisa Epstein's study of the largest U.S. industrial firms showed that the effects on firm performance are unclear, but that at least pretending to hop on the latest management bandwagon is a good way for a CEO to get a raise. Economists talk about how these *perverse incentives* can lead executives and organizations to take actions that are not in the best interests of the firm as a whole. Such incentives may help explain why, although mergers damage the performance of acquiring firms, companies keep doing them anyway. Executives in the acquiring firm may damage their own stock in the long term, but leading a larger firm can increase their pay and status. The investment bankers who broker these deals only make the big bucks if the deal closes. CEO John Thompson of Symantec, like most experienced executives, recognizes these incentives and so views advice from investment bankers with a grain of salt. He told a group of Stanford students that, yes, Symantec does a lot of acquisitions, but he is skep-tical of investment bankers' opinions because "candidly, their 'predictions' are driven by a desire for fees; organic growth is cheaper." [12]

The idea that changes can be good for some people or interests but not for others is not particularly startling—it is almost inevitable that any change will create some winners and some losers. From the board of directors' perspective, the challenge is to try and see who wins and who loses as a way of evaluating the proposed change perspective. From the point of view of senior leadership, or anyone else working inside the organization, the aphorism that "where you stand depends on where you sit" is always useful in understanding why people are taking a particular positions. And recognizing the trade-offs between individual and organizational interests in any particular change is important in thinking about what to do and how to do it. If you want to be an effective and ethical leader, you need to be aware that seemingly harmless, or even helpful, moves can be costly to your organization. For example, in one large firm we worked with, some senior executives quietly worried whether millions in fees were paid to a prestigious professional service firm because they actually needed the advice, or because the CEO saw working with the famous firm as a path to personal prestige and power.

5. Do You Have Enough Power to Make the Change Happen? If Not, You Might Forget About It

Power is sometimes seen as a dirty word, but it is a fact of organizational life. Support for an organizational change effort from senior management, even from the top dog, doesn't mean it will be implemented. The list of leaders who have tried but failed to change big organizations goes on and on, from Durk Jager at Procter & Gamble, to Jacques Nasser at Ford, to Jill Barad at Mattel, to Howell Raines at the *New York Times*. Leaders are sometimes shocked to discover how little power they have to push changes through an organization. Howell Raines, former executive editor of the *New York Times*, started his term in 2001 with the belief that he was doing the right thing: "A quiet but intense factional war was going on within the *Times*, between the senior editors who endorsed these improvements and traditionalists on the newsroom floor and among mid-level managers. The latter group wanted the paper to stay the way it was and took as an insult the animating idea behind our strategy: the idea that 'the world's greatest newspaper' is not nearly as good as it could be and ought to be."[13]

Raines was fired in 2003, partly because of the Jayson Blair plagiarism scandal that damaged the *Times'* reputation for careful and ethical reporting. As Raines now admits, however, he also lost his job because he never got the support of those traditionalists for the sweeping changes he tried to make. Raines didn't quite realize how much power they had, how his brusque bullying undermined his support from both groups, and especially how much he eroded his power by running so many *Times* articles and editorials railing against the Augusta National Golf Club's refusal to admit women. Not only did Raines insist on running front-page stories after much of his staff no longer saw the subject as newsworthy, he killed a column by Pulitzer Prize winner Dave Anderson that disagreed with a *Times* editorial about Augusta. So when things got tough during the Blair scandal, there was little support within the paper for Raines or his strategy.

As Jeffrey Pfeffer's book *Managing with Power* shows, people who make organizational change happen get realistic information about the power dynamics, figure out which groups are likely to support and oppose their initiatives, identify whose cooperation and support they must have to succeed, and use means ranging from gossip, to public forums, to attitude surveys, to careful observation of facial expressions to track concerns and shifts in the political wind.[14] The political landscape is not immutable, but there is no point in starting something that can't be successfully concluded. Successful organizational politicians are especially skilled at inventing ways to sidestep, neutralize, and even gain support from natural enemies.

We are working with software giant SAP on an initiative aimed at making its software easier to use and are accelerating reliance on user-centered design throughout the company. The Design Services Team (DST), which is spearheading this movement in the company, reports directly to SAP's board, has extensive contact with CEO Henning Kagermann and Chairman Hasso Platner, and has many resources at their disposal—all classic signs that a group has the power to turn ideas into action. Yet the team's leaders—Senior Vice President and DST founder Zia Yusuf and team co-heads Michael Heinrich and Matthew Holloway—believe support from the top and resources are not enough and that nothing will change unless there is a cultural change that puts end-users at the center of the software design process and gives them support from the powerful internal groups that actually develop the software. They've had key early successes by doing projects that are (intentionally) staffed largely by hard-nosed developers from groups that have traditionally downplayed user needs in favor of functionality or technical performance. These early projects not only have produced user-friendly software, they have changed the opinions of many hard-core developers, who now value user-centered design and tell their brethren, "I was cynical at first too, but this stuff works, it can help us design better software."[15]

6. Are People Already Overwhelmed by Too Many Changes?

Despite the wonders of the information age, organizations are still composed of human beings. Even the most brilliant group of people can only make so many decisions, learn so much, and do so many things at any given time. As Nobel Prize winner Herbert Simon pointed out, although this insight is so obvious that it seems trivial, economists and managers routinely use models that assume human beings have unlimited information-processing capacity. But people's ability to focus and make choices is limited. As a consequence, too many choices can actually cause people to freeze in their tracks and do nothing. For instance, a study of participation in retirement plans (40l(k)s) found that the more investment options people had, beyond a relatively small number, the less likely they were to enroll in the plan at all and the more likely that, if enrolled, they would leave their deposits invested in a money market account.[16] A study of all U.S. semiconductor firms between 1946 and 1984 found that, although having a large number of products on the market helps firms survive longer, introducing numerous products into the market all at once is dangerous. After one of these bursts of simultaneous product introduction, possibly because of the overload on both customers and employees, the chances that a firm would die increased an average of 40 percent.[17]

Much the same thing happens when companies introduce too many new management practices too fast. During research for our book, the *Knowing-Doing Gap*, we found the "flavor-of-the-month problem" was one of the biggest impediments to turning knowledge into action.[18] Senior executives would introduce new programs at such high rates that it was impossible for even the most skilled managers to keep pace, plus people didn't think they needed to take the changes seriously since a new flavor would be coming along soon. As we saw in the case of incentives, sometimes less is more.

Senior leaders who push for fewer changes and push for them harder are more likely to have success than leaders who introduce so many changes that people become confused about which matter most and least to the company and how to spread their time and money among the initiatives.

7. Will People Be Able to Learn and Update As the Change Unfolds?

We've emphasized throughout this book that traveling through life with an attitude of wisdom—the ability to act with knowledge while doubting what you know—is the single most important quality that a leader, adviser, or team can have for practicing evidence-based management. Updating on the basis of new information, either generated from the company's own experience or from external evidence, is an essential part of acting on the basis of facts. This means that part of deciding whether to embark on a course of change is finding out whether a beautiful and perfect solution is expected, or whether the proposal is seen as a decent starting point that will need to be changed, and perhaps even abandoned, as it unfolds and people learn from experience. If the change does not permit updating because of its essential characteristics—some things are very hard to undo—or if the organization does not readily or easily learn from experience, the risk of undertaking the change gets a lot higher.

We saw an attitude of wisdom in action in the mid-1990s when we went to a companywide meeting at IDEO, the renowned innovation company we talked about in chapter 4, at which then-CEO (and current Chairman) David Kelley announced a major reorganization. The company, especially its Palo Alto headquarters, had grown so fast that it was becoming increasingly difficult to manage a culture of innovation in a group of around 150 professionals who all reported directly to the senior team. Sorting out who would staff the 50 or so different design projects IDEO undertook each year was one of the worst headaches. At the start of the meeting, Kelley acknowledged that IDEO had become unwieldy and then introduced five leaders, each charged with heading a new "studio." Each leader made a pitch about "why you should join my studio." Unlike any reorganization we've ever seen, the affected people choose which group to join rather than being assigned. They listed their first, second, and third choices, but all the designers got their first choices. Kelley reminded them that IDEO's guiding philosophy was "enlightened trial and error outperforms the planning of flawless intellects." So Kelley encouraged the IDEO designers to see this new structural arrangement and their assignment as a changeable prototype, just like the products, services, and experiences they designed for clients. To reinforce this message, Kelley hung hundreds of little *Experiment* signs throughout the company and—in a move that shocked all of us who knew him—shaved off his trademark Groucho Marx–style mustache for the meeting. He told the people that "the changes we are trying are just like shaving off my mustache, they are temporary and reversible experiments."

8. Will You Be Able to Pull the Plug?

A more extreme version of updating is being able to terminate the experiment. A change poses lower risk if there is an option to discontinue if it becomes clear that the new idea, however well intentioned, was a mistake. That's because damage control is possible, as contrasted with an effort that, once under way, can neither be stopped nor undone. Unfortunately, such exits can be difficult because, once initiatives and programs are started, they take on a life of their own.

Many readers will be familiar with the concept of *escalating commitment*, the idea that once we make a choice, particularly if that choice is both public and consequential, we are reluctant to change. So, for instance, an early study by Barry Staw showed that people who made an initial investment decision and were given feedback that things were not going well tended to put even more resources into their chosen course of action. Decades of research have shown that escalation of commitment is a widespread phenomenon and one that is hard to avoid or overcome.[19]

A second process may be even more pernicious: the tendency to avoid looking at the consequences of past decisions. Note that escalation requires reviewing a decision and then piling on more resources; avoidance means people don't look back at all. We have observed many boards making major decisions, such as mergers, changes in pricing strategy, and hiring a new CEO. We have been almost completely unsuccessful in getting board members to go back and review those decisions, not so they can assign blame, but so they can actually learn something. There is, after all, no learning without reflection. The problem seems to be twofold. First, people like to feel good about themselves and their competencies. One way to avoid feeling bad is to avoid confronting your mistakes, and the best way to avoid confronting mistakes, other than not making any, is to avoid reviewing past actions. Second, there is the oft-expressed phrase that since what is done is done, the company needs to move forward and make the best of the situation it currently confronts. Although this is certainly true, and the expression "no use crying over spilled milk" is pragmatically useful, if people never understand how and why the milk got spilled in the first place, the odds of recurrence are higher than if learning had actually happened. In the worst cases, people make the same mistakes again and again, but pretend as if the same old problems are brand-new challenges.

Commitment pressures and lack of open reflection are especially prevalent in places where people feel insecure about their positions—in places infected with fear. Quality guru W. Edwards Deming's recommendation to "drive out fear" contains much wisdom. When fear and insecurity are rampant, reviews of past actions and decisions often degenerate into a game of blame and punishment, which squelches learning and continuous improvement.

Does Change Need to Be Difficult and Take a Long Time?

There is another important half-truth about organizational change (and if you believe it is the whole truth, change becomes a lot harder): that organizational change invariably takes a long time, is hard to accomplish, and is best if done slowly. It is common to hear leaders and their advisers lament that changing an organization's culture takes many years, if it can be done at all. This conventional, and flawed, idea is a big reason why profound change is so rarely attempted. This is a tough half-truth to disprove, because it has elements of self-fulfillment embedded in it. After all, if you expect change to be difficult and take a long time, it will.

This is a particularly dangerous half-truth because it is a roadblock to getting anything done. Consider three of these effects. First, there is the deadline effect. Remember when you were in school? If a paper was due December 10, when did you start it? Be honest, did you really start in October? Everyone knows we put things off until the last minute. The implication: if I tell you a culture change is going to take five years, when you are going to start? Perhaps Year Four! If you put off starting a change effort or devoting resources to it, the change will, of course, take longer to complete.

Second, there is the urgency effect. Crucial and pressing issues and problems are not postponed; conversely, if something is readily postponed, the message is that it must not be urgent or especially important. So when leaders tell their people that culture change will take a long time, they are conveying that it is not the highest priority. Do people push and expend extra energy to accomplish less important things? Not often. So once again, the message that change will take time, and its implication that it can't be that urgent, create an absence of energy around the change that makes it more difficult and time-consuming to implement.

And finally there is the perception-of-difficulty effect. If I tell you things are going to be difficult, or if I imply that things are going to be difficult by saying that they are going to take a long time, I have given you some good reasons to avoid the change or postpone it. Most of us prefer to do things that aren't difficult and risky. So, again the message creates its own reality.

But doesn't profound change take a long time? Actually no, it doesn't have to. Continental Airlines (as we described in chapter 5) went from worst to first in on-time performance and, more importantly, profoundly changed its employee and customer service culture in about a year.[20] Magma Copper changed its employee relations culture from one of labor strife and low productivity to one of cooperation and remarkable productivity gains in about 18 months. In 1989 Magma was near bankruptcy with everything about the company broken, and by 1992 the cover story of *Industry Week* celebrated its more than 50 percent gain in productivity and its financial recovery.[21] DaVita (formerly known as Total Renal Care), the largest operator of kidney dialysis centers in the United States, was almost bankrupt in 2000. Kent Thiry, the company's new CEO, transformed fundamental elements of the culture in less than two years. Within a few years, the stock price went from $2 to $40 a share and patient outcome measures rose to among the best in the industry. We could go on, but the point is clear: culture change does not necessarily need to drag on for years or be painful and difficult at every stage. It's all about how you approach it.

Even the best change decision will be a disaster if it is implemented poorly. The organizational change literature is vast, but as we plowed through the huge pile of cases, cautionary tales, and quantitative studies, four persistent lessons about change popped up. We found that, although there are times when change is slow and painful, organizations can change remarkably fast when the right conditions are in place. Despite all the warnings about resistance to change, the belief that "organizational change is difficult and takes a long time" is a dangerous half-truth. Renowned organizational researchers including James March and Karl Weick show that organizations are surprisingly adaptive and can change quickly and easily.[22] They warn that the organization may not change in ways that a particular group (including senior management) expect or want. A change program or initiative may have unintended effects, both positive and negative, or people may pursue it with more force than its sponsors ever imagined or wanted.

Yet there is a basic story underlying most successful change efforts. Change happens when:

1. People are *dissatisfied* with the status quo

2. The *direction* they need to go is clear (at least much of the time) and they stay focused on that direction

3. There is confidence conveyed to others—more accurately *overconfidence*—that it will succeed (so long as it is punctuated by reflective self-doubt and updating as new information rolls in)

4. They accept that change is a *messy process* marked by episodes of confusion and anxiety that people must endure

We call these elements the *big four*. To implement change effectively, a manager's job is to make sure that all these elements are in place, and when they are not, act to put them in place. Table 7-3 provides a brief summary of these four intertwined forces for change.

TABLE 7-3

The big four: making fast and effective change happen after the decision

1. Dissatisfaction	People need to be unhappy with the current state of affairs. If unhappiness with the status quo isn't there, create it.
2. Direction	Relentlessly communicate what the change is, why it is necessary, and what people ought to be doing *right now* with as much clarity as possible. If you aren't saying, writing, and modeling the same message over and over again, it probably isn't going to stick.
3. Overconfidence— punctuated by self-doubt and updating	Express *excessive faith* that the change will succeed and be worth the pain, time, and money in the end. Creating a self-fulfilling prophecy is one of the most powerful things you can do to increase the odds of success, regardless of the success rate experienced elsewhere. To avoid the dangers of operating on blind faith, however, confident actions need to be punctuated by episodes where people openly *discuss their doubts and uncertainties* and *update* to incorporate new facts into what the organization does.
4. Embrace the mess	Accept that there will always be errors, setbacks, miscommunication, frayed nerves, and frightening rumors when a person or organization tries to do something new, no matter how well the change is planned and implemented. Treat glitches as a normal part of the change process, learn from them, assume that everyone has the best intentions, and focus on how to fix the problem instead of whom to blame. Point at solutions instead of at each other.

1. Dissatisfaction

The motivational power of a "burning platform" is hard to dispute. The apparent difficulty and risk of taking on a major change can evaporate when there is convincing evidence—and widespread agreement—that the organization is in peril. When we tell people about Continental's success in transforming its culture and service in about a year, the typical response is, "It was easier for them, they were facing yet another bankruptcy and their potential disappearance." Similarly, DaVita had less than 90 days' worth of cash to run the business, was in default on most of the company's loan covenants, and faced immediate financial catastrophe. So it was not as difficult to get employees' attention and convince them of the need to change immediately. And the fact that General Motors closed its Fremont automobile assembly plant before it reopened as a joint venture with Toyota—called New United Motors Manufacturing (NUMMI)—provided indisputable evidence that there was a crisis, thus setting the stage for remarkable improvements in everything from employee absenteeism and substance abuse levels, to productivity and quality.

But the conclusion that deep changes are easier to do during a crisis isn't particularly obvious. There is evidence that, at least at first, the stress of a crisis can cause people, teams, and organizations to *freeze up*—to be so riddled with fear and anxiety that they cling to the past even more tightly.[23] Companies in crisis also often have little money to fund major change programs. Making change while pressed to the wall certainly increases some people's motivation, but they may have fewer resources of any kind to rely on in the effort. Plus customers and employees often have other options. Customers who abandon the company may further amplify financial problems and create a need to devote even greater time, money, and energy to marketing and sales efforts. And big changes can be more difficult to do as experienced people head for the door, something they are likely to do in times of company difficulty. Yet a persistent theme throughout the change literature is that, despite these impediments, dissatisfaction provokes people to question old ways of doing things and fuels motivation to find and install better new ways—especially when leaders can find ways to dampen fear and increase trust and psychological safety.

There is often ambiguity about whether an organization is actually in crisis. The question of what is satisfactory or unsatisfactory performance—and thus the sense of urgency and motivation fueled by dissatisfaction—is driven by what leaders say and do, not just objective facts. For many years, Andy

Grove was quite good at having Intel live by his mantra "only the paranoid survive," even though for much of this period the company had an overwhelming share of the microprocessor market. In contrast David Kearns, former CEO of Xerox, told one of us that when he first took over in the early 1980s, the company lacked a sense of urgency even though competitors were not only selling cheaper small copiers, Xerox's manufacturing costs for small copiers were higher than the retail prices for similar copiers sold by competitors. The lack of urgency was bolstered by two rationalizations from senior Xerox executives: first, that the small copiers from companies such as Canon and Ricoh competed in a different market segment and so weren't relevant to the main Xerox business; and second, that Xerox's manufacturing costs were falling, so eventually Xerox would catch up—ignoring that competitors were also making improvements all the while.

One of the reasons that stretch goals—or "big, hairy, audacious goals," to use the phrase from *Built to Last*—are so useful is that they generate a sense of striving and dissatisfaction with the status quo that is not easily met, which fuels continuous motivation.[24] We mentioned that when Kent Thiry became CEO of DaVita (then Total Renal Care) in 2000, the company was just months from bankruptcy and in default on many loans—so convincing people that they needed to do things differently wasn't difficult. But even in 2005, with the stock price up more than 20 times and the company doing well, Thiry was able to inspire aspiration for even greater things. He did this partly by endlessly repeating three pairs of questions and answers. Question 1: "What is DaVita?" Answer 1: "New." He then pointed out that even though the renamed company was now five years old, it was still new because it was making acquisitions and continually transforming itself and striving for higher levels of performance. Question 2: "Whose company is it?" Answer 2: "Ours." Thiry meant "ours" in that everyone in the company had both the opportunity and the responsibility to make the organization successful and what they wanted it to be. Finally, Question 3: "What could the company be?" Answer 3: "Special." This meant becoming the best dialysis company in the history of the world and providing the best clinical outcomes for patients. Thiry always expressed recognition and appreciation for what DaVita had achieved. But he repeated these three questions and answers again and again to keep alive the rumble of dissatisfaction that had saved the company and to inspire people to even greater accomplishments. This mindset stimulates the continuous improvement and ongoing change that drives continued success.

2. Direction

It is easy to get lost or distracted, to succumb in behavior to the saying, "the urgent drives out the important," or to lose focus on what actually matters for business success. So, accomplishing change rapidly requires a clear sense of direction and a focus on those critical activities necessary for success. Reactivity, a Silicon Valley start-up founded during the dot-com boom, is alive today largely because this is exactly what their senior team did to help the company navigate the dot-com bust.

John Lilly, Brian Roddy, and Bryan Rollins founded Reactivity in 1998. Unlike most start-ups at the time, Reactivity turned a $600,000 profit its first year by providing high-end Web consulting services to more than 80 companies. They also incubated other start-ups, the most publicized being a collaborative software company called Zaplet that ultimately received $130 million in venture capital before merging with MetricStream in 2004. Reactivity brought in $3 million in consulting revenue in 2000 and raised $23 million of venture funds, which it used to expand consulting and incubation services; grow to 70 people; open offices in Boston, Austin, and Seattle; and hire an experienced senior team. Glenn Osaka from Hewlett-Packard was brought in as CEO in January of 2001. Soon after Osaka arrived, the technology bust hit Silicon Valley. The venture capital funds that supported Reactivity's once lucrative consulting and incubation services evaporated by late 2001.

Unlike many struggling dot-coms, Reactivity didn't close. Rather Osaka, Lilly, and Roddy started "a major reset." By 2002, they had closed all offices except Silicon Valley, cut the company to 17 people, and voluntarily returned $12 million to investors. Why give back the money? The team believed that having too much money too early in the restart process would, as John Lilly put it, "make us dumb," tempting them to hire people they didn't need yet and think about ideas too long without testing them, and creating a false sense of security when urgency was required. For several months, the team brainstormed different possible directions for the company, weighing people's skills, potential market demands, and what was realistic given their limited funds. They decided that Reactivity should become a product-based company and use their substantial technical skill to become an enterprise software firm, developing sophisticated products to "enable secure XML and Web services." After Osaka, Lilly, and Roddy decided—with the board's constant backing and guidance—to make this drastic change, they identified the few things that really mattered to the firm's survival: developing the products, getting customers, and later getting additional venture capital. They quickly stopped everything else the firm was doing and for the next few years focused their own and every other employee's attention on doing a small number of key things.

We remember watching Osaka explain to a software designer that he had to stop bringing in consulting work because, although it would generate some cash in the short term, it would distract them from developing and selling the products that were the only hope for saving the company. As Lilly put it, "The point we focused on through the transition was that customers and revenue were ultimately all that mattered. Everyone who stayed through the transition did selling work, including making cold calls and talking with customers. That was a hard thing for a lot of the engineers. That was the message we focused on." This clear direction and relentless focus enabled Reactivity to get through the tough times, develop award-winning renowned XML products, recruit an impressive list of customers, and receive several additional rounds of "restart" financing.[25] As we showed in *The Knowing-Doing Gap* and explore further in the next chapter on leadership, being specific about the few things that matter most is a hallmark of effective leadership.

3. Overconfidence—Punctuated by (Private) Self-Doubt and Continuous Updating

People like to associate with success—successful people, successful organizations, and successful projects inside organizations. This tendency is sometimes called *basking in reflected glory* and is illustrated by a study showing that college students were more likely to wear clothing with school colors and logos on it on Mondays following the football team's victories than on Mondays following a defeat.[26] What this means for mobilizing support to make change rapidly is simple: those leading the change need to project confidence in its ultimate success. Perhaps the starkest example of such confidence occurred during the serious mechanical problems that befell the Apollo 13 space mission, when the phrase "failure is not an option" (because the astronauts would die) was uttered. Talented individuals are more likely to want to work on things that look as if they are going to be successful, and to the extent that more talent and support gets attracted to projects, the projects will be more successful. So, once again, we see the operation of a self-fulfilling prophecy. Moreover, emotions are contagious, including the emotions of confidence and enthusiasm. So, belief in success helps motivate and inspire others, and creates a climate where effort, and thus success, is more likely.[27]

The thoughtful reader will already have noted the apparent contradiction. On the one hand, confidence and belief that a change effort will be successful are helpful for ensuring success, but on the other hand, we advocate updating, abandoning doomed efforts, and learning from experience as it accumulates. How can confidence and enthusiasm—and belief in the ultimate success of the endeavor and the team's abilities—be reconciled with the need to also be realistic, to admit setbacks, and to learn from those problems so that companies don't persist with failing trajectories?

The answer is for leaders to act with confidence, but not necessarily believe they know as much or are as certain as they appear. As we've shown and will explore further in the next chapter, striking a balance between confident action and constructive self-doubt is part of being a wise leader. In the late 1980s, Pfeffer saw this balance in action when he observed Dr. Frances Conley, the first tenured female neurosurgeon at Stanford. Dr. Conley was reviewing films of a malignant brain tumor with her surgical fellows. Now, and even more so then, malignant brain tumors are usually death sentences. Treatment options were limited and there was much uncertainty about whether to use surgery, radiation, or various drugs. In talking with the neurosurgeons she was training, Conley was candid about the options, the strengths and weaknesses of each, and openly confronted the uncertainty about what to do. But when she and her team went to visit the patient, they conveyed a different demeanor. Without denying the seriousness of the illness, the team confidently told the patient what they had decided was the best course of treatment. When Pfeffer asked about this shift in tone, Conley emphasized the importance of a patient's mental state on survival and the will to live, and the so-called *placebo effect*—the well-documented finding (especially in pharmaceutical research) that just believing that something (even a sugar pill) is working can produce health improvement.[28] Conley also emphasized that it was important to be confident because she didn't want the patient running for the door and into the hands of a less capable team. As Conley and her team demonstrated that day, it is both possible and constructive to project confidence, even while fully recognizing uncertainties, limitations, and the need to learn more.

The lesson for managers is clear: you can privately describe doubts and uncertainties and fully recognize the limitations of your knowledge and abilities, while still projecting the confidence required to get others to commit their energy and effort. We dig further into the nuances of this lesson in the next chapter on leadership, as the ability to strike this balance is also a hallmark of skilled leaders.

4. Embrace the Mess

There are many paradoxes associated with how managers think about change, be it introducing new products or changing management practices. An important one to recognize and get beyond is the following. If you ask any scientist, engineer, or manager the likelihood that a new technology will go from laboratory to market without setbacks and changes in direction, they will tell you it almost never happens. Similarly, people recognize that implementing changes in management practices require improvisation and that things seldom go completely as planned. Nonetheless, you can find many articles and books that hold out the hope of planned and controlled change, and you encounter many managers who have trouble dealing with the inevitable false steps, setbacks, redirections, and ambiguity that are inherent in doing anything new. This problem comes partly from the fear of failure, which drives managers to search for (and sometimes find) greater predictability and control over events. This search for certainty, even when none exists, also comes from an educational system that emphasizes problems that have right or wrong answers and which does not do much to prepare people to confront and live with ambiguity. And this discomfort also comes from the sometimes reasonable belief that if only the managers knew more, hired more consultants, and thought more, they could somehow resolve all of the ambiguity that confronts them.

In a world of uncertainty, not only the ability to reduce that uncertainty, but also the ability to live with it, and perhaps embrace it, are critical skills for leaders. But these are rare skills. Instead of searching fruitlessly for perfect certainty, which is never attainable, leaders who want to accomplish change reasonably quickly embrace the mess, do the best they can with the knowledge and evidence at hand, learn as they go, and take action in the meantime. Again, medicine provides an interesting and applicable model. As most doctors will tell you, the reason they refer to the *practice* of medicine is because medicine is just that, learned and performed through practice. It is never certain, and foremost in the practitioner's mind are the limitations of knowledge coupled with the need to take (often rapid) action.

What to Do About Change

Organizations actually change all the time. When leaders talk about *resistance to change*, what they usually mean is that subordinates (or perhaps board members, stockholders, or the media) aren't doing what leaders want them to do.[29] As we show in this chapter, sometimes that resistance is well-founded, well-intentioned, and actually helpful in keeping companies from doing dumb things. Even presumably good changes carry substantial risks because of the disruption and uncertainty that occur while the transformation is taking place. That's why the aphorism "change or die" is empirically more likely to be "change and die."

The best evidence suggests that companies can make things worse by believing that change takes a long time, which can result in changes that *do* take a long time. If the process of change can be disruptive, it follows that the longer the process goes on, the more risk there is that bad things will happen. Much like pulling off a bandage, whatever needs to be done is often better done quickly. And this idea of accomplishing change as quickly as possible is not just an academic pipe dream. There are numerous companies that made profound changes in their cultures and values, let alone in their operations and management practices, in a year or two, not the five plus years we typically hear discussed as the time required.

Because change is risky and there are advantages to getting it done quickly, we have offered guidelines and questions for leaders who are contemplating whether or not to embark on some change and, if they do decide to go forward, how to get it done in a quicker and better fashion. These thoughts on how to direct the change process set the stage for our next chapter on evidence-based leadership. One of the main assumptions throughout the business world is that change is, and should be, led from the top. Whether or not that is true—whether or not leaders are in control of their organizations and ought to be—is the next topic we discuss.

Are Great Leaders in Control of Their Companies?

WE ARE OBSESSED with leadership. Thousands of studies and books are already devoted to it, and we still want more. In 1990, Bernard Bass published the *Handbook of Leadership*, which ran over 1,000 pages and contained over 7,500 references to past research on the topic.[1] Even that heroic effort omitted much leadership research. In 2004, the four-volume *Encyclopedia of Leadership* was published. It runs 2,120 pages, contains hundreds of articles written by over 400 "leading scholars and experts," and will cost you a staggering $595.[2] This massive tome also covers only part of the territory. Our search of Business Source Premier, a database of management periodicals, revealed that nearly 15,000 peer-reviewed articles have been published on leadership since 1975. When we put the word *leadership* in Amazon.com's book search engine, over 110,000 listings popped up.[3] The people who buy business books and magazines seem to have an insatiable appetite for this topic.

So much is written about leaders because we believe that our fate, and the fate of our organizations, is in their hands and ought to be. We talk and act as if leaders are all-powerful deities and devils who wield complete command over even the largest organizations and that the organizations are better off for this fact. A *Fortune* magazine story about former Kellogg

CEO (and subsequently U.S. Secretary of Commerce) Carlos Gutierrez is typical. The title ballyhoos Gutierrez as "The Man Who Fixed Kellogg." The opening paragraph lists at least 10 ways that Gutierrez fixed Kellogg during his five-year reign. Every sentence portrays him as the sole master of this big company, crediting him alone with everything from motivating employees, to the decision to promote the *Spider-Man* films, to reviving old cereal brands, to putting some "snap, crackle, and pop into Kellogg's stock."[4] *Fortune* described the powers of Xerox CEO Ann Mulcahy in much the same way, as "the working mother who gets a job that she never dreamed of and now has the fate of a company in her hands." And *Business Week* titled its story "Anne Mulcahy Has Xerox by the Horns."[5] Nor is this glorification of leader potency just a U.S. phenomenon. A U.K.–based *Financial Times* article about CEO of General Motors Rick Wagoner begins, "Rick Wagoner's aura envelops the entire planet. His every move sends ripples around the globe. His every decision affects the actions of millions in countless nations."[6]

Compensation committees, which set executive pay, reflect and reinforce these beliefs—that who heads a company, and what that leader does, are among the most potent determinants of company performance. The CEOs of America's 500 largest companies were paid a total of over $3.3 billion in 2003, an 8 percent raise over 2002.[7] If CEOs deserve what they get, they must be getting more important and more deserving all the time. In 1980, the average CEO in America made 42 times as much as the average blue collar worker, a ratio that rose to 85 times as much in 1990, and to a whopping 531 times as much by 2000.[8] When Harvard Business School leadership researcher Rakesh Khurana asked corporate directors if CEOs are worth all that money, they reacted with anger and surprise, as if he had raised a taboo subject. Khurana found that directors held "virtually religious" convictions on the subject, which led them to dismiss any evidence showing that CEO quality is *not* a primary and potent cause of firm performance.[9]

It is not just that people believe leaders have almost total control of their organizations. Many people believe that leaders *should* have complete control. Every reader of this book is familiar with the typical organization chart and its hierarchy of authority. Most people believe that leaders in more senior positions—those higher up the chain of command—not only have the right, but also have the responsibility, to make important decisions about and for those serving under them. People in higher positions are presumed to know what should be done and how to do it better than their underlings; after all, the selection process that put them in those roles should assure that only the most qualified and able reach higher ranks. So decisions made by senior leaders will presumably be wiser and better decisions than if these decisions were made by underlings. When the capital markets imploded after the Enron catastrophe, AES, the large independent electric power producer, got into financial difficulties; much of the blame was attributed to AES's highly decentralized style of operations. The assumption was that if top managers had made more decisions, the company would have done better, even though most of the its worst decisions were made, or at least ratified, by the board of directors—the board just wanted to blame others for the choices it made.

Making decisions and exercising power over others are also among the rewards that many people seek and enjoy by attaining higher-level positions. We, as human beings, almost instinctively obey authority, and in our very obedience, reinforce the idea that leaders ought to be making the decisions that we then obey.[10] But this idea that we are well served to have leaders in control of their organizations is also a half-truth. In some cases, it is helpful for leaders to be in control of their organizations. But in many instances, organizations have failed because of excessive centralization and too much influence and control on the part of the leader.

This chapter explores both of these half-truths: that leaders are in control and that they ought to be. Each is sometimes true, but also sometimes false. In understanding these half-truths, we can provide a more nuanced view of leadership and offer some useful guidelines for those who occupy leadership roles in organizations.

Leaders Make a Big Difference

History is filled with leaders who made a big difference in the world: Gandhi and his work for Indian independence from Britain; Martin Luther King Jr. and his efforts to bring civil rights to African-Americans and economic justice to all citizens; Queen Elizabeth I and her persistence and skill in fostering unity throughout the British kingdom; Winston Churchill and his words and deeds that helped England maintain its fighting spirit during World War II; and Lyndon Johnson who, as president, passed legislation creating Medicare, numerous cabinet departments and federal agencies, and social welfare programs such as Head Start that last to this day. Other leaders had profoundly negative effects—Joseph Stalin and Adolph Hitler each consigned millions of people to their deaths.

Leaders make a difference on a smaller organizational scale, as well. As leadership researcher Robert Hogan and his colleagues point out, "The fact that Lincoln's army was inert until Ulysses S. Grant assumed command . . . is, for most people, evidence that leadership matters."[11] So is the 1910 race to the South Pole between the Norwegian team led by Roald Amundsen and the English team lead by Robert Falcon Scott. Amundsen drove his men to prepare, develop experience, and refine their equipment, resulting in a smooth trip to the Pole with few setbacks. In contrast, "Scott's incompetence cost him the race, his life, and the lives of three team members."[12]

Moreover, beyond these case studies, systematic quantitative research demonstrates that leadership *can* influence organizational performance. A study of all National Basketball Association teams over a four-year period, for example, found that although simply changing coaches didn't matter, bringing in a new coach enhanced team performance when that new coach had prior professional coaching experience, a strong historical win-loss record, and a track record of improving past teams. A study of 50 United Methodist ministers who had worked at 132 different churches over a 20-year period showed similar effects. Simply changing ministers didn't affect church performance, but bringing in a minister with a history of boosting members and donations in his previous parishes produced the same positive effects when he was transferred to a new congregation.[13] As we discussed in chapter 4, Lawrence Kahn examined how managers of major league baseball teams affected their teams' overall win-loss records and whether better managers could help players perform above their potential (as measured by each player's past performance). Kahn found that better managers helped both their teams and individual players perform better.[14]

One of the most sophisticated studies of the leadership-performance link was conducted in the automobile industry. The authors estimated productivity equations to ascertain the growth in both labor and capital productivity in six companies over a 40-year period. The study found effects of top management on all of the companies except Toyota (because it had a system that made performance robust and largely independent of who occupied senior leadership positions) and that these effects were significant. For instance, Don Petersen, Ford's CEO during much of the 1980s, increased productivity growth some 3.1 percent annually above the average for all Ford executives.[15] This is perhaps because, as he told us, Ford was so desperate at the time that they decided to put someone in charge who actually knew something about cars and trucks, rather than a bean counter. CEO and presidential charisma also appears to positively affect performance and to make a difference.[16] And, by contrast, having an arrogant CEO causes companies to pay excessive prices when acquiring new companies, which then damages long-term performance.[17] Studies of leadership effects conducted at the smaller group or unit level, including studies of flight crews and military units also show that when the appropriate indicators of effectiveness are examined, leader action and experience make a difference in how the units perform.[18]

Even leadership studies that find comparatively small performance effects can be interpreted as showing that leadership matters quite a bit. Although studies of firm performance and the allocation of municipal budgets, for example, show that leaders' effects are dwarfed by temporal or year effects as well as the effects of the environment, a relatively small percentage effect attributed to the leader can still be large in absolute terms. A small percentage of a large number is a big number, or as Everett Dirkson, the late Republican Senate leader was reported to have said, "a billion here, a billion there, and pretty soon you're talking about real money."

Leaders not only affect financial indicators of performance such as sales, profits, productivity, or budget allocations, they also affect their organization's interpersonal climate and the satisfaction and mental well-being of those they lead. The evidence strongly suggests that leaders can certainly make a big difference to individuals when they are abusive or ineffective, or both. Researchers have been studying organizational climate for more than 50 years and routinely find "that 60% to 75% of the employees in any organization—no matter when or where the survey was completed and no matter what occupational group was involved—report that the worst or most stressful aspect of their job is their immediate supervisor." These studies also show that "abusive and incompetent management create billions of dollars of lost productivity each year."[19] Study after study demonstrates that bad leaders destroy the health, happiness, loyalty, and productivity of their subordinates.

Particularly in smaller organizations, leaders can and do exercise control and if they make bad decisions, can create financial disaster for the companies they lead. That is why venture capitalists are much more willing to fund start-ups with experienced leaders who have good track records. We have witnessed firsthand how poor leaders can drive skilled and motivated people out of their organizations and into the arms of competitors, or perhaps even worse, cause people to withhold discretionary effort even while remaining in their jobs. We once interviewed a senior executive who was so demoralized by his boss's stubbornness and poor decisions that he gave up trying to argue and instead carefully implemented every decision exactly as his controlling and detail-oriented superior instructed. This executive learned to take pleasure in how badly things turned out—he called it "engaging in malicious compliance." Such effects can be particularly disastrous for young or small organizations that do not have large financial cushions, accumulated brand equity, or customer bases to fall back on. In short, the fact that leaders affect both morale and financial performance seems self-evident.

Except When They Don't

Nonetheless, leaders and managers often have far less influence over performance than most people think. As Mike Ditka, a former National Football League player and coach has stated, "Coaches get too much credit and too much blame."[20] One study of the performance of 167 companies over a 20-year period sought to allocate variation in performance to the effects of industry, year (time period, which presumably measures general economic conditions), company-specific effects, and the impact of changes in leadership. Not surprisingly, the conclusion was that company and industry had much larger effects on variation in sales, profits, and profit margins than did changes in leadership.[21] When Jeffrey Pfeffer published a review of research on leadership back in 1977, he found that although leaders do have some impact, their actions rarely explain more than 10 percent of the differences in performance between the best and the worst organizations and teams. Scores of more recent studies confirm that the link between leadership and performance is modest. Scholars who conduct and evaluate the best peer-reviewed studies argue over how much leadership matters and when it matters most. But when they put their often petty differences aside, most agree that the effects of leadership on performance are modest under most conditions, strong under a few conditions, and absent in others.[22] Studies of leaders from large samples of CEOs in public companies, to university presidents, to managers of college and professional sports teams show that organizational performance is determined largely by factors that no individual—including the leader—can control.[23]

Even the most powerful executives have little influence over macroeconomic trends, the price of international currency and oil, wars and terrorism, organizational history, and the weather. That is why although stock prices sometimes move dramatically in the short term when a CEO is fired or hired, there are seldom long-term effects on market value.

Those who have studied the investment impact contend that the replacement of a corporate boss is often like that of a baseball team manager: after a knee-jerk sense of relief comes a realization that it won't do much good if the new guy has to lead the same bunch of bums whose losing streak got the previous manager axed. In the same way, a company can have new leadership but still be burdened by a poor reputation, an unprofitable business mix, and a shortage of clear ways to extricate itself from its malaise.[24]

There are a number of reasons why leaders may make only a small difference in how well companies do. One reason is that they often operate within constraints that they can't change easily or at all—the existing people, products, markets, and general economic conditions. There is also evidence that leadership effects are modest because the people who are allowed to hold and keep leadership positions are pretty similar to each other. In theory, different leaders could have a big impact if they saw the world in different ways, if there were wildly varying skill sets and competence levels among leaders, and if there were big differences in how those leaders who are hired and remain did their jobs. In practice, however, leaders don't exhibit such differences because they are selected for similarity in education and outlook. Many leaders wind up thinking similarly and making similar decisions as a result. And organizations do not have unfettered access to any leader who might be potentially available. Leaders who appear to be successful will be more highly sought after and are more likely to take positions at larger, already more successful organizations. So, another reason why leaders may make less difference in practice than in theory is that poorly performing organizations may have limited access to those leaders who would be most able to make a big difference.

Particularly in large organizations, people are heavily screened for credentials, competencies, and backgrounds similar to those of other CEOs (e.g., there are currently only eight female CEOs in the *Fortune* 500 and seven of these women have MBAs). Many organizations also choose internal candidates, people who have worked their way up the ranks. As renowned management theorist James March pointed out, this too drives out differences: "Assuming that all promotions are based on similar attributes, each successive filter further refines the pool, reducing variation among managers. On attributes the organization considers important, vice presidents are likely to be significantly more homogeneous than first-level managers."[25] The result is what statisticians call a *restriction of range* in the observed population of senior executives. March concluded:

Management may be extremely difficult and important even though managers are indistinguishable. It is hard to tell the difference between two different light bulbs also; but if you take all the light bulbs away, it is difficult to read in the dark. What is hard to demonstrate is the extent to which high performing managers (or light bulbs that endure for an exceptionally long time) are something more than one extreme end of a probability distribution generated by essentially equivalent individuals.[26]

What the evidence indicates is that leaders can and do make an important difference in organizational and group performance, although the effects are not as large as usually assumed nor as important as many other factors. It seems clear that leaders have some chance of making things better, but they can also make things much worse by taking actions that increase employee turnover and diminish employee motivation, as well as encourage lying and stealing, and causing numerous other organizational problems. This all suggests that avoiding bad leaders may be a crucial goal, perhaps more important than getting great leaders.

Why the "Leaders Make a Big Difference" Half-Truth Persists

Leadership certainly matters. But the belief that leaders have massive influence over performance turns out to be a half-truth. As leadership researcher James Meindel put it, our culture romanticizes leaders, anointing them with "esteem, prestige, charisma, and heroism" that outstrips the weight of the evidence.[27] Why does this irrational faith in the power of potent individuals persist?

One reason is a matter of perception. More than 30 years ago, Gerald Salancik conducted a simple experiment: a person was asked to control a model train as it traveled around a track. An observer watched the person try to control the train. Unbeknownst to both, the experimenter kept changing the power going to the train, making it speed up and slow down unexpectedly, which caused it to derail. The person running the train soon recognized that he or she had little control. The observer perceived something different. The observer could not and did not see the fluctuations in speed that were outside of the control of the person running the train, but instead saw a person who couldn't keep a model train on the tracks. As the person running the train was visible and salient, the observer attributed the train's performance to that person's effort and ability, not to the unexplained and invisible factors that actually caused the derailments.[28] In just this fashion, when we look at organizations, we see the people who are in charge; we don't see the constraints that affect both their behavior and the company's performance. So the salience of individual action affects how we interpret events.

We discussed this general effect of overattributing outcomes to the causal agency of individuals in chapter 4. This *fundamental attribution error* has been replicated in numerous studies, although it is more pronounced in Western cultures with their emphasis on the individual, compared to Asian or other cultures that emphasize the effects of groups and institutions more.[29] Our attribution of potency to individuals, including those in leadership roles, is a consequence of perceptual biases and what is salient to us. We see the people acting, but the constraints under which they are acting are largely invisible to us.

Another reason we give leaders too much credit or blame is that all humans need to make sense of the onslaught of confusing information thrown at us. So we use *cognitive shortcuts* to interpret what we see and experience in comforting and efficient ways. Placing excessive faith in leadership is one of those shortcuts. The long list of complex and ever shifting possible causes of organizational performance creates the disconcerting feeling that the organizations we join, are served by, and observe from the outside are difficult—even impossible—to control, which fuels fears that what happens to us and to the people we care about is also difficult to predict and control. The complexity also means that the causes of organizational performance are difficult to communicate in efficient ways. Our culture's romance with leadership may reflect flawed beliefs, but it helps people translate this mess into simple terms that we can understand, cope with, and communicate to others. Even a renowned leader like former GE CEO Jack Welch couldn't change the firm's history, nor could he be everywhere at once. But research shows that it makes most of us feel better and requires less mental effort on our part to pretend that Welch was in complete control. A while ago, for example, we were talking with former GE executive Spencer Clark, who had led a large business during Jack Welch's reign. Clark joked, "Jack did a good job, but everyone seems to forget that the company had been around for over a hundred years before he ever took the job, and he had 70,000 other people to help him."[30]

A related bias is that we often generalize from the performance of the unit to the qualities of the leader, and then infer that since performance was good (or bad), the leader must be also. People conclude that good companies have good managers, and bad companies have bad managers, regardless of other facts. Particularly when performance is either very good or very bad, leadership is erroneously seen as especially critical and powerful.[31] This effect has been produced in controlled experiments that compare high- versus low-performing teams. Members attribute team performance to their leaders even when the game is rigged so that leadership doesn't matter.[32] These *attributional errors* are not made just by inexperienced observers. Harvard leadership researcher Rakesh Khurana found that executive search committees almost always ranked candidates that way, too.

Venture capitalist Steve Dow often sees the reverse effect when a competent CEO leads a struggling firm. Start-ups have notoriously high failure rates, no matter how well they are managed. Dow has been a general partner at Silicon Valley's Sevin Rosen since 1983 and served on dozens of boards over the years. He tells us that many board members, especially young venture capitalists who lack operational experience, are quick to talk about replacing the CEO at the first hint of trouble. Dow asks them, "Now, suppose *you* were CEO, what would you do differently than the one we have right now?" Dow says that most of the time they can't think of much, if anything, they would change. Like everyone else, until they think about it carefully, these venture capitalists can't separate the CEO's performance from the firm's performance.

Yet another reason leaders get too much credit or blame for what goes on boils down to money, power, and prestige. Senior executives, and just about everyone they come into contact with, have powerful incentives to *act as if* leaders are in control of organizations and ought to be. Leaders have enormous incentives for perpetuating the myth that they are in control, including the nearly $10 million per year that the average CEO of the largest 200 U.S. firms was paid in 2003.[33] If they came clean and admitted their limited powers, it would weaken their claim on these dollars, along with the royal treatment and hero worship that so many expect and get. Elite executive search firms like Korn/Ferry, Heidrick & Struggles, and Spencer Stuart have the same incentives, since the fees they charge their corporate clients are based on the executive's compensation (typically one-third of the first year cash compensation). The more senior executives make, the more the search firms make. Finally, regardless of the actual influence of leaders over organizational performance, senior managers still have great discretion over how their firm's resources are distributed. They can hand out raises and promotions, hire and fire high-priced consultants and attorneys, and allow or forbid media access. In short, leaders spend their days among people who have every incentive to flatter and fawn over them, and who devote careful attention to their every whim, further fueling the half-truth that leaders are lords and masters of all that transpires around them, including how well their organizations do.

Should Leaders Be in Control of Their Organizations?

Ask almost any organizational leader in the private or the public sector "Do you have as much power, control, or influence as you think you need over your organization?" and the answer is almost invariably *no*. Business journalists and some academics may think that leaders have enormous influence on what goes on, but the leaders themselves, living and managing as best they can, recognize all too well the limits on their ability to make things happen. Richard Kovacevich, the CEO of Wells Fargo Bank, once described his job as basically making speeches and shaking hands. With more than 120,000 employees, he doesn't feel he can move the organization either as rapidly or as much as he might want to, and he certainly recognizes the limits of his direct and immediate influence on what goes on. Robert Sutton once consulted to the CEO of a *Fortune* 100 company who was continually frustrated because middle managers (whom he called "the trolls") ignored initiatives and orders from the senior team, even when there were financial incentives for changing their behavior—he lamented that they were in charge, not him. Similarly, when he was president of the United States, Richard Nixon constantly complained about people in the State Department and CIA—career civil servants—whose behavior did not bend to his will. Even U.S. presidents, at the moment the most powerful people in the world, can't always get the bureaucracy to do what they want.

Which raises the question: *should* leaders be in more complete control of their organizations? Even if the all-powerful CEO-as-potentate is a myth, in reality maybe the prevalence of the myth speaks to some potentially desirable state of affairs that is simply not realized frequently enough in practice. The answer to this question depends, of course, on whose perspective you take.

From the point of view of leaders, be they CEOs, deans (or associate deans) of schools, university presidents, or heads of nonprofit or governmental agencies, more control is almost always seen as better. That's because of what we described earlier as the self-enhancement bias—the idea that, in order to see ourselves in the best possible light so we can feel better about ourselves and feed our egos, we consistently overestimate our own skills and abilities.[34] In the world of organizational decision making, what all this means is that we believe activities we have performed, or even been tangentially involved in influencing, are better than those where we have had less proximate involvement.

Consider the following experiment by Jeffrey Pfeffer and his colleagues. Research subjects, all Stanford MBAs, were told they would be the supervisor of a subordinate who would be working on a rough draft for an advertisement for a Swatch watch in the next room. These supervisors were randomly assigned to one of three treatments. Those in the first group were told that, because they were so busy, they would only see the final advertisement. Supervisors in the second group were told that they would see an intermediate version of the advertisement and answer a standardized checklist that could be used to provide feedback, but were also told that, just as in the real world, communication difficulties and time constraints would mean their feedback would not be given to the subordinate. In the third and final group, supervisors filled out exactly the same checklist after seeing the same intermediate draft, and were told their comments would be seen by the subordinate. In reality, the feedback provided by supervisors had no effect on the final product; supervisors in all three groups saw the identical final advertisement. They were then asked to rate the quality of the final product, as well as their own skill as a supervisor. You might guess the results, but Pfeffer and his colleagues were surprised by the magnitude. Supervisors in the third group, who believed that their comments influenced the final advertisement, rated that identical product about twice as highly as the other supervisors who believed that they had no influence, and gave similarly inflated ratings to their own ability as managers.[35] The mere act of believing that they had engaged in supervision led them to believe that the final product was twice as wonderful (and they were twice as wonderful), even though their actions had no actual impact!

Not only do leaders overestimate their positive effects on followers, the belief that leaders ought to be in control is a dangerous half-truth because when they wield too much influence and control over followers, bad things often happen to their companies and their employees. No leader is omniscient. Even the smartest, most experienced, most dedicated individual is, in the end, a human being with the biases and failings that this fact entails. One of the most consistent findings in the literature on decision making and performance is that the best groups perform better than the best individuals, because groups are able to take advantage of the collective wisdom and insight of multiple individuals, while individual judgments reflect the narrower insights and skills of just one person. On the insights and skills of a *single* person.[36] So decision quality is enhanced under most conditions when there are multiple, independent inputs.

Leaders make mistakes—all people do. But to the extent leaders exert tremendous control over their organizations, there are few or no checks or balances to reign in the errors. Most corporate disasters and financial scandals, including those perpetrated by Jeff Skilling and Andy Fastow at Enron, Al Dunlap at Sunbeam, Hank Greenberg at the large insurer AIG, and Dennis Koslowski at Tyco, happened not simply because these people were greedy, immoral, or unethical people, but because such people were in leadership positions with so much control that no one could challenge them or raise questions. Placing so much control in the hands of a single individual violates the principle of checks and balances, a principle designed to ensure that any single individual, no matter how mistaken or how flawed, cannot do unlimited damage.

Another problem arises when leaders have excessive control. One of the most persistent and powerful social psychological processes is that of commitment—we are more likely to carry through on decisions we have made and are therefore committed to. When leaders make decisions for us or on our behalf, they think the decisions are better—after all, they made them— but the rest of the people have no investment in actually carrying through on actions and choices they had no part in making. So ceding too much control to leaders may make those leaders feel better about the choices that get made, but almost certainly will leave the organization confronting substantial challenges in getting things implemented.

There is yet one more reason that it is a dangerous half-truth to believe that things will go better when leaders are firmly in control. As Dennis Bakke, former CEO of the independent power producer AES, reminds us in his book *Joy at Work*, life is not just about performance, effectiveness, and efficiency.[37] The very essence of being a sentient human being is the ability to make choices and take actions—to be responsible, in control of at least some aspects of our own life, and engaged in actively creating the world in which we live. To cede those tasks to others, even others who are benign and possibly even wiser than us, is to deny the full experience of being fully human and fully alive. A huge behavioral science literature—studies of everyone from nursing home patients, to assembly line workers, to surgical nurses, to software developers—shows that having both perceived and actual control over what happens in our lives is essential to the mental and physical health of all human beings, and it causes us to try harder, too.[38] So while leaders may think that things are better if they have more control over their organizations, considerations of decision quality, commitment and implementation, and the essence of what it means to be a healthy human being suggest that too much control in the hands of too few people is probably not good for either organizations or the people who work in them.

What Should Good Leaders Do?

We have seen that leaders neither have as much control over things as many people believe, nor should they. Yet people who occupy leadership positions need to figure out how to exercise their responsibilities. And although leaders aren't omnipotent, what they do does matter. Given the evidence on leader effects and effective leader behavior, there are some sensible suggestions that can guide behavior, or more accurately, show how to design and think about behavior.

The fundamental guidelines we propose emerge from four paradoxes that leaders face:

1. Everyone expects leaders to matter a lot, even as they have limited actual impact. Leaders need to act as if they are in control, project confidence, and talk about the future, even while recognizing and acknowledging the organizational realities and their own limitations.

2. Because leaders succumb to the same self-enhancement tendencies as everyone else, magnified by the adulation they receive, they have a tendency to lose their behavioral inhibitions and behave in destructive ways. They need to avoid this trap and maintain an attitude of wisdom and a healthy dose of modesty.

3. Because the desirability of exercising total control is itself a half-truth, effective leaders must learn when and how to get out of the way and let others make contributions. So sometimes the best leadership is no leadership at all.

4. Leaders often have the most positive impact when they help build systems where the actions of a few powerful and magnificently skilled people matter least. Perhaps the best way to view leadership is as the task of architecting organizational systems, teams, and cultures—as establishing the conditions and preconditions for others to succeed.

Our argument here is much like that in other chapters: by recognizing both parts of the half-truth and negotiating the middle ground appropriately, leaders, managers, and everyone else involved in an organization can construct the most effective course of action.

Act and Talk As If You Are in Control and Project Confidence While Talking About the Future

Boards of directors, search committees of all stripes, human resource management departments, and just about anyone who completes performance evaluation, will likely succumb to the belief that leaders are in control and ought to be. So they hire, praise, hold on to, and promote leaders who seem to be in control of events. This means that you will never get or keep a leadership position if you can't convince others that you are in control—even when you don't have much control. It also means that *pretending you are in control* of organizational performance can help leaders gain *actual control* over at least some aspects of that performance.

Andy Grove, cofounder and former CEO and chairman of Intel, confessed as much right after he retired. Grove was asked how he kept his people motivated given his conclusion that "none of us have a real understanding of where we are heading. I don't." Grove answered, "Well, part of it is self-discipline and part of it is deception." He added, "And the deception becomes reality. Deception in the sense that you pump yourself up and put a better face on things than you start off feeling. But after a while, if you act confident, you become more confident. So the deception becomes less of a deception."[39]

Consider the case of Steve Ciesinski, formerly CEO of Resumix, a $30 million company that provided résumé-processing software to make better and more efficient hiring decisions. Spun out of Ceridian as part of a leveraged buyout, Resumix faced two daunting problems as the 1990s drew to a close. First, it had a highly leveraged capital structure that made new investments difficult and a board composed mostly of relatively young venture capitalists who had funded the buyout and who wanted to manage by the numbers with little consideration of the human element. Second, the company had a client-server based application that needed to move to a Web-based application to be competitive, while it still needed to continue to provide good service to the existing customer base on the old system and technology.

In order to keep Resumix's 450 customers and 240 employees committed to the company and to tasks absolutely essential for survival—let alone success—Ciesinski could not simply say, "Things are difficult, capital is scarce, we are facing many competitive challenges, and the way forward is not easy to discern." Customers would abandon the company and would not buy upgrades or services, rendering financial survival precarious. Employees—remember this was during the Internet boom—would head for the exits for better opportunities, making it impossible to create and sell new and better versions of the product and deliver great customer care. Ciesinski was straightforward with his people about the competitive and financial realities, but at the same time, he projected a sense of confidence both about what needed to be done and that the company had the ability to do it. This confidence permitted Resumix to retain key employees, including technical employees, which let it continue the evolution of the product. The confidence and the product road map shown to the customers retained customer loyalty, thereby maintaining licensing and service revenues. The result: Ciesinski was able to sell the company for more than $100 million to HotJobs (subsequently purchased by Yahoo!), providing a handsome return to shareholders and the employee option-holders. None of this would have been possible without projecting both a sense of what needed to be accomplished as well as the belief that it was feasible. In that way, confidence becomes self-fulfilling just as Grove suggested, setting in motion behaviors that in fact make things better whereby the confidence is justified.

What this means is that part of a leader's job is to behave in ways that cause others to believe in the possibility of success of both the organization and the leader. To maintain the impression that you, as a leader, are in control—and to take some actual control as well—you need to start and sustain the "Leadership Control Cycle" shown in figure 8-1. There are five intertwined parts of the cycle:

1. Leaders talk and act if they are in control.

2. Key players believe that leaders' words and deeds can have a strong impact on the organization.

3. Changes happen to the organization (e.g., in performance, reputation, employee turnover, or structure).

4. Organizational changes are attributed to leaders (regardless of objective impact that leaders actually have on organizational changes).

5. Leaders believe that their words and deeds actually shape organizational action and performance (although wise leaders don't believe in their own powers and superiority too much).

Fortunately, leadership research provides guidance about what it takes to start and sustain this cycle, especially about the kinds of talk and action that

FIGURE 8-1

The leadership control cycle

fuel perceptions leaders have—or will soon have—control over the organization and enhanced organizational performance.

Take Credit and Some Blame

One of the most obvious and most strongly supported ways that leaders amplify the perception that events are controllable and that they are confident of success is by taking credit when good things to happen to the organization. Study after study shows that companies headed by CEOs who credit favorable financial performance to what they *and their people* did will perform better down the road than companies that are equally successful by the same financial measures but do not make such claims. Many leaders, especially modest ones, use the word *we* and insist that others inside the company get credit for good things that happen. Peter Drucker asserted that effective executives "think and say *we*."[40] Jim Collins concludes, "Level 5 leaders look out the window and assign credit—even undue credit."[41] Using words like *we* and *us* can help leaders gain more effective control over events because such inclusive language creates excitement and sparks action among followers. But strategic use of the word *we* also amplifies impressions that the leader is in command of followers—so long as the focus is on how the leader's own skill, effort, and smarts made good things happen rather than luck or events that were outside of his or her control.

Things get stickier for both leaders and companies when it comes to explaining inevitable setbacks and downturns. On the one hand, there is much research on the "optimistic coping style" and "self-serving attributions." Optimists enjoy better mental and physical health and live longer.[42] They are also more persistent in the face of failure. And research on winning versus losing U.S. presidential candidates shows that in 80 percent of elections between 1900 and 1984 winners avoided talking about negative events, and when setbacks were raised, were more likely than losers to deny blame and point fingers at others and events they couldn't control.

On the other hand, it turns out that company executives are different from politicians. Leaders who claim that "it isn't my fault" and "I couldn't have done anything about it" aren't doing themselves or their organizations any favors over the long haul. Deflecting blame might help them keep their jobs for a time, enjoy better mental health, and persist in the face of failure. But ducking the heat shatters the illusion of control. Investors, customers, employees, and the press conclude that leaders who don't take responsibility for mistakes and setbacks lack the power to make things better. Controlled experiments by Fiona Lee and her colleagues show that hypothetical managers who took responsibility for bad events like pay freezes and failed projects were seen as more powerful, competent, and likeable than managers who denied responsibility.[43]

The wisdom of acknowledging blame is confirmed by two studies that tracked *Fortune* 500 firms over long periods. Both were careful studies designed to rule out alternative explanations. Gerald Salancik and James Meindl examined 18 *Fortune* 500 firms over 18 years. They found that, especially in firms with wild swings in performance from year to year, performance was superior down the road when executives attributed both *good* and *bad* performance to internal actions.[44] Similarly, Fiona Lee and her colleagues examined yearly stock price changes in 14 companies over a 21-year stretch. They found that taking blame for setbacks wasn't just effective in companies with wild performance swings. In years when senior management blamed their firm's troubles on internal and controllable factors, stock prices were consistently higher the next year, compared to when executives denied responsibility for setbacks.[45]

Dell CEO Kevin Rollins illustrates how to take blame. When the company missed quarterly revenue projections by several hundred million dollars—even though profits were up 28 percent and revenue grew 15 percent—he blamed himself, stating that "we executed poorly on managing overall selling prices." Rollins then went on to explain how he and his team were taking steps to fix the problem. And taking blame was not a one-time thing for him. Several years earlier, when he was COO, Rollins became concerned that the culture had become tainted with greed, and he blamed himself and other senior executives for setting the wrong tone. He then launched some steps—including evaluations by subordinates—to deal with the problem.[46]

Talk About the Future

Because the past is over and can not be changed, leaders who want to project confidence and the impression that they are in control of events talk optimistically about the future, often emphasizing that today's sacrifices will pay dividends down the road. President Abraham Lincoln's Gettysburg Address provides an eloquent illustration of this principle. Lincoln gave this famous 278-word speech during the U.S. Civil War on the Gettysburg battlefield on November 19, 1863, where 50,000 soldiers had just died in the most deadly battle in American history. Lincoln's final sentence tied those horrible sacrifices to a better future. "It is rather for us to be here dedicated to the great task remaining before us that from these honored dead we take increased devotion to that cause for which they gave the last full measure of devotion that we here highly resolve that these dead shall not have died in vain, that this nation under God shall have a new birth of freedom, and that government of the people, by the people, for the people shall not perish from the earth."

A corporate analogue can be seen in the case of General Electric. During his early years as CEO, Jack Welch was nicknamed "neutron Jack" because he had overseen massive layoffs and numerous plant closings in his efforts to cut costs and get GE out of all but the most potentially profitable businesses. Welch was feared and despised in many corners of GE and criticized in the business press for being so heartless. Perhaps to help distract attention from current pain and to get people focused on creating a more successful future for the company, Welch focused attention on that future in GE's 1989 annual report: "We want GE to become a company where people come to work every day in a rush to try something they woke up thinking about the night before. We want them to go home from work wanting to talk about what they did that day, rather than try and forget. We want factories where the whistle blows and everyone wonders where the time went, and someone wonders aloud why we need a whistle."[47]

Such forward-looking language not only fuels a sense of control, it can create direction and energy that leaders can use to shape subsequent events. As Robert Eccles and Nitin Nohria point out in their book *Beyond the*

Hype, such language may seem calculating and fake given all the jobs that Welch eliminated at GE, but there is evidence that Welch's forward-looking and upbeat rhetoric did inspire confidence among his people and investors, and ultimately was translated into specific GE work practices.[48]

Be Specific About the Few Things That Matter, and Keep Repeating Them

One of the major challenges faced by leaders who want to convince others that they are in control, and want to gain actual control, is the onslaught of conflicting and small details that demand attention. Warren Bennis identified the constant demands on leaders to devote attention to things that are urgent, but not important, as one of the main reasons that "leaders can't lead."[49] After all, it is difficult to convince others that you are in control when you race from one (usually trivial) emergency to another. And it is difficult to gain objective control when you switch from one unrelated topic to another, as your people can't figure where to focus their efforts and attention (versus what can be ignored, or at least delayed, for now). As we showed in *The Knowing-Doing Gap*, leaders can help manage these demands by deciding on the few crucial things that matter most *right now* and relentlessly communicating about those few things.[50] Longtime Toyota CEO Taiichi Ohno believed that senior management's effectiveness depended on having close and constant contact with what happened on the factory floor, because Toyota's renowned production system was the most important factor in its success. Ohno made this clear by asserting, "Toyota managers should be sufficiently engaged on the factory floor that they have to wash their hands at least three times a day."[51]

Believing That You Are Powerful Can Wreck Your Organization

One of the paradoxes of being effective in a leadership role is that you must instill confidence in others to motivate effort and convince them that the future will be bright if they act in a cooperative, coordinated fashion to accomplish things. Yet even as you are instilling that confidence in others and projecting that you know what you are doing, it is imperative to avoid succumbing to your own hype, believing your own press, and as a consequence, suffering the downsides of believing in your own omnipotence.

Our Stanford colleague Professor Deborah Gruenfeld has long been fascinated with the effects of simply putting people in a position of power. Gruenfeld was in the magazine business before becoming an academic. One CEO she dealt with now and then was Jan Wenner, editor of *Rolling Stone* magazine. Gruenfeld describes how during their meetings he would often stop and take a big bite of a raw onion, followed by a swig of vodka straight from the bottle. Werner never offered Gruenfeld any onion or vodka, and in fact, neither of them ever commented on his unusual habit. Once Gruenfeld became an academic and started studying power, she realized that, although he was more colorful than many powerful people, Werner's focus on his own pleasures and apparent obliviousness toward his less-powerful guests was consistent with much rigorous research on people in power. Gruenfeld and her colleagues show that when people are put in positions of power, they start talking more, taking what they want for themselves, ignoring what other people say or want, ignoring how less-powerful people react to their behavior, acting rudely, and generally treating any situation or person as a means for satisfying their own needs—and that being put in position of power blinds them to the fact that they are acting like jerks.[52]

There are ways, of course, to partly avoid the problems of believing one's own hype, and they all entail reducing the differences in how people are treated—for instance in pay and perquisites. At Cisco Systems everyone—even senior leaders—flies coach. When Ko Nishimura was CEO of contract manufacturer Solectron, he did not have a reserved parking place and sat in an open office. Leaders can also reduce power differences and shatter illusions of their superiority by surrounding themselves with people who don't hesitate to tell them they are wrong and why. They don't shoot the messenger. They find ways to bypass the filtering of bad news and contrary opinions that occurs as information travels up the hierarchy. An extensive body of research shows that, even if you aren't to blame in any manner, simply delivering bad news to someone will cause them to blame you for it and to experience negative feelings toward you. This is one of the reasons that, as news travels up hierarchical levels, each messenger changes it a bit to tell the boss a happier and happier story.[53] This so-called *mum effect* helps explain what Nobel Prize–winning physicist Richard Feynman learned when investigating the 1986 explosion of the *Challenger* space shuttle. Feynman asked a group of engineers to estimate the probability that the shuttle's main engine would fail. Their estimates ranged from 1-in-200 to 1-in-300. When Feynman asked NASA's boss to make the same estimate, he proposed a failure rate of 1-in-100,000. Feynman asserted that this was just one of the many illustrations that managerial isolation from reality was rampant throughout NASA, a problem that persisted after the *Challenger* explosion, according to the independent panel that studied why the *Columbia* shuttle disintegrated on re-entry in 2003.[54]

Leaders can also reduce power differences by selecting, training, and promoting senior managers who see themselves as *serving* rather than *dominating* others in the organization. For example, A. G. Lafley, the CEO of Procter & Gamble, believes that P&G's success depends on spreading good ideas throughout this vast company, and has emphasized that managers will get credit for both giving and taking ideas, and for doing everything they can to help others in the company succeed not just themselves. He didn't try to spark cooperation by making tiny adjustments in the pay system or adding "cooperation" to a long list of factors considered in promotion decisions. Lafley simply made clear—by saying it again and again, and doing it in one promotion decision after another—that managers who failed to share their ideas across businesses and within teams simply would not get promoted to the next level. This message has done more than reduce unnecessary power differences and destructive status games at P&G. Lafley's relentless message that innovation comes from sharing the ideas hiding in different corners of the company has led to dozens of new successful products, from tartar-fighting IAMS pet food, to teeth whiteners, to an osteoporosis drug called Actonel.[55]

Figure Out When, and How, to Get Out of the Way

The Western cultural stereotype of leadership is not only that leaders are in control and should be but also that they ought to do certain things—ask questions, provide guidance, give lots of positive and negative feedback, and provide lots of information and direction that help guide what their subordinates do, presumably in this process making the organization more effective. Stanford researcher Elizabeth Gerber found that although leaders are given wildly varying advice, nearly everyone from gurus to management consultants to academic researchers maintains that the best leaders make their presence felt as strongly as possible. General George S. Patton plays to this fantasy perfectly; he was advertised as a man of constant action who seemed to be everywhere at once during battle, racing from one squad of soldiers to another, shouting orders and encouragement, and belittling cowards and praising heroes. Or think of how California governor Arnold Schwarzenegger rode his Hollywood persona into politics, drawing on his action-figure roles to appeal to a false but appealing fantasy of how he could stride into Sacramento and use his superpowers to save the state from its various woes.

Of course there are times when leaders are wise to use this in-your-face style of leadership, such as when they do know more about the work than team members, when their people need resources, when they are stuck on a problem or have interpersonal problems, when they need to understand the company's goals, or when they need links to other parts of the company that only the leader can provide. If you look at the best evidence, however, there are more times when intruding on and evaluating underlings—or just watching them work—damages performance. There are also many other times when, even though leaders may believe they are making things better, they are simply useless. The first step that effective leaders need to take is not to ask "What can I do?" Rather they should ask "Am I needed at all? Will my actions, or even my presence, do more harm than good?" The best leaders know when and how to get out of the way.

Phil Jackson has been the most successful coach in the National Basketball Association during the past 15 years, winning multiple world championships with the Los Angeles Lakers and the Chicago Bulls. Jackson is known for intervening far less than other coaches and for being especially skilled at managing players with great talent like Shaquille O'Neal and Michael Jordan. Jackson realizes that sometimes getting out of the way of his great players and letting them do their jobs is just as important as making suggestions, calling time-outs, and shouting encouragement. Jackson understands that leadership entails getting things done through other people, and sometimes the best way to do that is to let those people use their knowledge and talents without interference.

How can a leader tell when it is best to get out of the way, or best to start hanging around where his or her people work, asking questions, and giving people advice and feedback? There are three basic rules. First, if you know less about the work than the people you are managing, get out of the way unless you want to learn something from them. Second, when a group does creative work, a large body of research shows that the more that authority figures hang around, the more questions they ask, and especially the more feedback they give their people, the less creative the work will be. Why? Because doing creative work entails constant setbacks and failure, and people want to succeed when the boss is watching—which means doing proven, less creative things that are sure to work![56] This is one reason why William Coyne, executive vice president of R&D at 3M for over a decade, says that a big part of his job is simply leaving his people alone and making sure that other executives did, too. As he puts it, "After you plant a seed in the ground, you don't dig it up every week to see how it is doing."[57]

In practice, convincing leaders to get out of the way is difficult because their power and earnings are related to how many people they oversee, because so many people believe that a decision made by a leader is better than one made by a subordinate, and because so many leaders believe that they make better decisions than their subordinates and believe that if they watch, question, and nag their subordinates, those underlings will perform better. Even though you might think that, under pressure to be more efficient, organizations would want as little hierarchy and unnecessary supervision as possible, this is not always so. Yet one of the most effective ways to ensure less intrusion in the work of others is to have fewer leaders and fewer hierarchical levels. The famous Lincoln Electric Company, for example, has always had very wide spans of control, which ensures that supervisors cannot get too involved in the work of others. When former CEO Don Hastings was vice president of sales, he had 37 regional sales managers reporting to him.[58]

When people in your organization complain that they need more help and resources to provide supervision and oversight, instead of reorganizing or adding more staff, question whether or not the additional oversight they want is actually going to be helpful or harmful. Ask yourself if it will merely increase the power of the people making the requests, drive out creativity, and lead to annoying and wasteful interactions where the judgment of once empowered employees will be constantly questioned. As the founder of one *Fortune* 500 company lamented to us, the "professional management" that now runs his firm created a world where everything was hard to do because, "the people who check your work have their work checked by other people, and then the people who check the checkers are checked by more checkers."

Build Systems and Teams: Leaders as Architects or Designers

One of the main lessons from organization theory and leadership research is that leaders exercise the greatest personal influence over a company or group when it is young, small, or both. That is why company founders have such a strong and often enduring impact on the long-term success of a company, as well as its culture, values, and way of operating.[59] That is also why some of the strongest links between leadership skill and performance are seen in churches, cockpit teams, surgical teams, and basketball—the leader can directly interact with, persuade, and teach key members and outsiders. As organizations become larger and more complex, however, leadership becomes a less direct and less dramatic process. The task becomes more about building an effective team rather than about the magic powers of any given CEO to make decisions and take personal control. It also becomes a task entailing building reliable systems that work the same way over and over again, rather than becoming a heroic savior who steps in and saves the day.

The image of the leader as an architect comes through in a number of popular management books in which the job of creating a culture and set of practices in which people can be successful, innovative, and productive is described.[60] The fact that Toyota can succeed over decades, even as the value of the Japanese yen fluctuates, there are changes in preferences for cars of different sizes, and technology and competitive conditions change, and that the company shows no *leadership effect*—or changes from succession—speaks to building a robust set of interrelated management practices and philosophies that provide advantage above and beyond the ideas or inspiration of single individuals.

The mind-set required for this task entails, in part, something we have already discussed—being willing to let go and let other people perform, develop, learn, and make mistakes. It is hard to build a system where others can succeed if the leader believes he or she needs to make every important decision and knows better than anyone else what to do and how to do it. It is in finding a balance between guidance and listening, between directing and learning, that those in leadership roles can make their most useful contributions to organizational performance.

Getting Beyond the Half-Truths of Leadership

All of the half-truths we have discussed in this book are harmful to the organizations and people who succumb to them. But perhaps some of the most dangerous half-truths are those that beset ideas about leadership. In this chapter, we considered two prominent half-truths—that leaders are in control of their organizations and ought to be. We provided evidence that these ideas are partly right but also frequently incorrect, and then we provided some guidelines for leaders to negotiate an environment filled with conflicting demands and expectations. We conclude this chapter by considering a few other key misapprehensions about leadership that cause leaders and their organizations trouble.

One mistake people make is to believe that leadership is a skill that they can learn by reading, sitting through talks, or taking classes. This chapter contains evidence and advice that can help leaders and managers do a better job of practicing their craft, in part by not falling prey to some dangerous half-truths about leadership. But the fact is that no book, consultant, class, or series of classes, including an MBA, can teach anyone how to lead a small team, let alone a big organization. It is a craft you can learn only through experience. This lesson about leadership is evident throughout history, and remains true despite all the training and business knowledge that has been amassed. As historian David McCullough's lovely book *1776* shows,

George Washington had never led an army into battle when he took command of the Continental Army in 1775. Washington suffered from indecision and made terrible choices that killed thousands of soldiers during 1776. Yet he persisted, exuded calm and confidence throughout, eventually learned how to do the job well enough to begin scoring major victories by the end of 1776, and continued to become a more effective military leader until the American Revolutionary War ended in 1781.[61] The analogy we have made to medicine throughout this book is apt because, although learning how to judge research and learning about the best and worst practices and drugs can help doctors do a better job of serving their patients, no doctor can learn how to practice medicine without years of experience—without learning by doing. Because leaders are expected to be in control and to change things, even while their actual powers are limited, and they often can be most effective by letting or helping others do their own work, it requires wisdom and experience to navigate the many conflicting demands and expectations they face. That's why, as Morgan McCall noted in his review of leadership development programs, the most successful programs develop people by providing them with leadership experience and feedback on that experience.[62]

A second, related myth about leadership is that a skilled leader can manage well in any company or industry. This belief has led to an excessive reliance on outside succession and the problems that sometimes ensue when people come in without sufficient grounding in the institutional specifics of the company they are running. Becoming an effective manager requires deep knowledge of your industry, organization, people, and the work they do. This is why, although many companies look to an outside CEO as their savior, companies that are performing reasonably well are better off promoting an insider to the top job. Bringing in an outsider typically bolsters performance only when the company is in financial trouble or senior management are stealing money or lying to shareholders, signs that the company needs new skills or values and a message needs to be sent that the bad old people are gone and good new people have arrived. A study by Rakesh Khurana and Nitin Nohria about CEO departures at *Fortune* 200 companies between 1980 and 1996 found that if the CEO was retiring voluntarily, then bringing in an outsider was linked to a fall in performance over the next three years. But when the old CEO was fired, bringing in an outsider was linked to performance increases.[63]

But what about when a leader does take a job in a new industry or new company? If you look at cases where leaders successfully move from one industry or company to another, they've usually taken the time to learn about the work their people do, their customers, and their products *before* they start making major changes. That's exactly what CEO Andrea Jung did during her first month at Avon in 1999, at a time when the company's sales and the stock price were plummeting, women were becoming less and less interested in selling cosmetics and the like to their friends or by knocking on doors, and the company's product line was tired and dull. One of the first things Jung did was go to work as an Avon Lady herself, "going door to door in [her] neighborhood," because she wanted to understand the selling experience. It was by ringing doorbells on New York's Upper East Side that she gained insight into Avon's larger business. She heard customer gripes over discontinued colors, mishandled orders, and confusing promotions. One customer chewed her out for showing up with a catalog that didn't offer her favorite skin cream. Once Jung comprehended the problems, she acted quickly, cutting old products, increasing Avon's R&D budget by nearly 50 percent, and developing new programs for recruiting larger numbers of Avon Ladies, plus selling products in stores—not just through direct sales— for the time in Avon's history.[64] But Jung didn't start making these changes until she took the time to understand Avon's customers, people, and the product line. Avon's sales and stock price have climbed steadily since Jung took the job, an accomplishment that *Fortune* described as "one of the great turnaround feats in recent memory."[65]

Bill George of Medtronic did much the same thing, but he spent months instead of weeks with customers. When George became CEO of this medical device company in 1991, he had no prior experience in the industry—unlike Jung, who had worked in related businesses at Neiman Marcus and Bloomingdale's. Medical devices are also technologically complex to learn, and forging relationships with the key customers—surgeons—is something that takes time. So George spent more than 50 percent of his time the first nine months watching surgeons install Medtronic devices in patients, learning about how doctors did their work, and hearing their questions and concerns about Medtronic's products. George also spent much of his first year at Medtronic manufacturing plants and in direct conversation with people in research and development. His dedication to learning how people in his company did their work was, we suspect, one reason that he was such a successful leader of Medtronic. George's behavior is the opposite of what we more typically see. New leaders, particularly those from outside, come in and want to make their mark. They try this by essentially doing the opposite of whatever the previous incumbent did, regardless of whether or not that was working, and certainly regardless of any evidence or advice. It is no wonder that so many new leaders do so much harm to their organizations.

Bill George's example also deflates another myth or half-truth about leadership—that leaders can come in and make a big, positive difference right away. In fact, just as George took his time to understand the particulars of the situation, there is evidence that often the best leadership performance comes after years of experimenting and learning. Danny Miller and Jamal Shamsie studied all of the major studio heads between 1936 and 1965, including legends such as Darryl Zanuck, Louis B. Mayer, and Jack Warner. Miller and Shamsie found that these 31 leaders experimented a great deal with different movie genres early in their years on the job, and that it took about 15 years before the average studio achieved its highest level of financial performance.[66]

Leadership is a difficult craft because the expectations are always so high, the blame so swift and harsh, and leaders have less impact over what happens to their organizations than most people imagine. But it is a craft that people can develop over time and that some are better at than others. By considering the various myths and half-truths about leadership, we see that there is evidence about the steps leaders can take to have a more positive effect on their organizations. The big lesson is that the best leaders are smart enough to act like they are in charge but wise enough not to let their power go to their heads or to take themselves too seriously.

Part Three

From Evidence to Action

9

Profiting from Evidence-Based Management

THIS BOOK tells a saga of missed opportunities, of too many companies and too many leaders who are more interested in just copying others, doing what they've always done, and making decisions based on beliefs in what ought to work rather than on what actually works—thereby failing to face the hard facts and use the best evidence to help navigate the competitive environment. There also is good news. We showed the advantages reaped by companies and leaders that *are* interested in evidence-based management and that use a different set of standards for sorting through ideas in the business marketplace. We have seen that evidence-based management is too often the exception rather than the rule, even when eschewing conventional wisdom and focusing on sound logic and facts yields tremendous gains—whether we are talking about work-life integration, selecting talent, structuring rewards, how much to emphasize strategy, managing change, or leadership.

Consider one more comparison between the gains that companies garner when they find, face, and act on the best facts, versus those that don't. There is compelling evidence that when companies use human resource practices based on the best research, they trump the competition. These findings are replicated in industry after industry, from automobiles, to textiles, to computer software, to baseball. Research on initial public offerings also shows that start-ups that place greater value on employees bolster their five-year survival rates.[1] Yet many companies still routinely use inferior people management practices. The problem isn't just that HR managers know what do but can't get their companies to do it. Like other leaders, many HR executives hold flawed and incomplete beliefs. They fall prey to second-rate evidence, logic, and advice, which produce suspect practices, and in the end, damages performance and people.[2] We wrote this book to show how managers can find and use evidence so their companies can avoid such dreadful journeys, where the best of intentions lead to the worst of destinations.

Leaders of for-profit companies aren't alone in ignoring data and making worse decisions as a result. Implementing evidence-based practices is an uphill battle in lots of domains. In public policy, "the disconnect between science and policy is nothing short of astonishing as pols [politicians] ignore science that doesn't yield the answer they want."[3] In law enforcement, psychologist Gary Wells has demonstrated repeatedly that when eyewitnesses are asked to pick a suspect from a traditional lineup, where all suspects stand shoulder-to-shoulder (or eyewitnesses see a "six-pack" of suspect photos all at once), they consistently make identification errors. Even when the real suspect is not in the lineup, witnesses often falsely finger the person who looks most like the suspect anyway. About three-quarters of the people exonerated by DNA evidence were falsely identified by eyewitnesses in lineups! Wells has shown that eyewitnesses make far fewer errors when presented one suspect at a time—and there is no particular expense or technology barrier to showing people pictures or suspects sequentially rather than all at once. Yet although Wells has spent 20 years campaigning to convince police departments to use sequential lineups, only *four* out of over 19,000 legal jurisdictions have implemented this evidence-based practice.[4]

Or take education. In early 2005, California governor Arnold Schwarzenegger proposed attacking school performance problems with merit pay for teachers. He didn't talk about evidence that supported this idea, perhaps because little exists. As we saw in chapter 1, decades of research have failed to produce evidence that merit pay in schools has positive effects on learning. Or consider health care, particularly patient safety and the prevention of unnecessary death and complications. Study after study confirms that when hospitals have a higher ratio of nurses to patients and limit nurses' work hours, patients have lower death rates and fewer complications and infections. Yet few of these insights have been implemented, and hospital administrators routinely resist mandated nursing staffing ratios and work hours.[5]

When it comes to public policy, education, and health care, much like management, ideology and false hope regularly trump the evidence—which wastes both money and lives.

When the late Peter Drucker was asked why managers fall for bad advice and fail to use sound evidence, he didn't mince words. "Thinking is very hard work. And management fashions are a wonderful substitute for thinking."[6] If you are willing to do the hard thinking required to practice evidence-based management, if you want to reap its benefits, you need to recognize your blind spots, biases, and your company's problems and take responsibility for finding and following the best data and logic. Progress in other fields suggests that this is more than a pretty dream from a pair of naïve academics. The evidence-based medicine movement is progressing, and even its harshest critics admit that acting on better data leads to better care. In education, too, there is growing pressure to base policies and practices on research.[7] Politics and ideology still run roughshod over sound decisions at times. Yet there are success stories, like the Chicago Consortium on School Research, a group of independent researchers whose rigorous studies have changed ineffective policies and practices in Chicago schools and provided hard data about the drawbacks of politically motivated policies like incentive pay for teachers and flunking kids who don't meet grade-level standards.[8] Implementing an evidence-based approach can bolster management practice and organizational performance in much the same way. But there is much work to be done.

Implementation Principles

We've emphasized that evidence-based management isn't just a list of techniques that you can memorize, mimic, and install. It is a perspective for traveling through organizational life, a way of thinking about what you and your company know and what you don't know, what is working and isn't, and what to try next. It isn't a one-time fix that will magically solve all your problems. But there are effective steps that you can take every day to sustain the right mind-set—to keep facing the hard facts, avoid falling prey to dangerous half-truths, and spot and reject total nonsense. We call these implementation principles for practicing evidence-based management.

These principles aren't mysterious or complicated, but you can't gain a competitive advantage unless you actually *use* them. A formidable impediment to evidence-based management is that people won't even try it because they doubt its value. They conclude that evidence-based management doesn't work, or if it does work in a few weird companies, it would be impossible to implement in their own company. When leaders believe it is impossible to obtain competitive leverage *and* it is impossible to do it via better inferences and data, they set in motion a self-fulfilling prophecy that undermines performance—and puts the company at a disadvantage compared to companies that believe in and use evidence-based methods. We wrote this book for managers who want to learn, use, and spread evidence-based management in their companies, to do what it takes to get and sustain that advantage. We've identified nine implementation principles to help people and companies that are committed to doing what it takes to profit from evidence-based management.

1. Treat Your Organization as an Unfinished Prototype

Companies that succeed through evidence-based management develop the right mind-set. Their people learn even as they act on what they know. We've talked a lot about this "attitude of wisdom" in *Hard Facts*. Philosophers and psychologists define wisdom as knowing what you know and what you don't know, and finding a midpoint between overconfidence and insecurity. Psychologist John Meacham writes, "I have concluded that the essence of wisdom is to hold the attitude that knowledge is fallible and to strive for a balance between knowing and doubting."[9]

Leaders who practice the attitude of wisdom think and act as if their organization is an unfinished prototype not something that is "not broke, so they won't fix it." They don't treat it as something they will ruin with dangerous new ideas, that is too much of a mess to fix, or is impossible to change because there will be too much resistance. Think of some of the wisest companies and people we've seen: Cisco's constant refinement of its merger process; Enterprise Rent-A-Car's experimentation with customer loyalty measures; Harrah's use of data to find the truths about succeeding in the casino business; David Kelley's treatment of IDEO as a prototype that he constantly tinkered with in his head; Usama Fayyad's group at Yahoo! running controlled experiments with millions of Web site visitors; Anne Mulcahy's hundreds of big and small changes at Xerox; Andy Grove confidently leading Intel in the direction he thought was best *for now*, but changing directions when confronted with better facts.

Amazon.com is yet another example, because its management philosophy emphasizes constant experimentation and learning from results. As CEO Jeff Bezos explains, people throughout Amazon realize that their job is to "maximize invention per unit of time" and to "minimize the cost of experiments with small teams." These small teams have few constraints, but all are expected to track their experiments carefully. Amazon uses "the Internet to collect hard facts about what's working and what's not," not only to make better decisions, but because "that prevents in-fighting and also eradicates hierarchical rank."[10]

Or take home shopping network QVC. It's a bit smaller than Amazon, but twice as profitable, and ranks third among U.S. broadcasters (behind NBC and ABC) in revenue. QVC products are hawked live on television and are available for immediate purchase. The products include virtually everything from recipe books, to jewelry, to clothes, to Dell computers. QVC had over 7 million customers in 2004, and 93 percent of its revenue came from repeat customers. The products QVC sells are selected through a process of constant experimentation, punctuated by evidence-based reflection about why some sell and others don't. As a product is being sold on the air, producers make minute-by-minute adjustments in camera angles, lighting, and the host's dialog, persisting with changes that seem to increase sales and dropping changes that seem to dampen sales. More reflection and learning occur at daily 9:00 a.m. postmortems, where QVC employees watch videos of yesterday's broadcasts to try and figure out why some product pitches succeeded and others failed. To illustrate, they considered if the prior day's least successful product—Tranquility Yoga Wear—failed because of a poor pitch by the TV host or because it was a bad product. In this case, they decided it was the product, so it was liquidated on the QVC Web site (which has grown to the sixth-largest U.S. Internet retailer).[11]

QVC's decisions are data driven, but the data are fluid; the company acts on the best data that producers can get at the moment even while they continually experiment with camera angles or dialog. A key implication of treating an organization as an unfinished prototype is that many times trying something half-baked, based on the best data you can get and doing so quickly, is better than waiting to get perfect information or to find the perfect solution, where every tiny detail has been considered and analyzed at the cost of much delay. After all, by the time you have completed an in-depth study, the issue may have passed, all the executives may have been fired for inaction, and the company may be dead. An organizational change agent once complained to us that too many academics forget that it is often better to get a little evidence now than a massive amount much later. He teased us, "You professors seem to forget that, when you go to the doctor for a blood test, they don't drain your whole body and look at every cell, a little sample is enough."

He had a good point. A manager's job is to act on the best available evidence and to keep updating. All of the evidence will never be in. In every field, be it airline safety, medicine, the military, or a private company, conditions and circumstances change and new knowledge is acquired all the time. Leaders deal with uncertainty—that's what they have to do. When they face a patient who needs help, doctors prescribe treatments and medicines based not on perfect information or knowledge, but on the best evidence available at that moment. That evidence—and the best treatment—changes over time. In much the same way, evidence-based management means acting on what you know at a moment in time, based on the best available data you have, even as you try to create the conditions for learning more—which means seeing the truth as a moving target—in other words, seeing both your organization and your knowledge about how to manage it as unfinished but useful prototypes.

2. No Brag, Just Facts

In chapter 1, we told you about DaVita, which operates more than 600 dialysis centers in 37 states. One of the company's mantras is "no brag, just facts." This guiding principle focuses people's attention on the forces that drive the quality of care they provide, along with the efficiency and profitability of their business operation. DaVita also emphasizes "no brag, just facts" because it wants to stamp out the self-promotion and puffery that might help individual employees and the company succeed in the short term or the company feel better about performance, but can undermine patient care and operational efficiency over the long term by not dealing with reality.

"No brag, just facts" is the best slogan we know for guiding and inspiring an evidence-based management movement. It is the antidote to the smart talk, self-aggrandizement, and bullshit-based decisions that pollute so much of business life. As Yale's Harry Frankfurt defines it, bullshit means that a person makes assertions with "complete disregard for whether what he's saying corresponds to facts."[12] If there is to be an evidence-based management movement, at least in your company, it means doing just the opposite. Rather than tolerating half-truths and nonsense, it means that people will hold each other accountable for saying things that correspond to the facts, and as we've emphasized, will act on the best facts even when they are painful to hear. Think about it. "No brag, just facts" would have meant that Merck's executives would have faced the evidence about Vioxx rather than training salespeople to play "dodgeball," as they called it, to duck physicians' questions about risks of heart problems. It also would have meant that Hewlett-Packard would have studied how negatively consumers viewed Compaq products *before* making what turned out to be a bad merger. Or it would have meant, that once HP executives learned these facts, they would have seriously considered the implications for the proposed merger's success, instead of blaming the messenger. But it was "brag, not facts" at both Merck and HP—damn the evidence and full speed ahead. And look what happened.

3. Master the Obvious and Mundane

You may wonder how using better evidence can possibly produce better results—it seems too easy and self-evident. It sometimes reminds us of the old joke about the two economists walking down the street who spot a $20 bill lying on the sidewalk. The first says, "Look, a $20 bill. Let's pick it up." The second replies, "It can't possibly be a $20 bill—if a $20 bill were lying on the sidewalk, someone would have picked it up by now." Managers also avoid what's clearly in front of them; they simply presume they are already doing all they can to make good decisions, so there is no point in changing anything.

The guidelines for practicing evidence-based management and steps we've developed for managing in light of the six dangerous half-truths are rife with obvious and mundane common sense. But as we've seen, although much of what we suggest may seem like common sense, it is not common practice, and in fact common sense is in short supply. One obvious bit of advice, for example, is that if you are considering a program or practice, find out if others—another company, a consulting firm, or academics—have already gathered solid evidence about whether it works elsewhere, and if so, when, where, and why. We are struck by how many companies spend months or even years doing internal research, pilot programs, and experiments to decide whether to adopt some program or practice without first stopping to see if pertinent evidence already exists elsewhere. Ignoring data that isn't developed locally is just another manifestation of the not-invented-here syndromes. Certainly, as we've seen, experiments and pilot programs are useful, but before launching one, it is worth checking to see if you aren't reinventing the wheel. This idea may sound like blazingly obvious common sense—but it is so obvious that smart people forget to do it. We've made this suggestion to dozens of companies over the years, to everyone from General Electric executives to McKinsey consultants. In nearly every case, the first reaction was, "Oh, we hadn't thought of that." We've also had people reject this suggestion because it sounded too easy and obvious to be any good. Being a "master of the obvious" may not sound exciting and won't get you labeled as genius, but it can make and save your company a lot of money.

A related implication of taking an evidence-based approach is that dull, seemingly trivial, things can make big differences. Consider an experiment at the University of Missouri that compared decision making in 56 groups where the members *stood* during short (10- to 20-minute) meetings to 55 groups where members *sat* during meetings. Groups where members stood took 34 percent less time to make the assigned decision, and there were no significant differences in decision quality.[13] Whether people should sit or stand during meetings may seem downright silly at first blush. But do the math: How many employees do you have? How many 10- to 20-minute meetings do they have a year? Sure, there are times when people need to sit down during meetings, such as when emotionally hot issues are discussed, but there are plenty of times when standing is fine. Let's consider energy giant Chevron, which has over 50,000 employees. If each employee replaced one 20-minute sit-down meeting per year with a stand-up meeting, this research implies that each meeting would be about 7 minutes shorter and be just as effective. That would save Chevron over 350,000 minutes—nearly 6,000 hours—per year.

4. See Yourself and Your Organization as Outsiders Do

A big impediment to evidence-based management is that human beings, especially those with good mental health, often have inflated views of their own talents and prospects for success. This rampant optimism is a double-edged sword. The upside is that it creates positive self-fulfilling prophecies, which increase the odds of success. The downside is that excessive optimism causes people to downplay or not see risks, and to persist despite clear evidence they are traveling down the wrong path. One study found, for example, that over 80 percent of entrepreneurs surveyed estimated that chances were over 70 percent that their venture would succeed, and over 30 percent believed that their firm was certain to succeed—even though only about 35 percent of new businesses survive their first five years.[14] Max Bazerman's book on managerial decision making shows that outsiders often make more objective judgments than insiders do—so having a blunt friend, mentor, or counselor can help you see and act on better evidence.[15] This is one reason why Kathleen Eisenhardt's study of successful versus unsuccessful Silicon Valley start-ups found that in companies that survived and thrived, the CEO usually had a trusted counselor on the team—while CEOs of unsuccessful firms usually did not. These counselors were typically 10 to 20 years older than the CEO, with broad industry experience, and were most valuable for helping CEOs recognize when they were traveling down the wrong path and a shift in strategic direction was needed.[16]

There is an old joke that when you hire a consultant, she looks at your watch and tells you what time it says. Unfortunately, human biases are so strong that companies may be wise to hire consultants for just that purpose, as sometimes leaders are unable or unwilling to see what is obvious to everyone else. But leaders who can step out of their own shoes and see their companies *as if* they are outsiders will make better decisions. Aric Press, the editor of the *American Lawyer*, made this point when he suggested that law firms ought to use "jerk audits" to spot, reform, and weed out nasty, demeaning lawyers. "At a minimum, what I'm suggesting is that you ask yourselves this question: Why do we put up with this behavior? If the answer is 2,500 value-billed hours, at least you will have identified your priorities without incurring the cost of a consultant."[17]

5. Power, Prestige, and Performance Make You Stubborn, Stupid, and Resistant to Valid Evidence

Ah ego, the great destroyer. Certainly, fear and lack of courage have sunk companies, but excessive confidence and certainty are more common and destructive. Many leaders fall prey to this problem because they believe they can only achieve and reflect greatness if they never admit they made an error, don't know something, or have a shred of doubt. In the late 1990s, Microsoft lost a famous antitrust trial. A *Fortune* article asked, "Here's the great mystery of the Microsoft trial: How can a company this smart put on a defense this dumb?"[18] The answer seems to be that overconfidence is a dangerous side effect of being a monopoly. Microsoft executives were so sure of their position, so sure they were right, that they seemed unable to see things from others' perspectives, so as a consequence, they were unwilling or unable to take the proceedings seriously enough.

Coca-Cola under Douglas Ivester suffered a similar problem for similar reasons. Coke is also among the most powerful and recognizable brands in the world. Like Microsoft, it has enjoyed market dominance for decades, and in the late 1990s had come off a period of remarkable financial performance. When people in Europe believed that contaminated Coke had made them ill, Ivester's initial response was insulting and inadequate, which cost the company dearly in lost business and image. Convinced that he was right, Ivester simply told his own people and French officials, "There is no health issue" and "There is nothing wrong with Coca-Cola."[19]

Fortune asked, "Why didn't Ivester speak out? Go on television? Tell European consumers the facts or at least show a little empathy and feel their pain?" Perhaps Ivester didn't because he was "adamant about standing firm." Perhaps he didn't because "people who know Ivester will say he believes that he can manage his way through any situation."[20] In other words, many of the problems that Ivester and Coca-Cola suffered were due to hubris and its ugly ripple effects: arrogant people don't bother to listen, ask for advice and help, or take others' perspective because they *know* they are smarter then everyone else. As we have already discussed, CEO hubris causes companies to overpay for acquisitions, too.

Consider another variant of this problem. A new CEO comes in and vows to put his or her stamp on the organization. Instead of taking the best from the past and then building on it, many new executives break completely from the past to demonstrate their difference and make their own mark, even if some of the old ideas and practices they discard are effective. Plus, CEOs have pet theories, often acquired through experience or stemming from their beliefs or ideologies. Regardless of the reasons, many new CEOs arrive confident, powerful, and determined to be different, so it is out with the old and in with new, even if the old was based on hard facts.

Hewlett-Packard provides a case in point. HP was once a well-run organization, in part because its people were so interested in fact-based management. In the early 1990s, although HP executives believed in differentiated rewards and pay-for-performance, they decided to test these systems before actually implementing them. So HP businesses experimented with 13 different pay programs. "Most of these involved team- and skill-based pay systems; some involved gain sharing and some cash incentives or bonuses."[21] The company's goal "was to learn from these 'experiments' and use the data to decide whether to encourage broader use of pay-for-performance at Hewlett-Packard."

The findings were consistent. "The local managers who enthusiastically initiated these pay-for-performance programs ran into difficulties in implementation and maintenance and were ready to abandon them so they could allocate their efforts elsewhere." As a result: "based on the experiences reported by management at these 13 sites, Hewlett-Packard executives decided to discontinue experimentation with the alternative pay-for-performance programs."[22] These experiments did find that pay motivated performance, just as past research shows. But the costs weren't worth the benefits. The lost trust in the company, damaged employee commitment, shift of focus away from the work and toward pay, infighting about pay levels, and difficulty of managing these programs meant they simply weren't worth the trouble—a conclusion shared by senior executives who initially supported such schemes, division managers who implemented them, and employees who lived through the experiments.

It sounds like a happy ending, but it wasn't. Carly Fiorina believed in pay-for-performance and more dispersed rewards between the best and worst performers—so when she took over as CEO, she forced the system throughout HP, disregarding the evidence gathered by the company itself. The HP story is all too common. CEO whim, belief, ego, and ideology, rather than evidence, direct what too many companies do and how they do it. As we described in chapter 8, and as the Microsoft, Coca-Cola, and HP examples show, wise leaders should begin by assuming—no matter how flexible, smart, and open to facts they've been in the past—that the mere act of stepping into a powerful position can transform them into stubborn, dumb, and evidence-resistant jerks.

6. Evidence-Based Management Is Not Just for Senior Executives

Evidence-based management is too important to leave exclusively to senior leaders. The best organizations are places where everyone has permission, or better yet, the responsibility to gather and act on quantitative and qualitative data, and to help everyone else learn what they know. Recall Amy Edmondson's research on drug-treatment errors in chapter 4. Nurses in the best units felt obligated—by pressures from supervisors and peers—to catch their own mistakes and those of others and to help everyone learn from errors. Nurses in the best units, measured by patient outcomes, talked openly about mistakes since "mistakes are serious because of the toxicity of the drugs, so you are never afraid to tell the nurse manager." Nurses in the worst units were, by contrast, afraid to report errors because "heads will roll."[23] Or think of the chilling similarity between the *Challenger* and *Columbia* tragedies, where in both cases engineers had evidence that a problem was likely, yet people with more power but less knowledge ignored their warnings and sometimes bullied those who made them. Worse yet, many others at NASA, and their contractors, had been taught that the norm was to keep silent, even when they had crucial facts. As the Columbia Investigation Board found, people who were "marginal and powerless" had "useful information or opinions" that they didn't express.[24]

What was the foundation of the astounding turnaround of the NUMMI automobile plant in Fremont, California, which went from one of the worst plants in the world under General Motors to one of the best under Toyota management, with nearly the same workforce? One big difference between the old and the new system was that, under the Toyota system, assembly workers were actively involved in and responsible for tracking their own quality and productivity, coming up with ideas about how to improve them, and designing experiments to test their ideas—all with remarkably light management oversight.[25] Or consider Google and 3M, companies with vastly different cultures, workforces, technologies, and histories (Google is barely five years old and 3M is approaching its 100th birthday). Yet both thrive through the creativity of their people. Technical staff in both organizations are given the time, resources, plus trust and responsibility, to tinker with their own ideas that might help the company.

The theme that cuts across all of these settings is that when managers treat employees as if a big part of their job is to invent, find, test, and implement the best ideas, then managers make fewer mistakes, organizations learn more, and more innovation happens. This conclusion isn't backed just by selective case studies. Much research shows that when companies use more of each employee's intelligence and talents, they make more money.[26] This research reflects one of the biggest differences between the underlying assumptions made under old-fashioned "scientific management" and modern "evidence-based management." A cornerstone of Fredrick Winslow Taylor's classic book on *Scientific Management* and a host of related work at the turn of the 20th century was that superior performance depended on smart managers who did all the thinking and compliant workers who did just as they were told—it was as if managers and workers were from different species, one with big brains and the other with tiny brains.[27] Many of Taylor's methods for designing work systems were big advances, but evidence amassed since then shows that his assumptions about the most effective relationship between managers and workers were flawed. The upshot is that it is essential to teach *everyone* the practices and mind-set of evidence-based management.

7. Like Everything Else, You Still Need to Sell It

We've shown that a big roadblock to evidence-based management is that the kinds of information that managers (and all people) are drawn to, remember, and try to use are often the reverse of what it takes to practice evidence-based management—case studies about successes rather than systematic information about good and bad outcomes, and particularly a bias for the new and novel. Unfortunately, new and exciting ideas grab attention even when they are vastly inferior to old ideas. We celebrate geniuses and superstars even though knowledge moves forward through communities that swarm down on ideas and knock them back and forth. And vivid, juicy stories and case studies sell better than detailed, rigorous, and admittedly dull data—no matter how wrong the stories or how right the data. A way out of this dilemma is to use evidence about what sells best to sell the best evidence. This means using many of the same tricks as purveyors of bad practices to further evidence-based management.

One tactic is to find widely admired gurus and stars who use the attention they receive to promote evidence-based practices, to emphasize that they are not lone geniuses but that their ideas reflect work by a community of people, and thus deny that they are magical people with magical powers. We don't have to invent such people; they already exist. Dr. David Sackett is Exhibit A. As we saw in the opening chapters, Sackett is touted as the father of modern evidence-based medicine. Yet he responds to such flattery by emphasizing that he is given too much credit and his colleagues are not given enough. Sackett has also repeatedly warned of the dangers of becoming an "expert" because it can mean you stop learning and others place too much weight on your knowledge. He also continually presses for research methods and standards that advance evidence-based medicine. It likely isn't possible to stop the hero worship that pervades business culture, but we can advance evidence-based management with antiheroes who use approaches reminiscent of Sackett's, people like Harrah's Gary Loveman and Amazon.com's Jeff Bezos.

Another trick is to make valid evidence come to life—so people will be drawn to it and act on it. The idea is to use a two-step process. First, you identify an organizational problem or preferred practice based on solid, if unexciting, evidence. Second, you use vivid stories, cases, or better yet, create vivid experiences to grab management attention and spark organizational action. Some years ago, Pfeffer was teaching an executive program on the importance of managing people and culture. He wanted to make the point that, particularly in service industries, people make the difference. So he asked everyone in the class with a cell phone to call United Airlines' reservations and to put their hands up (and disconnect the call) when they were tired of listening to *Rhapsody in Blue*. He then asked people to dial 1-800-I FLY SWA, Southwest Airlines' phone line, but to be prepared since the call would likely be answered on the first ring. Many people made conversation with the agent who answered, and some even bought tickets for trips, such as weekend jaunts to Las Vegas, that they didn't know they wanted to take. The point was made, and the difference in the service experience was transformed from a set of ideas and statistics to a vivid experience.

Better ideas don't automatically triumph in the end. New technologies and practices that win in the marketplace for ideas usually have tireless and skilled champions. One of Thomas Alva Edison's collaborators, Francis Jehl, complained repeatedly that Edison was more of a skilled pitchman than inventor, and that his "genius" was most reminiscent of master huckster P. T. Barnum. Yet Edison's invention factory would never have been funded, and few customers would have bought his company's inventions, without his ability to sell.[28] Steve Wozniak was the technical genius behind the early Apple computers, but venture capitalist Arthur Rock would not have funded the company and Apple would not have gained its cult-like following without Steve Jobs' ability to ignite human imagination. Charles Darwin not only wrote hundreds of letters to promote his theory of evolution, a team of renowned proponents vigorously promoted his ideas too—close friends of Darwin who "instinctively moved together."[29] These so-called *four musketeers*, geologist Charles Lyell, biologist Thomas Henry Huxley (known as "Darwin's bulldog"), botanist Joseph Hooker, and American botanist Asa Gray, gave speeches, engaged in public debates and correspondence with critics, and wrote numerous articles—and in doing so, spread and sold the ideas in *Origin of Species*.

8. If All Else Fails, Slow the Spread of Bad Practices

In a perfect world, leaders would seek out and find the best evidence, and never implement policies and practices that clashed with sound evidence. But we don't live in a perfect world. Unfortunately, as we've seen, many managers and other employees face pressures to do things that aren't only untested, but are known to be ineffective. In such cases, a challenge—a genuine moral dilemma—can arise because if they follow orders from superiors, people can knowingly harm their organizations, colleagues, and customers. We hesitate to recommend what might be called *evidence-based misbehavior*. But a case can be made that when leaders are wrong—and people don't have the power to reverse their commands—that ignoring orders, delaying action, or implementing programs incompletely may be best for all involved.

James March shows that although resistance to change is typically portrayed as an irrational refusal to do something, which hampers performance, it can protect decision makers and organizations from folly. If you have done all you can to persuade superiors that a practice is wrong, and they insist on going ahead with it anyway, you might openly defy their directives. But such insubordination can get you fired. That might not only be bad for you, but if someone who enthusiastically implements this practice replaces you, your organization can suffer. An alternative approach is to quietly ignore bad practices and do what you think is right.

In the mid-1980s, Robert Sutton saw this tactic used in a large bank that was closing over 100 branches in California. Sutton wanted to learn about effective versus ineffective ways of closing organizations and apparently so did the bank. So the retail action team that oversaw the closings picked four branches that they considered *good* closings and four that they considered *bad* closings (especially in terms of the percentage of customers retained). Sutton then interviewed each branch manager. There was a clear pattern. Managers at each successful closing had largely ignored the procedures developed by the retail action team and developed their own practices instead. But they weren't ignoring the official procedures to be malicious; they were doing it, as James March would say, to protect their bank from folly, because the action team's procedures were cumbersome and ineffective. One manager held up a thick book of procedures and policies put together by the retail action team, and bragged that the key to his success was ignoring everything in the book! In contrast, managers at each bad closing lamented that they had tried to follow the official procedures closely and doing so had hampered their ability to convince customers to transfer to other branches. When Sutton began presenting his findings to the retail action team, he was quickly shown the door, and his follow-up phone calls were not returned.

If you can't openly refuse or discreetly ignore a bad policy, a related practice is to drag your feet as long as possible, and when you can't do that any longer, implement it in as few corners of the organization as possible. Again, it is far better to make and implement sound decisions, but a fact of organizational life is that more powerful people sometimes require their underlings to do dumb things. Frankly, we would hesitate to even bring up these rather grubby "evidence-based misbehavior" tactics if we hadn't seen the difficult position that school administrators were put in as a result of severe political pressures—in many cases directly from mayors—to end social promotion and start flunking kids who didn't meet grade-level standards. As we saw in chapter 2, although the idea of only advancing qualified students to the next grade sounds good, there is overwhelming evidence that social promotion is the lesser of two evils, as it results in better test scores and graduation rates, and is far less costly than flunking kids.

A couple years ago, Sutton had conversations with senior administrators from two large school districts, both of which were in the middle of ending social promotion (again, both districts had suffered through unsuccessful attempts in past years). Sutton asked them if they knew that every shred of evidence showed that they were implementing a bad practice. Both administrators had virtually the same answer. Yes, they knew the literature well and had tried to talk politicians out of ending social promotion—but they had failed because it was a policy that so many voters supported. So both felt forced to go ahead and implement the policy in their schools. *But* they were both doing it as slowly and incompletely as they could. Indeed, both explained—in defensive and somewhat angry tones—that in a perfect world free of politics, they wouldn't have to act that way, but that their subtle resistance would result in the least damage to their schools and students. The message was that either they resisted that way, or they would be fired and replaced by someone who believed in ending social promotion and would do far more harm. In short, resistance and foot-dragging isn't always futile. A case can be made that evidence-based misbehavior is the best you can do for your organization at times.

9: The Best Diagnostic Question: What Happens When People Fail?

As we were finishing the final revision of *Hard Facts, Dangerous Half-Truths, and Total Nonsense*, we stopped to reflect on how the ideas in this new book meshed with our last book, *The Knowing-Doing Gap*. We considered the most crucial lessons that we had gleaned from writing these two books, from studying companies and talking to so many managers, and trying to help them spot and implement evidence-based practices. We concluded that when we wanted to learn a lot about a company quickly—wanted a fast hint about whether an organization's leaders had the attitude of wisdom, whether a company used practices that were supported by the best evidence, and whether conditions were ripe for turning all that knowledge into action—we both asked the same diagnostic question: *what happens when people fail?*

We wish it were possible to live in a world where mistakes, setbacks, and errors never happen. We despise our own failures, it wounds us when people we care about suffer setbacks, and we even find ourselves feeling bad for people we dislike when they make mistakes. Failure hurts, it is embarrassing, and we would rather live without it. Yet there is no learning without failure. As we've seen, there is always a learning curve when an organization tries something new or trains people—including doctors and managers—to do something new. If you look at how the most effective systems in the world are managed, a hallmark is that when something goes wrong, people face the hard facts, learn what happened and why, and keep using those facts to make the system better.

The U.S. civil aviation system is the safest in the world and has become even safer over time because of the accident and incident reporting system it has used for years. This system permits pilots (and others) to report anonymously to the Federal Aviation Administration incidents such as near misses and equipment problems that could potentially have been disastrous. The agency then follows up on these reports, looking for regular patterns that require corrective action to remove the root causes of the problems. For instance, taxiing procedures for airplanes on runways have been changed in response to many near collisions.

We've also seen that there is no innovation without failure. Most organizational change efforts have a high failure rate—from mergers, to new product introductions, to technological change efforts. But the rub is that the only thing more dangerous than changing an organization is never changing it at all. Learning from past and current change efforts is crucial to treating organizations as unfinished prototypes, and such learning depends on creating a climate of psychological safety where people can openly talk about things that went wrong and might go wrong. We've also seen that great leaders, including George Washington, didn't learn their jobs without making mistakes and that even the most experienced leaders will continue to make mistakes. The difference is that bad leaders make the same mistakes again and again, while good leaders, who create conditions for learning, make new and different mistakes. And it is the leaders of large companies who admit when they make mistakes, and show that they've learned from it, who help their companies perform best over the long haul, not those who only take credit for good news and blame others or bad luck for setbacks.

The most succinct and useful advice we know about how to handle failure comes from medicine, where the motto is *forgive and remember*.[30] Forgive, so that people are willing to talk about and admit the errors that are inevitable in any human endeavor, and remember, so that the same mistakes don't occur repeatedly. Organizations that forgive and forget keep making the same mistakes over and over again. Organizations that remember—but blame, stigmatize, and punish losers—create a climate of fear. So the game becomes avoiding personal punishment and humiliation, not helping others learn or fixing the system. Forgiving but remembering failure promotes learning without creating a climate of fear. Remembering also helps because when the same people keep making the same mistakes again and again (and others don't), it is a sign that these people need more training or are better suited for a different job.

This means that, if you want to take a first step towards practicing evidence-based management and closing knowing-gaps, find out: What happens to people who fail in your organization? Do you ever admit your own mistakes? Does your organization forgive and remember when people make mistakes, and does it use that information to keep making things better?

And don't just listen to what your friends tell you, or even to people who are still in your company. Collect some anonymous evidence. Find out if you actually learn something from bad hiring decisions, failed product development efforts, botched mergers, and mistakes and setbacks that plague successful projects as well. Talk to people who you usually disagree with, don't like, don't know, who have quit, and perhaps even those you've fired. Collect the evidence and confront the hard facts.

A Different Perspective on Leadership

The myth of the superhuman über-executive persists, but it's total nonsense. There isn't a shred of evidence that great leaders have magical powers that result in superior decisions and strategies, devised with little or no help from the mere mortals they tower over, inspire, and command. Research on what leaders actually do reveals that they live in a messy, uncertain world of give and take, with interruption piled on top of interruption, and they spend their days bouncing from one short and often unplanned interaction to another, where they attempt to motivate, coach, and influence people to get things done.[31] *Hard Facts, Dangerous Half-Truths, and Total Nonsense* shows that as leaders travel through their messy work lives, one of their most crucial chores is to display and promote curiosity—so that they and their followers will keep learning new skills, coming to grips with the best logic and evidence and applying what they know (for now) to change their organizations for the better. Leaders breed such curiosity by having both the humility to be students and the confidence to be teachers. And the best leaders know when and how to switch between these roles.

Taking the student role is crucial for learning the craft of management, but that is just the start. CEO "Wim" Roelandts, for example, displayed great skill in guiding the semiconductor company Xilinx through a huge drop in revenue in 2001. Roelandts and his senior team reversed the company's slide, emerged from the downturn as the industry leader in their segment, and did it all without layoffs—and stayed in the top 10 on *Fortune*'s "Best Place to Work" rankings throughout the ordeal. Leaders don't develop that kind of skill overnight. Roelandts spent 29 years at HP, and his first management job entailed overseeing only a single employee, so "luckily, all the early mistakes I made affected only one person." HP increased his management experience and responsibility over the years, and eventually he managed the computer systems organization, which had 20,000 people and $6 billion dollars in yearly sales.[32] The best leaders are lifelong students because they are curious and driven to keep learning what works best for their companies.

We saw this in the way Bill George spent over 50 percent of his first nine months as CEO of Medtronic watching and asking questions as surgeons installed his firm's medical devices. Ann Mulcahy also displayed the attributes of a good student when she became COO of Xerox in 2000 and realized that neither she nor other senior executives had quite come to grips with the dire straits the company was in and that they also did not understand enough about Xerox's businesses to make sound decisions. So Mulcahy set out to learn about the company she had worked for since 1976. To illustrate, Mulcahy did not have a background in finance and the CFO was of little help, so "folks in the controller's department would spend hours with me just making sure that I was prepared to answer all the ugly, tough questions from the bankers."[33] We have also seen this curiosity and drive for constant improvement from Hasso Platner, chairman and cofounder of software giant SAP. When Platner became interested in user-centered design, he and other SAP executives and managers from the Design Services Team took workshops from IDEO and got extensive coaching to learn how to do—not just to talk about—user-centered design.

Medical students are told—half jokingly—that learning a surgical procedure entails four steps: "hear one, see one, do one, teach one." The message the saying conveys, however, is completely serious. Once a surgeon learns something useful, he or she is obligated to teach it to colleagues. We would add that is a hallmark of successful teams and organizations in general. Such teaching can happen through classes, like the workshops on user-centered design that those SAP managers took from IDEO. These managers then taught and advised development teams throughout SAP in the logic and methods of user-centered design, leading those teams to produce over 100 user-friendly prototypes in 100 days. When we think of managers and leaders who best exemplify the mind-set required for practicing evidence-based management, a deep belief and commitment to teaching is usually a big part of the story. It is no accident that Jack Welch spent so much time teaching at GE's executive education center at Crotonville. Like those managers from SAP's Design Services Team, after Welch learned Six Sigma methods, he then taught quality classes to GE insiders and coached people throughout the company on how to use the methods.

Or consider DaVita, which is under constant pressure from Medicare, private insurers, and hospitals to cut the costs of its dialysis services. Many of DaVita's over 600 dialysis centers are run by registered nurses who have built devoted teams and have deep experience in nephrology, which is crucial for providing excellent patient care. But these facility leaders often didn't know much about running a business. So COO Joe Mello and CEO Kent Thiry responded to their lack of business acumen by building DaVita University (DVU), an extensive set of training and communication programs that touch all management activities. New facility administrators come to DVU to learn basic skills such as Microsoft Excel, as well as the basics of the business of running a facility—including profit and loss, budgeting, and scheduling labor. DVU then offers extensive additional training in other business skills. DaVita's ability to deliver the highest-quality care in the industry, while continually improving its labor productivity over the past five years, is the direct result of this continuous learning by facility leaders—who not only learn to do their own jobs better, but to coach their people how to be more effective managers and decision makers. And the teaching at DaVita University is not done by outside consultants, but by DaVita people, who in turn develop their leadership skills and knowledge through the teaching experience.

This commitment to teaching is also seen in leaders who take it upon themselves to teach their skills and values to future managers. Andy Grove has taught a strategy class at the Stanford Business School for years, and Grove's students report that he constantly presses them to disagree with him, defend their positions, and learn how to evaluate the logic and evidence behind their ideas. Bill George has retired from Medtronic and now teaches leadership to Harvard MBAs. And Gary Loveman's success in traveling in the *other* direction bolsters this view that great leaders are great teachers. Loveman went from being an untenured associate professor at Harvard Business School, managing an administrative assistant and a few research assistants, to running an organization with about 40,000 people. Many people assumed that his lack of management experience would doom him to fail. It turns out, however, that Loveman's academic background and experience helped him prepare for a leadership role.

Consider what leaders need to do. As we've shown, the search for the corporate savior—that lone, brilliant individual who can by force of will and breadth of intellect solve all organizational problems—is a bad bet. The business world is turbulent, constantly in flux, and intensely competitive. Adaptability, flexibility, and constant learning are indispensable under such conditions, in large part because a good answer today might be a bad one tomorrow. And in well-run organizations, searching for evidence and logic about better and worse business practices, running small experiments and learning from them, and always questioning, evolving, and learning by doing and from experience is not only some activity conducted by the CEO, but should be a perspective on management—a mind-set—used throughout the organization.

This is why Loveman, as an outstanding academic, had some essential qualities of a great CEO. The best classroom teachers don't lecture students on what they should know, but ask questions that guide students to learn on their own. After all, students learn far more when they think for themselves. And in the process of learning and teaching about the social or the physical sciences, considering theory, evidence, and how to learn from experiments and experience are big parts of the lesson that the best teachers and students master. Even though Loveman may not have managed many people before becoming COO of Harrah's, he had much experience directing conversations that engender intellectual curiosity, teaching people how to think and ask questions, and working with evidence and data. Inquiry is what research and science are about, and asking questions is central to the Socratic method used in teaching at places like Harvard Business School.

As CEO Kent Thiry of DaVita says, "a question well asked is half-answered." That is why, when we observed Thiry and Loveman in action, we saw leaders who continually asked questions of themselves and others, who were always inquiring, who never left well enough alone, and constantly pressed to impart this spirit of learning, curiosity, and inquiry throughout their companies. Leaders don't have to know everything, nor can they. Their job is to create a place where people constantly learn and teach new things, where people keep discovering what works and what doesn't, and to keep nudging their people to think intensely and face the hard facts along the way.

This task of leadership is not something that can be delegated to others. Executives have fallen into the habit of relying on consultants to reduce complexity and to do much of their hard thinking, contracting out reflection and seeking "insights and recipes that are punchy, succinct, explicit, and plausible."[34] The essential tasks of leadership cannot, or at least should not, be subcontracted. Building an evidence-based perspective into how people think and operate is among the most crucial of these tasks. There has been far more talk than action about building systems that cause people to learn and act on what is known, rather than what they believe or hope to be true. These gaps between the rhetoric about learning and actual organizational practices, the disconnect between what is known and what is applied in management practice, and the inconsistency between the need for reflective practices and how few managers actually stop and take time to reflect—and encourage their people to do it too—aren't, however, unsolvable problems. These and so many other discontinuities between action and the hard facts provide rich opportunities for those leaders and companies that actually implement an evidence-based approach. The question remains: Who will have the courage and wisdom to do it?

Notes

Chapter 1

1. For example, see Anne B. Fisher, "The Decade's Worst Mergers," *Fortune*, April 30, 1984, 262–270.

2. David R. King et al., "Meta-Analyses of Post-Acquisition Performance: Indicators of Unidentified Moderators," *Strategic Management Journal* 25 (2004): 187–200.

3. Charles O'Reilly, "Cisco Systems: The Acquisition of Technology Is the Acquisition of People," Case HR-10 (Palo Alto, CA: Stanford Graduate School of Business, 1998).

4. Julie Creswell, "When Bad Mergers Happen to Good Firms," *Fortune*, May 1, 2000, 46.

5. Founder and CEO of one of Siebel's failed acquisitions, e-mail to Jeffrey Pfeffer, August 2005.

6. O'Reilly, "Cisco Systems."

7. Scott McCartney and Michael J. McCarthy, "Southwest Flies Circles Around United's Shuttle," *Wall Street Journal*, February 20, 1996.

8. For a review of the evidence on the ineffectiveness of most layoffs, see Wayne F. Cascio, *Responsible Restructuring: Creative and Profitable Alternatives to Layoffs* (San Francisco: Berrett-Koehler, 2002).

9. Gretchen Morgenson, "When Options Rise to Top, Guess Who Pays," *New York Times*, November 10, 2002.

10. Matt Murray, "Option Frenzy: What Went Wrong?" *Wall Street Journal*, December 17, 2002.

11. Floyd Norris, "Stock Options: Do They Make Bosses Cheat?" *New York Times*, August 8, 2005.

12. Ibid.

13. Roger Martin, "The Wrong Incentive," *Barron's*, December 22, 2003, 30–31.

14. Dan R. Dalton et al., "Meta-Analyses of Financial Performance and Equity: Fusion and Confusion?" *Academy of Management Journal* 46 (2003): 13–27.

15. Lucian Arye Bebchuk, Jesse M. Fried, and David I. Walker, "Managerial Power and Rent Extraction in the Design of Executive Compensation," *The University of Chicago Law Review* 69 (Summer 2002): 751–846.

16. David R. Baker, "Silicon Valley Fights Fiercely for Options," *San Francisco Chronicle*, November 10, 2002.

17. Lisa E. Bolton and Chip Heath, "Believing in First Mover Advantage" (Palo Alto, CA: Stanford Graduate School of Business), 2005.

18. Andy Grove, "Taking on Prostate Cancer," *Fortune*, May 13, 1996, 54–72.

19. Kevin Patterson, "What Doctors Don't Know (Almost Everything)," *New York Times Magazine*, May 5, 2002, 77.

20. For a more complete review and discussion of evidence-based medicine, see David Sackett et al., *Evidence-Based Medicine: How to Teach and Practice EBM* (London: Wolfe, 2002); and William Rosenberg and Donald Anna, "Evidence-Based Medicine: An Approach to Clinical Problem-Solving," *British Medical Journal* 310 (1995): 1122–1126.

21. Gabrielle Bauer, "A Reluctant Policy Wonk: Dr. David Sackett, a Pioneer in Evidence-Based Medicine, Has No Time to Play King, but the World Seems Intent on Crowning Him," *The Medical Post*, August 22, 2002.

22. Rajiv Lal, "Harrah's Entertainment, Inc.," Case 9-502-011 (Boston: Harvard Business School, 2002).

23. Richard A. Hightower and Paul M. Sommers, "Do Contenders Really Outspend Non-Contenders in Major League Baseball?" Economics Discussion Paper 02-36 (Middlebury, VT: Middlebury College, 2002).

24. David Leonhardt, "Passing on Blue Chip Players Can Pay Off," *New York Times*, August 28, 2005.

25. Ibid.

26. Usama Fayyad and Nitin Sharma, interview with Robert Sutton, July 2005.

27. Richard J. Murnane and David K. Cohen, "Merit Pay and the Evaluation Problem: Why Most Merit Pay Plans Fail and a Few Survive," *Harvard Educational Review* 56 (1983): 2.

28. Ibid.

29. Brian Jacob and Steven D. Levitt, "Rotten Apples: An Investigation of Prevalence and Predictors of Teacher Cheating," working paper 9413, National Bureau of Economic Research, New York, 2002; see also Brian Jacob and Steven D. Levitt, "Catching Cheating Teachers: The Results of an Unusual Experiment in Implementing Theory," working paper 9414, National Bureau of Economic Research, New York, 2002.

30. Tony Bryk, conversation with Robert Sutton at the Center for Advanced Study in the Behavioral Sciences, Palo Alto, California, March 2003.

31. Numerous dangerous half-truths are advocated in the management literature, sold by consultants and academics, and reflected in the conventional wisdom accepted by many executives. This raises the question: how and why did we choose the half-truths examined here? We did do a survey of what several hundred managers—people who attended a number of our executive programs—believed to be true about organizational performance. That survey included every half-truth that we write about, along with many others. The six half-truths that we focus on here are all things that many, often nearly all, of these executives believed to be true—but they are not, strictly speaking derived only from those surveys. In the end, we examined the best evidence we could find, reflected on our experience in teaching and consulting over the years, and prioritized the half-truths that we found to be both widespread and particularly harmful when they are believed and used to guide organizational action. You may have your own favorites.

32. Melvin Konner, *Becoming a Doctor* (New York: Viking, 1987), xi.

Chapter 2

1. Alex Taylor III, "How Toyota Defies Gravity," *Fortune*, December 8, 1997, 100–108; Michael N. Kennedy and Allen Ward, *Product Development for the Lean Enterprise: Why Toyota's System Is Four Times More Productive and How You Can Implement It* (Richmond, VA: Oaklea Press, 2003).

2. Kevin Patterson, "What Doctors Don't Know (Almost Everything)," *New York Times Magazine*, May 5, 2002, 77.

3. Rakesh Khurana, *Searching for the Corporate Savior: The Irrational Quest for Charismatic CEOs* (Princeton, NJ: Princeton University Press, 2002).

4. This estimate is based on counts of business magazines and newspapers listed on Yahoo.com for a search done in October 2002.

5. This estimate is based on information provided on barnesandnoble.com and Amazon.com.

6. Peter Meyers, "Cranky Consumer: Rating Business-Book Summaries," *Wall Street Journal*, November 5, 2002.

7. Perseus Publishing, *Business: The Ultimate Resource* (Cambridge, MA: Perseus, 2002).

8. Compare, for instance, the recommendations that come from Jim Collins, *Good to Great* (New York: HarperCollins, 2001) with those from Tony Alessandra, *Charisma: Seven Keys to Developing the Magnetism That Leads to Success* (New York: Warner, 1998).

9. Bill Jensen, *Simplicity: The New Competitive Advantage in a World of More, Better, Faster* (New York: Perseus, 2001); Robert Axelrod and Michael D. Cohen, *Harnessing Complexity: Organizational Implications of a Scientific Frontier* (New York: Free Press, 2000).

10. Robert S. Kaplan and David P. Norton, *The Strategy-Focused Organization* (Boston: Harvard Business School Press, 2000); Henry Mintzberg, *The Rise and Fall of Strategic Planning* (New York: Free Press, 1993).

11. On small New York– and San Francisco–based consulting firms specializing in organizational and cultural change and strategy implementation, The Trium Group does do follow-up surveys to see if changes in knowledge, attitudes, behavior, and results come from its work with clients. Also, the firm has a three-tier pricing model in which clients *voluntarily* decide whether to pay more if the project has exceeded their goals and expectations, an agreed upon amount if it has met objectives, or less if the project did not deliver all that was expected. This provides an incentive for the company to do good work, not just sell business.

12. Darrell Rigby, "Management Tools and Techniques: A Survey," *California Management Review* 43 (Winter 2001): 139–160.

13. Jack Welch quote from *Workforce Magazine*, available on line at www.workforce.com/archive/feature/23/47/39/234742.php.

14. For a review of just some of the literature on this issue, see Alfie Kohn, *No Contest: The Case Against Competition* (Boston: Houghton Mifflin, 1986), particularly chapter 3, "Is Competition More Productive?" and chapter 10, "Learning Together."

15. Paul Lukacs, *American Vintage: The Rise of American Wine* (Boston: Houghton Mifflin, 2002).

16. Michael Porter and Gregory C. Bond, "Robert Mondavi: Competitive Strategy," Case 799-124 (Boston: Harvard Business School, 1999).

17. Ed Michaels, Helen Handfield-Jones, and Beth Axelrod, *The War for Talent* (Boston: Harvard Business School Press, 2001). The appendix makes clear that the dependent variable, total shareholder return, was for the years prior to the particular year the survey was done to gather the information on management practices. Performance data for the prior 10 years were correlated with current practices for the 77 firms participating in their 1997 survey; performance data for the prior three to five years were correlated with current performance for the 2000 survey. If the authors' temporal logic were applied to research on the link between smoking and lung cancer, the conclusion would be that lung cancer causes smoking.

18. Jerker Denrell, "Vicarious Learning, Undersampling of Failure, and the Myths of Management," *Organization Science* 14 (2003): 227–243.

19. Ibid., 229.

20. Glenn R. Carroll and Michael T. Hannan, "Automobile Manufacturers," in *Organizations in Industry*, eds. G. R. Carroll and M. T. Hannan (New York: Oxford University Press, 1995), 195–214.

21. Denrell, "Vicarious Learning," 228.

22. D. Eden and A. B. Shani, "Pygmalion Goes to Boot Camp: Expectancy, Leadership and Trainee Performance," *Journal of Applied Psychology* 67 (1982): 194–199; R. Rosenthal and D. B. Rubin, "Interpersonal Expectancy Effects: The First 345 Studies," *The Behavioral and Brain Sciences* 3 (1978): 377–386; Brian D. McNatt, "Ancient Pygmalion Joins Contemporary Management: A Meta-Analysis of the Result," *Journal of Applied Psychology* 85 (2000): 314–322.

23. For example, see Alexander G. Stajkovic and Fred Luthans, "Differential Effects of Incentive Motivators on Work Performance," *Academy of Management Journal* 44 (2001): 580–591; Richard W. Griffin, "Objective and Social Sources of Information in Task Redesign: A Field Experiment," *Administrative Science Quarterly* 28 (1983): 184–200; Gregory R. Oldham and Daniel J. Brass, "Employee Reactions to an Open-Plan Office: A Naturally Occurring Quasi-Experiment," *Administrative Science Quarterly* 24 (1979): 267–284.

24. See http://www.bain.com. We wrote to George Cogan, a senior partner at Bain, about this "correlation is not causation" problem. He readily acknowledged that this was so, and

pointed out that Bain's training materials emphasize that "we obviously cannot claim credit for these results" but this disclaimer is conspicuously absent from the Bain Web site. As we go to press, the claim that "our clients outperform the market 4 to 1" (up from 3 to 1) is the first thing visitors see when they go to www.bain.com, and the implication that Bain is responsible for this superior performance remains, accompanied by the statement "Companies that outperform the market like to work with us; we are as passionate about their results as they are." (Quotes from George Cogan are from an e-mail exchange with Robert Sutton on September 17, 2005.)

25. John Steinbeck, *The Log from the Sea of Cortez* (New York: Viking Press, 1941), 3.

26. G. MacKenzie, *Orbiting the Giant Hairball: A Corporate Fool's Guide to Surviving with Grace* (New York: Viking, 1996).

27. Andrea Gabor, "Quality Revival, Part 2: Ford Embraces Six Sigma," *New York Times*, June 13, 2001.

28. Keith H. Hammonds, "Grassroots Leadership—Ford Motor Co.," *Fast Company*, April 2000, 138–143.

29. Ibid.

30. See, for instance, M. A. Mone and W. McKinley, "The Uniqueness Value and Its Consequences for Organization Studies," *Journal of Management Inquiry* 2 (1993): 284–296.

31. See Andrew Hargadon, *How Breakthroughs Happen: The Surprising Truth About How Companies Innovate* (Boston: Harvard Business School Press, 2003).

32. Alfie Kohn, "Why Incentive Plans Cannot Work," *Harvard Business Review* (September–October 1993): 3–7; Jeffrey Pfeffer, "Six Dangerous Myths About Pay," *Harvard Business Review* (May–June 1998): 107–119; Egon Zehnder, "A Simpler Way to Pay," *Harvard Business Review* (April 2001): 3–8.

33. See http://www.gladwell.com.

34. A famous sociologist wrote a charming book that tries, but ultimately fails, to track down the originator of this saying. See Robert K. Merton, *On the Shoulders of Giants* (New York: Free Press, 1965).

35. See, for instance, Leslie Berlin, *The Man Behind the Microchip: Robert Noyce and the Invention of Silicon Valley* (New York: Oxford University Press, 2005). In spite of the title, the book details the large number of different people involved with this important technological invention, and Noyce's important but limited role in the entire enterprise.

36. "The 2002 HBR List: Breakthrough Ideas for Today's Business Agenda," *Harvard Business Review* (March 2002): 58–66.

37. James March, e-mail to Robert Sutton, November 2, 2002.

38. Russell L. Ackoff, "Management Gurus and Educators," *Reflections* 2 (2001): 66–67.

39. Stefan Stern, "Guru Guide," *Management Today*, October 2001, 82–87. Quote is from page 87.

40. Mary J. Benner and Michael L. Tushman, "Exploration, Exploitation, and Process Management: The Productivity Dilemma Revisited," *Academy of Management Review* 28 (2003): 238–256.

41. Richard J. Hackman, "On the Coming Demise of Job Enrichment," in *Man and Work in Society*, eds. E. L. Cass and F. G. Zimmer (New York: Van Nostrand Renhold, 1975), 97–115.

42. Michael A. Hitt and R. Duane Ireland, "Peters and Waterman Revisited: The Unended Quest for Excellence," *Academy of Management Executive* 1 (1987): 91–98.

43. See, for example, Billie Jo Zirger and Modesto A. Maidique, "A Model of New Product Development: An Empirical Test," *Management Science* 36 (1990): 867–884; for a review of much of this literature, see Shona Brown and Kathleen Eisenhardt, "Product Development: Past Research, Present Findings, and Future Directions," *Academy of Management Review* 20 (1995): 343–378.

44. Ambrose Bierce, *The Devil's Dictionary* (New York: Crowell, 1979), 112. (Originally published in 1911.)

45. Baruch Fischhoff, "For Those Condemned to Study the Past: Heuristics and Biases in Hindsight," in *Judgment Under Uncertainty: Heuristics and Biases*, eds. Daniel Kahneman,

Paul Slovic, and Amos Tversky (Cambridge, England: Cambridge University Press, 1982), 335–353.

46. Barry M. Staw, "Attribution of the 'Causes' of Performance: An Alternative Interpretation of Cross-Sectional Research on Organizations," *Organizational Behavior and Human Performance* 13 (1975): 414–432.

47. Robert B. Cialdini, *Influence: Science and Practice*, 4th ed. (Boston: Allyn & Bacon, 2001).

48. D. T. Miller, "The Norm of Self-Interest," *American Psychologist* 54 (1999): 1053–1060.

49. B. Frank and G. G. Schulze, "Does Economics Make Citizens Corrupt?" *Journal of Economic Behavior & Organization* 43 (2000): 101–113; H. Frank, T. D. Gilovich, and D. T. Regan, "Does Studying Economics Inhibit Cooperation?" *Journal of Economic Perspectives* 7 (1993): 159–171.

50. This research is summarized in Robert M. Hauser, "What If We Ended Social Promotion?" *Education Week*, April 7, 1999, 64–66.

51. Ibid.

52. Sheryl McCarthy, "Schools Repeat Social Promotion Problems," *Newsday*, March 28, 2002.

53. See John A. Meacham, "The Loss of Wisdom," in *Wisdom: Its Nature, Origins, and Development*, ed. Robert J. Sternberg (Cambridge, England: Cambridge University Press, 1990), 181–211; and John A. Meacham, "Wisdom and the Context of Knowledge: Knowing What One Doesn't Know One Doesn't Know," in *On the Development of Developmental Psychology*, eds. D. Huhn and J. A. Meacham (Basel, Switzerland: Krager, 1983), 111–134; see Robert J. Sternberg, "Implicit Theories of Intelligence, Creativity, and Wisdom," *Journal of Personality and Social Psychology* 49 (1985): 607–627.

54. Gabrielle Bauer, "A Reluctant Policy Wonk: Dr. David Sackett, a Pioneer in Evidence-Based Medicine, Has No Time to Play King, but the World Seems Intent on Crowning Him," *The Medical Post*, August 22, 2002.

Chapter 3

1. Libby Sartain with Martha I. Finney, *HR from the Heart* (New York: AMACOM, 2003).

2. Ibid., 18.

3. Ibid., 19.

4. Robert Sutton learned this when a senior faculty member first tried to tease him, and when that didn't work, seriously explained that Sutton and Pfeffer were too loud and laughed too much for a place like the Stanford Business School, where "serious thinking" goes on.

5. http://www.spectorcne.com/.

6. See Randall Stross, "Digital Domain: When Long Hours at a Video Game Stop Being Fun," *New York Times*, November 21, 2004; Matt Richtell, "Fringes vs. Basics in Silicon Valley," *New York Times*, March 9, 2005.

7. Kimberly Elsbach and Daniel Cable, "Passive 'Face Time' as Performance Relevant Information: Implications for Remote Workers," (paper presented at the Center for Work, Technology and Organization, Stanford University, Palo Alto, CA, February 2005).

8. Anat Rafaeli and Michael G. Pratt, "Tailored Meanings: On the Meaning and Impact of Organizational Dress," *Academy of Management Review* 18 (1993): 32–55.

9. Ibid, 43.

10. Indeed, future CEO Lou Gerstner showed up for his job interview wearing a blue shirt, challenging IBM's "white shirt" culture—and sending a message that being expected to dress alike was a sign that they thought alike. Gerstner loosened the dress code considerably under his reign. See Louis V. Gerstner, *Who Says That Elephants Can't Dance?* (New York: HarperBusiness, 2002).

11. There are numerous surveys that essentially show the same results. See, for instance, "U. S. Job Satisfaction Keeps Falling, the Conference Reports Today," news release, Conference Board, February 28, 2005, http://www.conference-board.org; "62% of Global Executives

Dissatisfied with Current Positions," press release, Korn/Ferry International, September 30, 2003, http://www.kornferry.com/; "Building a Highly Engaged Workforce: How Great Managers Inspire Virtuoso Performance, a GMJ Q & A with Curt Coffman," *Gallup Management Journal*, June 3, 2002, http://gmj.gallup.com/content/default.asp?ci=238.

12. Anat Rafaeli and Robert I. Sutton, "The Expression of Emotion in Organizational Life," in *Research in Organizational Behavior*, vol. 11, eds. L. L. Cummings and Barry M. Staw (Greenwich, CT: JAI Press, 1989), 1–42; Robert I. Sutton, "Maintaining Norms About Expressed Emotions: The Case of Bill Collectors," *Administrative Science Quarterly* 36 (1991): 245–268.

13. See, for example, Rebecca Abraham, "The Impact of Emotional Dissonance on Organizational Commitment and Turnover," *The Journal of Psychology* 133 (1999): 441–455; Patricia A. Simpson and Linda K. Stroh, "Gender Differences: Emotional Expression and Feelings of Personal Inauthenticity," *Journal of Applied Psychology* 89 (2004): 715–722; Emily A. Butler et al., "The Social Consequences of Expressive Suppression," *Emotion* 3 (2003): 48–67.

14. Rafaeli and Sutton, "The Expression of Emotion."

15. Robert I. Sutton, *Weird Ideas That Work: 11 and ½ Practices for Promoting, Managing, and Sustaining Innovation* (New York: Free Press, 2002), 35.

16. Sheila Anne Feeney, "Love Hurts," *Workforce Magazine*, February 2004, 38.

17. Sheila Puffer, "CompUSA's James Halpin on Technology, Rewards, and Commitment," *Academy of Management Executive* 13 (1999): 29–37.

18. Oliver Williamson, *Markets and Hierarchies* (New York: Free Press, 1975).

19. Benedict Carey, "Fear in the Workplace: The Bullying Boss," *New York Times*, June 22, 2004.

20. John A. Byrne, *Chainsaw: The Notorious Career of Al Dunlap in the Era of Profit-at-Any-Price* (New York: HarperBusiness, 1999), 5.

21. Peter Elkind, "The Fall of the House of Grasso," *Fortune*, October 18, 2004, 294.

22. Carey, "Fear in the Workplace."

23. Leslie Kaufman, "Questions of Style in Warnaco's Fall," *New York Times*, May 6, 2001.

24. Robert Lacey, *Ford: The Men and the Machine* (New York: Little, Brown, 1986), 130.

25. Ibid., 131.

26. Ibid., 134.

27. Sanford M. Jacoby, *Modern Manors: Welfare Capitalism Since the New Deal* (Princeton, NJ: Princeton University Press, 1997).

28. Ibid., 353.

29. Tim Sanders, "Love Is the Killer App," (presentation at the DigitalNow conference, Orlando, FL, March 31, 2005).

30. Arnold Bakker and Sabine A. E. Geurts, "Toward a Dual-Process Model of Work-Home Interference," *Work and Occupations* 31 (August 2004): 345–346.

31. See, for instance, E. E. Kossek and C. Ozeki, "Work-Family Conflict, Policies, and the Job-Life Satisfaction Relationship: A Review and Directions for Organizational Behavior–Human Resources Research," *Journal of Applied Psychology* 83 (1998): 139–149.

32. Alison M. Conrad and Robert Mangel, "The Impact of Work-Life Programs on Firm Productivity," *Strategic Management Journal* 21 (2000): 1225–1237.

33. Peter Nolan and Stephen Wood, "Mapping the Future of Work," *British Journal of Industrial Relations* 41 (2003): 170.

34. Conrad and Mangel, "The Impact of Work-Life Programs."

35. Robert D. Putnam, *Bowling Alone: The Collapse and Revival of American Community* (New York: Simon and Schuster, 2000), 283.

36. Ros Davidson, "You Are Being Watched," *Sunday Herald Online*, March 27, 2005, http://www.sundayherald.com/48616.

37. Arlie Russell Hochschild, *The Time Bind* (New York: Basic Books, 1997), 19.

38. Sharon Shinn, "Luv, Colleen," *BizEd*, March/April 2003, 19.

39. Jody Hoffer Gittell, *The Southwest Airlines Way* (New York: McGraw-Hill, 2003), 119.

40. Ibid.

41. Feeney, "Love Hurts," 38.

42. Michael G. Pratt and Jose Antonio Rosa, "Transforming Work-Family Conflict into Commitment in Network Marking Organizations," *Academy of Management Journal* 46 (2003): 395–418.

43. Ibid., 405.

44. From Sarahsmiley.com. Quote from http://www.sarahsmiley.com/asksarah.htm#How _should_senior_wives_relate_to_JO_wives_ (accessed April 16, 2005).

45. Olga Kharif, "Anne Mulcahy Has Xerox by the Horns," *BusinessWeek Online*, May 29, 2003, http://www.businessweek.com/technology/content/may2003/tc20030529_1642_tc111 .htm.

46. Erving Goffman, *The Presentation of Self in Everyday Life* (New York: Anchor Books Doubleday, 1959); Arlie Russell Hochschild, *The Managed Heart: Commercialization of Human Feeling* (Berkeley: University of California Press, 1983).

47. See, for example, Abraham, "The Impact of Emotional Dissonance"; Simpson and Stroh, "Gender Differences."

48. Sutton, *Weird Ideas That Work*.

49. Su Fen Lee, Cliff Redeker, Julie Shin, and Yilin Yeo, "Pixar: An Incredible Story of Creativity" (case study prepared for class on "Organizational Behavior and Management," in Stanford School of Engineering, Department of Management Science & Engineering, Palo Alto, CA).

50. Bill George, *Authentic Leadership: Rediscovering the Secrets to Creating Lasting Value* (San Francisco: Jossey-Bass, 2003).

51. Carey, "Fear in the Workplace," D6.

52. Bernard Tepper, "Consequences of Abusive Supervision," *Academy of Management Journal* 43 (2000): 178–190.

53. Shirleen Holt, "Giving the Goodies: Many Employees See Advantages in Maintaining Workplace Perks," *Seattle Times*, March 23, 2003.

54. Anne Miner, "Idiosyncratic Jobs in Formalized Organizations," *Administrative Science Quarterly* 32 (1987): 327–352.

55. Kossek and Ozeki, "Work-Family Conflict."

Chapter 4

1. For more information about IDEO, see Thomas Kelley, *The Art of Innovation* (New York: Doubleday, 2001) and http://www.ideo.com/.

2. This research resulted in papers including R. I. Sutton and A. Hargadon, "Brainstorming Groups in Context: Effectiveness in a Product Design Firm," *Administrative Science Quarterly* 41 (1996): 685–718; A. Hargadon and R. I. Sutton, "Building an Innovation Factory," *Harvard Business Review* (May–June 2000): 157–166; A. Hargadon and R. I. Sutton, "Technology Brokering and Innovation in a Product Development Firm," *Administrative Science Quarterly* 42 (1997): 716–749.

3. Benjamin Schneider, "The People Make the Place," *Personnel Psychology* 40 (1987): 437–453.

4. Ibid., 440.

5. Jim Collins, *Good to Great* (New York: HarperCollins, 2001).

6. Edwin A. Locke et al., "The Importance of the Individual in the Age of Groupism," in *Groups at Work*, ed. Marlene E. Tuner (Mahwah, NJ: Earlbaum, 2001), 501–528.

7. Ed Michaels, Helen Handfield-Jones, and Beth Axelrod, *The War for Talent* (Boston: Harvard Business School Press, 2001).

8. For example, in their 1997 sample of 77 companies, the authors report that companies were *first* rated as high or average performers based on return to shareholders during the prior decade, and *then* interviews and surveys were done to measure how these firms were "fighting" the talent wars. A change cannot be caused by something that occurs *after* it happens; yet the authors treated the business practices as "causes" and prior performance as "effect." Even if we

assume (as the authors might have) that the 1997 survey and interview data from these companies measured how they had managed talent during the prior 10 years, it is plausible—indeed far more likely—that better financial performance *caused* companies to use the practices that they recommend. Michaels and his colleagues report, for example, that the high-performing companies were more likely than average-performing companies to "pay whatever it takes to prevent losing top performers." Couldn't it be that firms with superior financial performance would simply have more money to lavish on top performers? Perhaps the most questionable claim in the book is made in *The War for Talent*'s last chapter, which tells leaders who follow their advice to "expect a huge impact in a year." We can't find any quantitative evidence in the book (or any other research) that seems to support this claim; rather it seems to be guided by stories about the authors' heroes. Given the limits of case studies we reviewed in chapter 2, and given that so much of the advice in the book is unsupported or clashes with past research, this claim simply isn't warranted.

9. Dean Keith Simonton, *Greatness: Who Makes History and Why* (New York: Guilford Press, 1994), 419–420.

10. This research was published by H. Sackman, W. J. Erikson, and E. E. Grant in 1968. It is described in Frederick P. Brooks Jr.'s *The Mythical Man Month* (Reading, MA: Addison-Wesley, 1995).

11. Frank L. Schmidt and John E. Hunter, "The Validity and Utility of Selection Methods in Personnel Psychology: Practical and Theoretical Implications of 85 Years of Research Findings," *Psychological Bulletin* 124 (1998): 262–274.

12. Ibid.

13. A pair of best sellers by Daniel Goleman and his colleagues—Daniel Goleman, *Emotional Intelligence: Why It Can Matter More Than IQ* (New York: Bantam, 1995); and Daniel Goleman, Richard Boyatzis, and Annie McKee, *Primal Leadership: Realizing the Power of Emotional Intelligence* (Boston: Harvard Business School Press, 2002)—have fueled much recent excitement about the power of emotional intelligence (EI) for predicting employee success. These books draw on past research and original evidence to argue that organization members who are skilled at detecting and managing emotions will have more successful careers and lead more successful organizations than counterparts who are otherwise similar, but who have lower "EQs." We find such claims to be appealing and they do seem consistent with earlier work on practical intelligence. And research may ultimately prove EQ's value for predicting which organization members will succeed and thus who to bring aboard your organization. Unfortunately, however, a spate of recent academic writing and research suggests that there is unclear evidence—and conflicting opinions—about what emotional intelligence is, how to measure it, and if the 19 elements of emotionally intelligent leaders identified by Goleman and his colleagues are original. A balanced summary of the current controversy can be found in a 2005 special issue of the *Journal of Organizational Behavior* that was devoted to emotional intelligence. See Paul E. Spector, "Introduction: Emotional Intelligence," *Journal of Organizational Behavior* 26 (2005): 409–410.

The upshot is that, even though it seems sensible that people, especially leaders, who are skilled at detecting others' emotions and managing their own feelings will be more successful, the value of bringing in emotional intelligence experts to assess and train your people remains questionable at the moment and the validity of "emotional intelligence" as a coherent concept is debatable.

14. Martin E. P. Seligman and Peter Schulman, "Explanatory Style as a Predictor of Productivity and Quitting Among Life Insurance Sales Agents," *Journal of Personality and Social Psychology* 50 (1986): 832–838.

15. Hank Gilman et al., "The Smart Way to Hire Superstars," *Fortune*, July 10, 2000.

16. Bradford D. Smart, *Topgrading* (New York: Prentice-Hall, 1999), 34.

17. Michaels, Handfield-Jones, and Axelrod, *The War for Talent*.

18. For reviews, see: R. B. Cialdini, *Influence: The Psychology of Persuasion* (New York: Quill, 1993); K.Y. Williams and C. A. O'Reilly, "Demography and Diversity in Organizations: A Review of 40 Years of Research," in *Research in Organizational Behavior*, vol. 20, eds. B. M.

Staw and L. L. Cummings (Stamford, CT: JAI Press, 1998): 77–140; J. Pfeffer, "Organizational Demography," in *Research in Organizational Behavior*, vol. 5, ed. L. L. Cummings and B. M. Staw (Greenwich, CT: JAI Press, 1983): 299–357; J. Pfeffer, *New Directions for Organization Theory: Problems and Prospects* (New York: Oxford, 1997).

19. See, for example, R. M. Kanter, *Men and Women of the Corporation* (New York: Basic Books, 1977); R. W. Eder and G. R. Ferris, *The Employment Interview: Theory, Research, and Practice* (Newbury Park, CA: Sage Publications, 1989); Thung-rung Lin, Gregory H. Dobbins, and Jiing-lih Farh, "A Field Study of Race and Age Similarity Effects on Interview Ratings in Conventional and Situational Interviews, *Journal of Applied Psychology* 77 (1992): 363–371.

20. Greg J. Sears and Patricia M. Rowe, "A Personality-Based Similar to Me Effect in the Employment Interview: Conscientiousness, Affect- Versus Competence-Mediated Interpretations, and the Role of Job Relevance," *Canadian Journal of Behavioural Science* 35 (2003): 13–24.

21. Michael Schrage, "The Rules of Collaboration," *Forbes ASAP*, June 5, 1995, 88.

22. Ira Miller, "Dark Horses Become Workhorses," *San Francisco Chronicle*, October 22, 2001.

23. Harold F. Rothe, "Output Rates Among Industrial Employees," *Journal of Applied Psychology* 63 (1978): 40–46.

24. F. D. Schoorman, "Escalation Bias in Performance Appraisals: An Unintended Consequence of Supervisor Participation in Hiring Decisions," *Journal of Applied Psychology* 73 (1988): 58–62.

25. Robert L. Cardy and Gregory H. Dobbins, "Affect and Appraisal Accuracy: Liking as an Integral Dimension in Evaluating Performance," *Journal of Applied Psychology* 71 (1986): 672–678; Barry M. Staw and Ha Hoang, "Sunk Costs in the NBA: Why Draft Order Affects Playing Time and Survival in Professional Basketball," *Administrative Science Quarterly* 40 (1995): 474–494.

26. Edward Rothstein, "Myths About Genius," *New York Times*, January 5, 2002.

27. Lawrence M. Kahn, "Managerial Quality, Team Success, and Individual Player Performance in Major League Baseball," *Industrial and Labor Relations Review* 46 (1993): 531–547.

28. See K. A. Ericsson and A. C. Lehman, "Expert and Exceptional Performance: Evidence of Maximal Adaptation to Task Constraints," *Annual Review of Psychology* 47 (1996): 273–305; K. A. Ericsson, *The Road to Excellence* (New York: Earlbaum, 1996). In addition, Robert Sutton spent many hours talking with K. A. Ericsson during the 2002–2003 academic year, when both served as Fellows at the Center for Advanced Study in the Behavioral Sciences in Palo Alto, California.

29. D. K. Simonton, *Origins of Genius: Darwinian Perspectives on Creativity* (New York: Oxford, 1999).

30. Atul Gawande, *Complications* (New York: Henry Holt, 2002), 19.

31. Richard Hackman, *Leading Teams* (Boston: Harvard Business School Press, 2002).

32. This study by Ralph Katz showed that the productivity of research and development teams continues to improve through the first three or four years that they work together, but teams that have had little change in personnel and little contact with outsiders who have new ideas suffer a drop in creative output. So, at least for creative work, shaking up things by moving members in and out and exposing them to outsiders appears to be wise. But even in this case, there does need to be a balance between stability and shaking things up, as teams did continue to improve for at least the first three years they were together. See R. Katz, "The Effects of Group Longevity on Project Communication and Performance," *Administrative Science Quarterly* 27 (1982): 81–104; R. Katz and T. J. Allen, "Investigating the Not Invented Here Syndrome: A Look at Performance, Tenure, and Communication Patterns of 50 R&D Project Groups," *R&D Management* 12 (1982): 7–19.

33. For a summaries of this and related research, see Earl L. Wiener, Barbara G. Kanki, and Robert L. Helmreich, *Cockpit Resource Management* (San Diego, CA: Academic Press, 1993); Richard Hackman, *Leading Teams* (Boston: Harvard Business School Press, 2002).

34. Kathleen M. Eisenhardt and Claudia Bird Schoonhoven, "Organizational Growth: Linking Founding Team, Strategy, Environment, and Growth Among U.S. Semiconductor Ventures, 1978–1988," *Administrative Science Quarterly* 35 (1990): 504–529.

35. Carol. S. Dweck, "Beliefs that Make Smart People Dumb," in *Why Smart People Can Be So Stupid*, ed. Robert J. Sternberg (New Haven, CT: Yale University Press, 2002), 24–41.

36. Ibid., 31.

37. This and other quotations about the investigations from Harold W. Gehman Jr. et al., *Columbia Accident Investigation Board: Report Volume I* (Washington, DC: Government Printing Office, 2003), http://www.caib.us/.

38. See, for instance, John Paul MacDuffie, "Human Resource Bundles and Manufacturing Performance: Organizational Logic and Flexible Production Systems in the World Auto Industry," *Industrial and Labor Relations Review* 48 (1995): 197–221; Frits K. Pil and John Paul MacDuffie, "The Adoption of High-Involvement Work Practices," *Industrial Relations* 35 (1996): 423–455; John Paul MacDuffie, "The Road to 'Root Cause': Shop Floor Problem Solving at Three Auto Assembly Plants," *Management Science* 43 (1997): 479–502.

39. M. B. Lieberman, L. Lau, and M. Williams, "Firm Level Productivity and Management Influence: A Comparison of U.S. and Japanese Automobile Manufacturers," *Management Science* 36 (1990): 1193–1215.

40. For a summary of the NUMMI experience, see Charles O'Reilly III and Jeffrey Pfeffer, *Hidden Value* (Boston: Harvard Business School Press, 2000).

41. Boris Groysberg, Ashish Nanda, and Nitin Nohria, "The Risky Business of Hiring Stars," *Harvard Business Review* (May 2004): 94.

42. Nelson P. Repenning and John D. Sterman, "Capability Traps and Self-Confirming Attribution Errors in the Dynamics of Process Improvement," *Administrative Science Quarterly* 47 (2002): 265–295.

43. Ibid., 287.

44. Brian D. Brio, *Beyond Success* (New York: Perigee, 1997), 30; John Wooden, *Wooden* (Chicago: Contemporary Books, 1997).

45. Richard J. Hernstein and Charles Murray, *The Bell Curve* (New York: Free Press, 1999).

46. Joshua Aronson, Carrie B. Fried, and Catherine Good, "Reducing the Effects of Stereotype Threat on African American College Students by Shaping Theories of Intelligence," *Journal of Experimental Social Psychology* 22 (2001): 1–13.

47. Staw and Ha, "Sunk Costs in the NBA."

48. Ibid., 487.

49. Lee D. Ross, "The Intuitive Psychologist and His Shortcomings," in *Advances in Experimental Social Psychology*, vol. 10, ed. L. Berkowitz (New York: Random House, 1977), 173–220.

50. See John A. Meacham, "The Loss of Wisdom," in *Wisdom: Its Nature, Origins, and Development*, ed. Robert J. Sternberg (Cambridge, England: Cambridge University Press, 1990), 181–211; and John A. Meacham, "Wisdom and the Context of Knowledge: Knowing What One Doesn't Know One Doesn't Know," in *On the Development of Developmental Psychology*, eds. D. Huhn and J. A. Meacham (Basel, Switzerland: Krager, 1983), 111–134; Robert J. Sternberg, "Implicit Theories of Intelligence, Creativity and Wisdom," *Journal of Personality and Social Psychology* 49 (1985): 607–627.

51. These data and insights are drawn primarily from two articles, Amy C. Edmondson, "Learning from Mistakes Is Easier Said Than Done: Group and Organizational Influences on the Detection and Correction of Human Error," *Journal of Applied Behavioral Science* 32 (1996): 5–28; and Anita L. Tucker and Amy C. Edmondson, "Why Hospitals Don't Learn from Failures: Organizational and Psychological Dynamics that Inhibit System Change," *California Management Review* 45 (2003): 55–72.

52. Gehman et al., Columbia Accident Investigation Board, 203.

53. Novations Group, "Uncovering the Growing Disenchantment with Forced Ranking Performance Management Systems," white paper (Boston, MA: Novations Group, August 2004).

Chapter 5

1. This statement comes from page 2 of the Cendant Corporation 2004 Proxy Statement, March 1, 2004. Similar statements can be found in many other proxy statements. Cendant and its chief executive, Henry Silverman, have been roundly criticized for excessive CEO compensation and for compensation that was not very closely tied to company performance (see, for instance, Gretchen Morgenson, "Two Pay Packages, Two Different Galaxies," *New York Times*, April 4, 2004. Nonetheless, incentive alignment is apparently an important goal and is taken as an article of faith that it is important in most proxy statements.

2. Jay R. Schuster and Patricia K. Zingheim, *The New Pay* (San Francisco: Jossey-Bass, 1992), ix.

3. Frederick W. Taylor, *Shop Management* (New York: Harper, 1903).

4. Edward P. Lazear, "Performance Pay and Productivity," *American Economic Review* 90 (2000): 1346.

5. See, for instance, B. F. Skinner, *Science and Human Behavior* (New York: Macmillan, 1953). Operant conditioning principles have been applied in management and organizational behavior by, among others, Walter Nord, "Beyond the Teaching Machine: The Neglected Area of Operant Conditioning in the Theory and Practice of Management," *Organizational Behavior and Human Performance* 4 (1969): 375–401; and Fred Luthans and Robert Kreitner, *Organizational Behavior Modification* (Glenview, IL: Scott, Foresman, 1975).

6. This expectancy theory of motivation is quite prominent in social psychology. An early formulation can be found in Victor H. Vroom, *Work and Motivation* (New York: John Wiley, 1964). Also, modern psychological research on decision making and negotiation reflect many of these assumptions about the power of financial rewards, but does show that cognitive biases "trip up" people in their quest to maximize valued outcomes, especially when it comes to maximizing financial gain. See Max H. Bazerman, *Judgment in Managerial Decision Making*, 6th ed. (Somerset, NJ: Wiley, 2006).

7. See, for instance, Andrea Gabor, *The Man Who Discovered Quality* (New York: Times Books, 1990).

8. Scott McCartney, "How to Make an Airline Run on Schedule," *Wall Street Journal*, December 22, 1995.

9. Edward P. Lazear, "The Power of Incentives," *The American Economic Review* 90 (2000): 410.

10. Robert L. Heneman, "Merit Pay Research," in *Research in Personnel and Human Resource Management*, vol. 8 (Greenwich, CT: JAI Press, 1990): 203–263.

11. One study by Hewitt Associates, reported that as of the late 1990s some 72 percent of all companies had variable pay for at least some groups of employees compared to 47 percent in 1990. See Rebecca Ganzel, "What's Wrong with Pay for Performance?" *Training*, December 1998, 34–40.

12. Ellen G. Frank, "Trends in Incentive Compensation" (information prepared for the authors from Hewitt Compensation Surveys, June 2004).

13. "Christmas Bonuses Give Way to Incentive Pay," *Edmonton Journal*, November 28, 2003.

14. "Garbage Truck Drivers Rushing to Finish Work Are Safety Risk," Associated Press, January 30, 2004.

15. Diana Jean Schemo, "When Students' Gains Help Teachers' Bottom Line," *New York Times*, May 9, 2004.

16. "Results-Oriented Cultures: Creating a Clear Linkage Between Individual Performance and Organizational Success," GAO-03-488 (Washington, DC: General Accounting Office, March 2003).

17. Christopher Lee, "Civil Service System on Way Out at DHS," *Washington Post*, January 27, 2005, http://www.washingtonpost.com/wp-dyn/articles/A39934-2005Jan26.html (accessed May 1, 2005).

18. Chip Heath, "On the Social Psychology of Agency Relationships: Lay Theories of Motivation Overemphasize Extrinsic Incentives," *Organizational Behavior and Human Decision Processes* 78 (1999): 25–62.

19. Ibid., 28.

20. Ibid., 38.

21. Watson Wyatt Worldwide company report, "Strategic Rewards: Maximizing the Return on Your Reward Investment," 2004, 11.

22. Michael Beer and Nancy Katz, "Do Incentives Work? The Perceptions of a Worldwide Sample of Senior Executives," *Human Resource Planning* 26 (2003): 30–44.

23. Ibid.

24. "At Emery Air Freight: Positive Reinforcement Boosts Performance," *Organizational Dynamics* 1 (1973): 42.

25. Ibid., 47.

26. Robert Rodin, *Free, Perfect, and Now* (New York: Simon and Schuster, 1999), 45.

27. Lazear, "Performance Pay and Productivity."

28. Ibid., 1353.

29. Ibid., 1354.

30. Ibid., 1352.

31. Ibid., 1358.

32. Ibid.

33. "Garbage Truck Drivers."

34. Ibid.

35. Transcript from National Public Radio, *All Things Considered*, October 30, 2003, 9:00–10:00 p.m. edition, p. 2.

36. Ibid.

37. Chip Cummins, Susan Warren, Alexei Barrionuevo, and Bhushan Bahree, "Losing Reserve: At Shell, Strategy and Structure Fueled Troubles," *Wall Street Journal*, March 12, 2004.

38. The image of the New York firefighters going up into the World Trade Center following the initial onset of the disaster of September 11, 2001, is probably overused. But it does raise the interesting issue of whether people could be induced to risk their lives for money, or if it is only a sense of duty, service, and professional calling that could produce acts of such heroism.

39. Lazear, "Performance Pay and Productivity," 1357.

40. Donald L. McCabe and Linda Klebe Trevino, "Cheating Among Business Students: A Challenge for Business Leaders and Educators," *Journal of Management Education* 19 (1995): 205–218; Donald L. McCabe and Linda Klebe Trevino, "What We Know About Cheating in College," *Change* 28 (1996): 29–33.

41. J. D. Brown, "Evaluations of Self and Others: Self-Enhancement Biases in Social Judgments," *Social Cognition* 4 (1986): 353–376; J. Kruger and D. Dunning, "Unskilled and Unaware of It: How Difficulties in Recognizing One's Own Incompetence Lead to Inflated Self-Assessments," *Journal of Personality and Social Psychology* 77 (1999): 1121–1134; D. T. Miller and M. Ross, "Self-Serving Biases in the Attribution of Causality: Fact or Faction?" *Psychological Bulletin* 82 (1975): 213–225.

42. "Many Companies Fail to Achieve Success with Pay-for-Performance Programs," *Hewitt Associates News & Information*, June 9, 2004.

43. Watson Wyatt, "Strategic Rewards," 12.

44. Gerald S. Leventhal, "The Distribution of Rewards and Resources in Groups and Organizations," in Leonard Berkowitz and Elaine Walster (eds.), *Advances in Experimental Social Psychology*, vol. 9, (New York: Academic Press, 1976), 92–259, provides a good summary of this research. See also G. S. Leventhal, J. W. Michaels, and C. Sanford, "Inequity and Interpersonal Conflict: Reward Allocation and Secrecy About Reward as Methods of Preventing Conflict," *Journal of Personality and Social Psychology* 23 (1972): 88–102.

45. *Hewitt Associates News & Information*, "Many Companies Fail to Achieve Success".

46. Sue Fernie and David Metcalf, "It's Not What You Pay, It's the Way You Pay It and That's What Gets Results: Jockey's Pay and Performance," discussion paper 295, London School of Economics, London, 1996; Harry J. Paarsch and Bruce S. Shearer, "The Response of Worker Effort to Piece Rates: Evidence from the British Columbia Tree-Planting Industry," *Journal of Human Resources* 35 (1999): 1–25; M. Ryan Haley, "The Response of Worker Effort to Piece Rates: Evidence from the Midwest Logging Industry," *Journal of Human Resources* 38 (2003): 881–890.

47. Gary Bornstein and Ido Erev, "The Enhancing Effect of Intergroup Competition on Group Performance," in *Using Conflict in Organizations*, eds. Carsten De Dreu and Evert Van De Vliert (London: Sage, 2003), 147–160.

48. R. G. Ehrenberg and M. L. Bognanno, "The Incentive Effects of Tournaments Revisited: Evidence from the European PGA Tour," *Industrial and Labor Relations Review* 43 (1990): 74S–88S; B. E. Becker and M. A. Huselid, "The Incentive Effects of Tournament Compensation Systems," *Administrative Science Quarterly* 37 (1992): 336–350.

49. Jeffrey Pfeffer and Nancy Langton, "The Effect of Wage Dispersion on Satisfaction, Productivity, and Working Collaboratively: Evidence from College and University Faculty," *Administrative Science Quarterly* 38 (1993): 382–407.

50. Phyllis A. Siegel and Donald C. Hambrick, "Pay Disparities Within Top Management Groups: Evidence of Harmful Effects on Performance of High-Technology Firms," *Organization Science* 16 (2005): 259–274.

51. D. M. Cowherd and D. I. Levine, "Product Quality and Pay Equity Between Lower-Level Employees and Top Management: An Investigation of Distributive Justice Theory," *Administrative Science Quarterly* 37 (1992): 302–320.

52. Matt Bloom, "The Performance Effects of Pay Dispersion on Individuals and Organizations," *Academy of Management Journal* 42 (1999): 25–40.

53. Jeffrey Pfeffer, "SAS Institute (A): A Different Approach to Incentives and People Management in the Software Industry," Case #HR6A (Stanford, CA, 1998), 8.

Chapter 6

1. The National Association of Corporate Directors, *Report of the NACD Blue Ribbon Commission on the Role of the Board in Corporate Strategy* (Washington, DC: NACD, 2004), 1.

2. Ibid.

3. See, for instance, Gordon E. Greenley, "Does Strategic Planning Improve Company Performance?" *Long Range Planning* 19 (1986): 101–109; S. Al-Bazzaz and P. M. Grinyer, "How Planning Works in Practice—A Survey of 48 U.K. Companies," *Long Range Planning* 13 (1980): 30–41.

4. See, for instance, Henry Mintzberg, *Rise and Fall of Strategic Planning* (New York: Free Press, 1993).

5. Whether or not this is a good or bad thing is debatable. See, for instance, Henry Mintzberg, *Managers Not MBAs* (San Francisco: Berrett-Koehler, 2004).

6. Neng Liang and Jiaquian Wang, "Implicit Mental Models in Teaching Cases: An Empirical Study of Popular MBA Cases in the United States and China," *Academy of Management Learning and Education* 3 (2004): 403, 405.

7. Torben Juul Andersen, "Integrating Decentralized Strategy Making and Strategic Planning Processes in Dynamic Environments," *Journal of Management Studies* 41 (2004): 1273.

8. Alfred P. Sloan, *My Years at General Motors* (New York: Currency, 1990).

9. See, for instance, Robert Burgelman, *Strategy Is Destiny: How Strategy-Making Shapes a Company's Future* (New York: Free Press, 2002); and Robert Sutton, *Weird Ideas That Work: 11 and ½ Practices for Promoting, Managing, and Sustaining Innovation* (New York: Free Press, 2002).

10. Greenley, "Does Strategic Planning Improve Company Performance?" 104–105.

11. C. Chet Miller and Laura B. Cardinal, "Strategic Planning and Firm Performance: A

Synthesis of More Than Two Decades of Research," *Academy of Management Journal* 37 (1994): 1650; J. A. Pearce, E. B. Freeman, and R. B. Robinson, "The Tenuous Link Between Formal Strategic Planning and Financial Performance," *Academy of Management Review* 12 (1987): 658–675.

12. Antonio-Rafael Ramos-Rodriguez and Jose Ruiz-Navarro, "Changes in the Intellectual Structure of Strategic Management Research: A Bibliometric Study of the *Strategic Management Journal*, 1980–2000," *Strategic Management Journal* 25 (2004): 981–1004.

13. Michael E. Porter, *Competitive Strategy: Techniques of Analyzing Competitors and Industries* (New York: Free Press, 1998).

14. See, for instance, Richard E. Caves, "Corporate Strategy and Structure," *Journal of Economic Literature* 28 (1980), 64–92; Porter, *Competitive Strategy*; Michael E. Porter, "The Structure Within Industries and Companies' Performance," *Review of Economics and Statistics* 61 (1979): 214–227.

15. Thomas H. Brush, Philip Bromiley, and Margaretha Hendrickx, "The Relative Influence of Industry and Corporation on Business Segment Performance: An Alternative Estimate," *Strategic Management Journal* 20 (1999): 519–547.

16. Jon Birger, "The 30 Best Stocks from 1972 to 2002," *Money*, Fall 2002, 88–95.

17. Charles E. Lucier and Amy Astin, "Toward a New Theory of Growth," *Strategy and Business* 1 (Winter 1996): 11.

18. Dwight L. Gertz and Joao P. A. Baptista, *Grow to Be Great* (New York: Free Press, 1995).

19. Robert A. Burgelman, "Intel Corporation in 1999," Case SM-70 (Palo Alto, CA: Stanford Graduate School of Business, revised October 12, 2004), 1.

20. Ibid.

21. Robert A. Burgelman and Andrew S. Grove, "Strategic Dissonance," *California Management Review* 38 (Winter 1996): 8–28.

22. Ibid., 11–12.

23. Robert A. Burgelman, "A Process Model of Strategic Business Exit: Implications for an Evolutionary Perspective on Strategy," *Strategic Management Journal* 17 (1996): 193–214; Burgelman and Grove, "Strategic Dissonance," 24.

24. Robert A. Burgelman, "Strategy as Vector and the Inertia of Coevolutionary Lock-in," *Administrative Science Quarterly* 47 (2002): 331.

25. For a discussion of these ideas, see, for instance, Nile W. Hatch and Jeffrey H. Dyer, "Human Capital and Learning as a Source of Sustainable Competitive Advantage," *Strategic Management Journal* 25 (2004): 1155–1178.

26. G. Bruce Knecht, "Banking Maverick: Norwest Corp. Relies on Branches, Pushes Service—and Prospers," *Wall Street Journal*, August 17, 1995.

27. Betsy Morris, "The Accidental CEO," *Fortune*, June 23, 2003, 42–47.

28. For a description of Dell's manufacturing prowess and process, see, for instance, Gary Rivlin, "Who's Afraid of China? How Dell Became the World's Most Efficient Computer Maker," *New York Times*, December 19, 2004.

29. Thomas R. Stewart and Louise O'Brien, "Execution Without Excuses: An Interview with Michael Dell and Kevin Rollins," *Harvard Business Review* (March 2005): 103–111.

30. Keynote speech by Steve Mariucci at Ernst & Young's "Northern California Entrepreneur of the Year" awards dinner, San Francisco, February, 2000.

31. Lawrence C. Rhyne's study of the relationship of planning to financial performance, for instance, explicitly notes the "control" function of planning and includes budgeting as part of his definition and measurement of strategic planning. See Lawrence C. Rhyne, "The Relationship of Strategic Planning to Financial Performance," *Strategic Management Journal* 7 (1986): 423–436.

32. Jeremy Hope and Robin Fraser, *Beyond Budgeting: How Managers Can Break Free from the Annual Performance Trap* (Boston: Harvard Business School Press, 2003), 5.

33. Ibid., 6.

34. Rivlin, "Who's Afraid of China?"

35. Clayton M. Christensen, *The Innovator's Dilemma* (Boston: Harvard Business School Press, 1998).

36. For cases about Kodak, see Giovanni Gavetti, Rebecca Henderson, and Simona Giorgi, "Kodak (A)," Case 9-703-503 (Boston: Harvard Business School, 2004); Giovanni Gavetti, Rebecca Henderson, and Simona Giorgi, "Kodak (B)," Case 9-704-489 (Boston: Harvard Business School, 2004).

37. Michael L. Tushman and Charles O'Reilly III, *Winning Through Innovation* (Boston: Harvard Business School Press, 1997).

38. Henry Mintzberg, "The Design School: Reconsidering the Basic Premises of Strategic Management," *Strategic Management Journal* 11 (1990): 184; Henry Mintzberg, "The Strategy Concept II: Another Look at Why Organizations Need Strategies," *California Management Review* 30 (1987): 26.

39. Steve Jobs, speech at DeAnza College's Flint Center, Cupertino, CA, May 6, 1998. This example is adopted from *Weird Ideas That Work*.

40. *Norwest: Sharing the Vision, Living the Values*, employee pamphlet, version 4/98, 8–9.

41. Darrin Earl, "Kelleher Visits McComb," *Texas Business Weekly*, February 5, 2003.

42. Kevin Maney, "10 Years Ago, eBay Changed the World, Sort of by Accident," *USA Today*, March 22, 2005.

43. Andrew Grove, interview by Clayton Christensen, presented at Harvard Business School Press Conference, Cupertino, CA, October 3, 2002.

44. Joyce Doria, Horacio Rozanski, and Ed Cohen, "What Business Needs from Business Schools," *Strategy + Business* (Fall 2003), 39–45.

45. Mintzberg, *Managers Not MBAs*; L. W. Porter and L. E. McKibbin, *Management Education and Development: Drift or Thrust into the 21st Century* (New York: McGraw-Hill, 1988); Jeffrey Pfeffer and Christina T. Fong, "The End of Business Schools? Less Success Than Meets the Eye," *Academy of Management Learning and Education* 1 (2002): 78–95.

46. Grove, Harvard Business School Press Conference.

Chapter 7

1. Michael Tushman and Charles A. O'Reilly III, *Winning Through Innovation: A Practical Guide to Leading Organizational Change and Renewal* (Boston: Harvard Business School Press, 1997); Robert J. Kriegel and Louis Patten, *If It Ain't Broke . . . Break It! And Other Unconventional Wisdom for a Changing Business World* (New York: Warner Books, 1991); Jeanie Daniel Duck, *The Change Monster: The Human Forces That Fuel or Foil Corporate Transformation and Change* (New York: Crown, 2001); Spencer Johnson, *Who Moved My Cheese?* (New York: Putnam, 1998).

2. From an advertisement for a speech by Michael Peter, founder of Identica Partnership, "Innotown" Conference, Norway, 2003.

3. From http://www.oracle.com/customers/index.html.

4. Barbara Palmer, "Oracle Financials Launch: 'Cut Colleagues a Little Slack,'" *Stanford Report*, August 20, 2003; Barbara Palmer, "Oracle Update: Better, but More Work Still Needs to be Done," *Stanford Report*, May 19, 2004; Dan Carnevale, "Cleveland State U. Sues PeopleSoft," *Chronicle of Higher Education*, April 9, 2004.

5. Amy Zuckerman, "ERP: Pathway to the Future or Yesterday's Buzz?" *Transportation & Distribution* 40, no. 8 (1999): 37–44.

6. Stratford Sherman and Rajiv M. Rao, "Secrets of HP's 'Muddled Team,'" *Fortune*, March 18, 1996, 116–120.

7. Clayton M. Christensen, Scott D. Anthony, and Erik A. Roth, *Seeing What's Next: Using the Theories of Innovation to Predict Industry Change* (Boston: Harvard Business School Press, 2004); Eric Abrahamson, *Change Without Pain: How Managers Can Overcome Initiative Overload, Organizational Chaos, and Burnout* (Boston: Harvard Business School Press, 2004).

8. See Gurumurthy Kalyanaram, William T. Robinson, and Glenn L. Urban, "Order of Market Entry: Established Generalizations, Emerging Generalizations, and Future Research,"

Marketing Science 11 (1995): G2212–G221. These authors conclude that, because existing studies present such inconsistent findings, there is no clear relationship between the order of market entry and firm performance or survival. More recent research continues to present a murky picture, as do popular writings that mistake early entrants for first entrants. For example, Amazon.com, the leader in online books sales, is often portrayed as the first online bookstore when, in fact, at least three other firms moved into this niche before Amazon.

9. Stephen Kerr, personal communication with author, March 29, 2005. Kerr was involved in implementing an early version of Work-Out in a business at GE and ultimately became the firm's chief learning officer.

10. Jeffrey Pfeffer and Robert I. Sutton, *The Knowing-Doing Gap: How Smart Companies Turn Knowledge into Action* (Boston: Harvard Business School Press, 2000).

11. James D. Westphal and Edward J. Zajac, "Substance and Symbolism in CEO's Long-Term Incentive Plans," *Administrative Science Quarterly* 39 (1994): 367–391.

12. Barry M. Staw and Lisa D. Epstein, "What Bandwagons Bring: Effects of Popular Management Techniques on Corporate Performance, Reputation, and CEO Pay," *Admiminstrative Science Quarterly* 45 (2000): 523–556.

13. Howell Raines, "My Times," *Atlantic Monthly*, May 2004.

14. Jeffrey Pfeffer, *Managing with Power: Politics and Influence in Organizations* (Boston: Harvard Business School Press, 1992).

15. Robert I. Sutton and Elizabeth Gerber, "The Birth of a Broker" (presented at the National Academy of Management Meetings, Honolulu, Hawaii, August 2005).

16. Sheena S. Iyengar and Wei Jiang, "The Psychological Costs of Ever Increasing Choice: A Fallback to the Sure Bet" (unpublished manuscript, Columbia University, 2005).

17. William P. Barnett and John Freeman, "Too Much of a Good Thing? Product Proliferation and Failure," *Organization Science* 12 (2001): 539–558.

18. Pfeffer and Sutton, *The Knowing-Doing Gap.*

19. Barry M. Staw and Jerry Ross, "Behavior in Escalation Situations: Antecedents, Prototypes and Solutions," in *Research in Organizational Behavior 9*, eds. L. L. Cummings and Barry M. Staw (Greenwich CT: JAI Press, 1987): 39–78.

20. Gordon Bethune, *From Worst to First: Behind the Scenes of Continental's Remarkable Comeback* (New York: Wiley, 1998).

21. George W. Bohlander and Marshall H. Campbell, "Problem-Solving, Bargaining, and Work Redesign: Magma Copper's Labor-Management Partnership," *National Productivity Review* 12 (1993), 531. See also William H. Miller, "Metamorphosis in the Desert," *Industry Week*, March 16, 1992, 30.

22. See James G. March, "Footnotes to Organizational Change," *Administrative Science Quarterly* 26 (1981): 563–577; Karl Weick, "Emergent Change as a Universal in Organizations," in *Breaking the Code of Change*, eds. Michael Beer and Nitin Nohria (Boston: Harvard Business School Press, 2000), 223–241.

23. Barry M. Staw, Lance E. Sandelands, and Jane E. Dutton, "Threat-Rigidity Effects in Organizational Behavior: A Multilevel Analysis," *Administrative Science Quarterly* 26 (1981): 501–524; Robert I. Sutton and Thomas D'Aunno, "Decreasing Organizational Size: Untangling the Effects of People and Money," *Academy of Management Review* 14 (1989): 194–212.

24. Jim Collins and Jerry I. Porras, *Built to Last: Successful Habits of Visionary Companies* (New York: HarperCollins, 1994).

25. This information comes from Robert Sutton, who served as a Reactivity Fellow between 2000 and 2001 and visited the company perhaps 20 times during this period, from two interviews conducted with John Lilly in 1999 and 2000, from conversations with Tom Byers, and from several detailed e-mail exchanges between John Lilly and Robert Sutton to check facts and elaborate details in early 2005.

26. R. B. Cialdini et al., "Basking in Reflected Glory: Three (Football) Field Studies," *Journal of Personality and Social Psychology* 34 (1976): 366–375.

27. Behavioral scientists have done extensive research of such "interpersonal expectancy"

effects. The classic article is Robert K. Merton, "The Self-Fulfilling Prophecy," *Antioch Review* 8 (1948): 193–210. The widespread evidence for such effects is summarized in R. Rosenthal and D. B. Rubin, "Interpersonal Expectancy Effects: The First 345 Studies," *Behavioral and Brain Sciences* 3 (1978): 377–386. Since that review, hundreds of other studies on nuances of the self-fulfilling prophecy have been published.

28. M. Talbot, "The Placebo Prescription," *New York Times Magazine*, January 9, 2000.

29. James G. March, "Footnotes to Organizational Change," *Administrative Science Quarterly* 26 (1981): 563–577.

Table 7-1

a. Tim Loughran and Anand M. Vijh, "Do Long-Term Shareholders Benefit from Corporate Acquisitions?" *Journal of Finance* 52 (1997): 1765–1790; Sara B. Moeller, Frederik P. Schlingemann, and Rene M. Stultz, "Wealth Destruction on Massive Scale? A Study of Acquiring Firm Returns in the Recent Merger Wave," *Journal of Finance* (forthcoming); David R. King et al., "Meta-Analyses of Post-Acquisition Performance: Indicators of Unidentified Moderators," *Strategic Management Journal* 25 (2004): 187–200; John Enberg et al., "The Effects of Mergers on Firms' Costs: Evidence from the HMO Industry," *Quarterly Review of Economics and Finance* 44 (2004): 574–600.

b. Amy Zuckerman, "ERP: Pathway to the Future or Yesterday's Buzz?" *Transportation & Distribution* 40 (1999): 37–44; M. Williamson, "From SAP to 'Nuts!'" *Computerworld* 31 (1997): 68–69; E. L. Appleton, "How to Survive ERP," *Datamation* 43 (1997): 50–53; J. King, "Dell Zaps SAP," *Computerworld* 31 (1997): 2. For a summary of major studies in IT project failure rate, see http://www.it-cortex.com/Stat_Failure_Rate.htm.

c. James N. Baron and Michael T. Hannan, "Organizational Blueprints for Success in High-Tech Start-Ups: Lessons from the Stanford Project on Emerging Companies," *California Management Review* 44 (2002): 8–36.

d. Mary J. Benner and Michael L. Tushman, "Exploitation, Exploration, and Process Management: The Productivity Dilemma Revisited," *Academy of Management Review* 28 (2003): 238–256; Mary J. Benner and Michael L. Tushman, "Process Management and Technological Innovation: A Longitudinal Study of the Photography and Paint Industries," *Administrative Science Quarterly* 47 (2002): 676–706; Mark J. Zbaracki, "The Rhetoric and Reality of Total Quality Management," *Administration Science Quarterly* 43 (1998): 602–636; James D. Westphal, Ranjay Gulati, and Stephen M. Shortell, "Customization or Conformity? An Institutional and Network Perspective on the Content and Consequences of TQM Adoption," *Administrative Science Quarterly* 42 (1997): 366–394.

e. Tom Davenport, "The Fad That Forgot People," *Fast Company*, November 1995, 70–75. Also Michael Finley, "It's Hammer Time! Michael Hammer Reengineers Reengineering," 2001, http://www.mfinley.com/experts/hammer/hammer.htm.

f. Wayne F. Casio, *Responsible Restructuring* (San Francisco: Berrett-Koehler, 2002); Darrell Rigby, "Debunking Layoff Myths" (Boston: Bain & Company, 2002), available at http://www.bain.com/bainweb/PDFs/cms/Marketing/6759.pdf; D. M. Gordon, *Fat and Mean: The Corporate Squeeze of Working Americans and the Myth of Managerial Downsizing* (New York: Free Press, 1996); Jeffrey D. Ford, "The Administrative Component in Growing and Declining Organizations: A Longitudinal Analysis," *Academy of Management Journal* 23 (1980): 615–630.

g. Joseph A. DiMasi et al., "The Cost of Innovation in the Pharmaceutical Industry," *Journal of Health Economics* 10 (1991): 107–142; Fahri Karakaya and Bulent Kobu, "New Product Development Success: An Investigation of Success and Failure in High-Technology and Non-High-Technology Firms," *Journal of Business Venturing* 9 (1994): 49–68; Melissa A. Schilling and Charles W. L. Hill, "Managing the New Product Development Process: Strategic Imperatives," *Academy of Management Executive* 12 (1998): 67–81.

h. Dun & Bradstreet, *Industry Norms and Key Business Ratios* (Philadelphia, PA: Dun & Bradstreet, 1994); John Freeman, Glenn R. Carroll, and Michael T. Hannan, "The Liability of

Newness: Age Dependence in Organizational Death Rates," *American Sociological Review* 48 (1983): 692–710; Josef Bruderl and Rudolf Schussler, "Organizational Mortality: The Liabilities of Newness and Adolescence," *Administrative Science Quarterly* 35 (1990): 530–547.

Chapter 8

1. Bernard Bass, *Bass & Stogdill's Handbook of Leadership* (New York: Free Press, 1990).

2. George Goethals, Georgia J. Sorenson, and James MacGregor Burns, *Encyclopedia of Leadership* (Thousand Oaks, CA: Sage, 2004).

3. Both these searches were conducted on November 8, 2004. The exact number of peer-reviewed "leadership" articles found on Business Source Premier was 14,121 and, when the "peer reviewed" restriction was removed, the number rose to 48,461. The exact number of leadership entries produced by the Amazon.com search was 116,527. No doubt there were duplicate entries produced by this second search, but it is still a huge number of books.

4. Matthew Boyle, "The Man Who Fixed Kellogg," *Fortune*, September 6, 2001, 218.

5. Betsy Morris, "The Accidental CEO," *Fortune*, June 23, 2003, 42–47; Olga Kharif, "Anne Mulcahy Has Xerox by the Horns," *BusinessWeek Online*, May 29, 2003, http://www.businessweek.com/technology/content/may2003/.

6. Tessa R. Salazar, "World's Biggest Automaker Revs Up Asia Pacific," *Philippine Daily Inquirer*, January 19, 2005.

7. "The Best and Worse Bosses: Executive Pay," *Forbes*, May 10, 2004, 214. Or see http://forbes.com/executivepay/forbes/2004/0510/124.html.

8. Rakesh Khurana, *Searching for a Corporate Savior* (Princeton, NJ: Princeton University Press, 2002).

9. Ibid., 110.

10. Stanley Milgram, *Obedience to Authority* (New York: Harper, 1983).

11. Robert Hogan, Gordon J. Curphy, and Joyce Hogan, "What We Know About Leadership: Effectiveness and Personality," *American Psychologist* 49 (1994): 493–50.

12. Ibid., 494.

13. Jeffrey Pfeffer and Alison Davis Blake, "Administrative Succession and Organizational Performance: How Administrative Experience Mediates the Succession Effect," *Academy of Management Journal* 29 (1986): 72–83; Jonathon E. Smith, Kenneth P. Carson, and Ralph A. Alexander, "Leadership: It Can Make a Difference," *Academy of Management Journal* 27 (1984): 765–776.

14. Lawrence M. Kahn, "Managerial Quality, Team Success, and Individual Player Performance in Major League Baseball," *Industrial and Labor Relations Review* 46 (1993): 531–547.

15. M. B. Lieberman, L. L. Lau, and M. D. Williams, "Firm-level Productivity and Management Influence: A Comparison of U.S. and Japanese Automobile Producers," *Management Science* 36 (1990): 1193–1215.

16. See, for example, David A. Waldman and Francis J. Yammarino, "CEO Charismatic Leadership: Levels-of-Management and Levels-of-Analysis Effect," *Academy of Management Review* 24 (1999): 266–288; R. J. House, W. D. Spangler, and J. Woycke, "Personality and Charisma in the U. S. Presidency: A Psychological Theory of Leadership Effectiveness," *Administrative Science Quarterly* 36 (1991): 364–396.

17. Mathew L. A. Hayward and Donald C. Hambrick, "Explaining the Premiums Paid for Large Acquisitions: Evidence of CEO Hubris," *Administrative Science Quarterly* 42 (1997): 103–127.

18. T. R. Chidester et al., "Pilot Personality and Crew Coordination," *International Journal of Aviation Psychology* 1 (1991): 25–44; G. J. Curphy, "An Empirical Investigation of the Effects of Transformational and Transactional Leadership on Organizational Climate, Attrition, and Performance," in *Impact of Leadership*, eds. K. E. Clark, M. B. Clark, and D. P. Campbell (Greensboro, NC: Center for Creative Leadership, 1993), 177–188.

19. Hogan, Curphy, and Hogan, "What We Know About Leadership," 494.

20. http://www.nj.com/weblogs/eagles/.

21. S. Lieberson and J. F. O'Connor, "Leadership and Organizational Performance: A Study of Large Organizations," *American Sociological Review* 37 (1972): 117–130.

22. Some researchers seem to conclude that leadership has no impact on performance, dismissing the hundreds of careful studies that show leadership can affect group and organizational performance under certain conditions. For example, researchers Glenn Carroll and Michael Hannan seem to dismiss the importance of leadership because a substantial number of studies (mostly conducted by them and their students) show that changing CEOs has no statistically significant effects on organizational death rates. See Glenn Carroll and Michael T. Hannan, *The Demography of Corporations and Industries* (Princeton, NJ: Princeton University Press, 2000). We agree leadership effects are overstated, but too many other rigorous field studies and experiments have documented conditions under which leadership skill and actions do have significant effects. For numerous examples, see George Goethals, Georgia J. Sorenson, and James MacGregor Burns, *Encyclopedia of Leadership* (Thousand Oaks, CA: Sage, 2004).

23. J. Pfeffer, "The Ambiguity of Leadership," *Academy of Management Review* 2 (1977): 104–112.

24. Conrad de Aenlle, "See You, Carly, Goodbye, Harry. Hello, Investors," *New York Times*, March 13, 2005.

25. James G. March, "How We Talk and How We Act: Administrative Theory and Administrative Life," in *Leadership and Organizational Cultures*, eds. Thomas J. Sergiovanni and John E. Corbally (Urbana, IL: University of Illinois, 1984), 18–35.

26. Ibid., 27.

27. James R. Meindl, Sanford B. Ehrlich, and Janet M. Dukerich, "The Romance of Leadership," *Administrative Science Quarterly* 30 (1985): 78–102.

28. Michael R. Wolfson and Gerald R. Salancik, "Observer Orientation and Actor-Observer Differences in Attributions for Failure," *Journal of Experimental Social Psychology* 13 (1977): 441–451.

29. Lee D. Ross, "The Intuitive Psychologist and His Shortcomings: Distortions in the Attribution Process," in *Advances in Experimental Social Psychology*, vol. 10, ed. Leonard Berkowitz (New York: Random House, 1977), 173–220.

30. Former GE executive Spencer Clark, personal communication with author, Stanford University, Stanford, CA, August 2003.

31. See Meindl, Ehrlich, and Dukerich, "The Romance of Leadership." Their finding that people are especially likely to give leaders excessive credit and blame when performance is at extreme levels helps explain why leadership was seen by both insiders and outsiders as crucial to the performance of the "good to great" companies studied by Jim Collins and his team.

32. See, for example, Roberto Weber, "The Illusion of Leadership: Misattribution of Cause in Coordination Games," *Organization Science* 12 (2001): 582–598.

33. Patrick McGeehan, "Executive Pay: A Special Report; Is C.E.O. Pay Up or Down? Both," *New York Times*, April 4, 2004.

34. A good summary of this literature can be found in Jeffrey Pfeffer and Christina T. Fong, "Building Organization Theory from First Principles: The Self-Enhancement Motive and Understanding Power and Influence," *Organization Science* 16 (2005): 372–388.

35. Jeffrey Pfeffer, Robert B. Cialdini, Benjamin Hanna, and Kathleen Knopoff, "Faith in Supervision and the Self-Enhancement Bias: Two Psychological Reasons Why Managers Don't Empower Workers," *Basic and Applied Social Psychology* 20 (1998): 313–321.

36. See, for instance, James H. David, "Social Interaction and Performance," in *Group Performance* (Reading, MA: Addison-Wesley, 1969).

37. Dennis W. Bakke, *Joy at Work: A Revolutionary Approach to Fun on the Job* (Seattle, WA: PVG, 2005).

38. See Martin E. Seligman, *Learned Optimism* (New York: Free Press, 1998); Robert I. Sutton and Robert L. Kahn, "Prediction, Understanding, and Control as Antidotes to Organizational Stress," in *Handbook of Organizational Behavior*, ed. Jay Lorsch (Englewood Cliffs, NJ: Prentice-Hall, 1987), 272–285.

39. From the transcript of a talk given by Andy Grove given at a Harvard Business School Publishing conference, Cupertino, CA, October 3, 2002.

40. Peter F. Drucker, "What Makes an Effective Executive," *Harvard Business Review* (June 2004): 58.

41. Jim Collins, "Level 5 Leadership," *Harvard Business Review* (January 2001): 66–67.

42. C. Peterson, Martin E. P. Seligman, and G. E. Vaillant, "Pessimistic Explanatory Style Is a Risk Factor for Physical Illness: A Thirty-Five Year Longitudinal Study," *Journal of Personality and Social Psychology* 55 (1988): 23–27.

43. Fiona Lee and R. Robinson, "An Attributional Analysis of Social Accounts: Implications of Playing the Blame Game," *Journal of Applied Social Psychology* 30 (2000): 1853–1879; F. Lee and Larissa Tiedens, "Who's Being Served? 'Self'-Serving Attributions and Their Implications for Power," *Organizational Behavior and Human Decision Processes* 84 (2001): 254–287.

44. Gerald Salancik and James Meindl, "Corporate Attributions as Strategic Illusions of Management Control," *Administrative Science Quarterly* 29 (1984): 238–254.

45. Fiona Lee, Christopher Peterson, and Larissa Z. Tiedens, "Mea Culpa: Predicting Stock Prices from Organizational Attributions," *Personality and Social Psychology Bulletin* 30 (2004): 1–14.

46. Gary Rivlin, "He Naps, He Sings, He Isn't Michael Dell," *New York Times*, September 11, 2005.

47. GE, *Annual Report*, 1989.

48. Robert G. Eccles and Nitin Nohria, *Beyond the Hype* (Boston: Harvard Business School Press, 1992), 33.

49. Warren Bennis, *Why Leaders Can't Lead: The Unconscious Conspiracy Continues* (San Francisco: Jossey-Bass, 1997).

50. Jeffrey Pfeffer and Robert I. Sutton, *The Knowing-Doing Gap: How Smart Companies Turn Knowledge into Action* (Boston: Harvard Business School Press, 2000).

51. Clay Chandler, "Full Speed Ahead," *Fortune*, February 7, 2005, 78–84.

52. Dacher Keltner, Deborah H. Gruenfeld, and Cameron Anderson Power, "Approach and Inhibition," *Psychological Review* 110 (2003): 265–284.

53. Mark R. Leary, *Self-Presentation: Impression Management and Interpersonal Behavior* (Boulder, CO: Westview, 1996).

54. Howard S. Schwartz, *Narcissistic Process and Corporate Decay* (New York: New York University Press, 1992), 89; Harold W. Gehman Jr. et al., *Columbia Accident Investigation Board: Report Volume I* (Washington, DC: Government Printing Office, 2003). Available at http://www.caib.us/.

55. Patricia Sellars, "P&G: Teaching an Old Dog New Tricks," *Fortune*, May 31, 2004, 166–180.

56. Robert I. Sutton, *Weird Ideas That Work: 11 and ½ Practices for Promoting, Managing, and Sustaining Innovation* (New York: Free Press, 2002).

57. Ibid., 127.

58. "The Lincoln Electric Company," Case 376-028 (Boston: Harvard Business School, 1975).

59. James N. Baron and Michael T. Hannan, "Organizational Blueprints for Success in High-Tech Start-Ups: Lessons from the Stanford Project on Emerging Companies," *California Management Review* 44 (2002): 8–36.

60. For example, Jim Collins and Jerry I. Porras, *Built to Last* (New York: HarperBusiness, 1994); Michael L. Tushman and Charles A. O'Reilly III, *Winning Through Innovation* (Boston: Harvard Business School Press, 1997).

61. David McCullough, *1776* (New York: Simon & Schuster, 2005).

62. Morgan McCall, *High Flyers* (Boston: Harvard Business School Press, 1998).

63. Rakesh Khurana, *Searching for a Corporate Savior* (Princeton, NJ: Princeton University Press, 2002); also see Katherine Zoe Andrews, "The Performance Impact of New CEOs," *Sloan Management Review* 42 (Spring 2001): 14.

64. Katrina Booker, "It Took a Lady to Save Avon," *Fortune*, October 15, 2001, http://www.fortune.com/fortune/subs/article/0,15114,367458-2,00.html.

65. "The Diversity List," *Fortune*, August 22, 2005, 89–100.

66. Danny Miller and Jamal Shamsie, "Learning Across the Life Cycle: Experimentation and Performance Among the Hollywood Studio Heads," *Strategic Management Journal* 22 (2001): 725–745.

Chapter 9

1. Theresa M. Welbourne and Alice O. Andrews, "Predicting the Performance of Initial Public Offerings: Should Human Resource Management Be in the Equation?" *Academy of Management Journal* 39 (1996): 891–919.

2. Michael J. Burke, Fritz Drasgow, and Jack E. Edwards, "Closing the Science-Practice Knowledge Gaps: Contributions of Psychological Research to Human Resource Management," *Human Resource Management* 43 (2004): 299–304.

3. Sharon Begley, "Inertia, Hope, Morality Score TKOs in Bouts with 'Solid Science,'" *Wall Street Journal*, June 6, 2003.

4. Ibid.

5. Ann Page, ed., *Keeping Patients Safe: Transforming the Work Environment of Nurses* (Washington, DC: National Academies Press, 2004).

6. Tom Davenport, "Peter F. Drucker—A Meeting of the Minds," *CIO Magazine*, September 15, 1997, 2, http://www.cio.com/archive/091597/.

7. Sharon Begley, "To Improve Education, We Need Clinical Trials to Show What Works," *Wall Street Journal*, December 17, 2004.

8. See http://www.consortium-chicago.org/aboutus/u0001.html.

9. John A. Meacham, "The Loss of Wisdom," in *Wisdom: Its Nature, Origins, and Development*, ed. Robert J. Sternberg (New York: Cambridge University Press, 1990), 181.

10. Helen Chang, "Customer Focus Keeps Amazon Experimenting, Bezos Says," October 2003, http://www.gsb.stanford.edu/news/headlines/vftt_bezos.shtml.

11. Elizabeth Esfahani, "A Sales Channel They Can't Resist," *Business 2.0*, August 25, 2005, 91–96.

12. Harry G. Frankfurt, *On Bullshit* (Princeton, NJ: Princeton University Press, 2005).

13. Allen C. Bluedorn, Daniel B. Turban, and Mary Sue Love, "The Effects of Stand-Up and Sit-Down Meeting Formats on Meeting Outcomes," *Journal of Applied Psychology* 84 (1999): 277–285.

14. A. Cooper, C. Woo, and W. Dunkelberg, "Entrepreneurs' Perceived Chances for Success," *Journal of Business Venturing* 3 (1988): 97–108.

15. Max H. Bazerman, *Judgment in Managerial Decision Making*, 6th ed. (Somerset, NJ: Wiley, 2006).

16. Kathleen M. Eisenhardt, "Making Fast Strategic Decisions in High-Velocity Environments," *Academy of Management Journal* 32 (1989): 543–576.

17. Aric Press, "In-House at the American Lawyer," *American Lawyer*, April 2004, http://www.americanlawyer.com/newinhouse0404.html.

18. Joseph Nocera, "Curtain Call," *Fortune*, July 19, 1999, 98.

19. Patricia Sellers, "Crunch Time for Coke," *Fortune*, July 19, 1999, 76.

20. Ibid., 74.

21. Michael Beer and Mark D. Cannon, "Promise and Peril in Implementing Pay for Performance," *Human Resource Management* 43 (Spring 2004): 6–7.

22. Ibid., 11.

23. Amy C. Edmondson, "Learning from Mistakes Is Easier Said Than Done: Group and Organizational Influences on the Detection and Correction of Human Error," *Journal of Applied Behavioral Science* 32 (1996): 5–28

24. Harold W. Gehman Jr. et al., *Columbia Accident Investigation Board: Report Volume I* (Washington, DC: Government Printing Office, 2003), http://www.caib.us.

25. Charles A. O'Reilly III and Jeffrey Pfeffer, *Hidden Value* (Boston: Harvard Business School Press, 2000).

26. Jeffrey Pfeffer, *The Human Equation: Building Profits by Putting People First* (Boston: Harvard Business School Press, 1998).

27. F. W. Taylor, *The Principles of Scientific Management* (New York: Harper, 1911).

28. Andre Millard, *Edison and the Business of Invention* (Baltimore, MD: John Hopkins University Press, 1990).

29. Janet Browne, *Charles Darwin: The Power of Place* (New York: Knopf, 2002), 130.

30. Charles L. Bosk, *Forgive and Remember* (Chicago: University of Chicago Press, 1979).

31. Henry Mintzberg, *The Nature of Managerial Work* (New York: Harper and Row, 1973); John Kotter, *The General Managers* (New York: Free Press, 1982); Rakesh Khurana, *Searching for a Corporate Savior* (Princeton, NJ: Princeton University Press, 2002).

32. Thomas Delong and Christina Darwall, "Xilinx, Inc. (A)," Case 9-403-136 (Boston: Harvard Business School, 2003), 3.

33. Bill George and Andrew N. McLean, "Anne Mulcahy: Leading Xerox Through The Perfect Storm," Case 9-405-050 (Boston: Harvard Business School, 2005), 8.

34. Arndt Sorge and Arjen van Witteloostuijn, "The (Non)sense of Organizational Change: An *Essai* about Universal Management Hypes, Slick Consultancy Metaphors, and Health Organization Theories," *Organization Studies* 25 (2004): 1207.

Acknowledgments

Hard Facts, Dangerous Half-Truths, and Total Nonsense reflects the culmination of our noisy, intense, and fun working relationship and friendship. But we never could have learned so much about evidence-based management, or ever finished this book, without the help and support of many people and organizations along the way. We've had between the two of us a total of over 200 different coauthors over the years. Jeffrey Pfeffer has been especially strongly influenced by the late Jerry Salancik, Bob Cialdini, Charles O'Reilly, Jim Baron, Morten Hansen, and Jerry Davis. Robert Sutton has been most strongly influenced by Robert Kahn, Tom D'Aunno, Larry Ford, Anat Rafaeli, Barry Staw, Kim Elsbach, and Andy Hargadon. We thank these smart and diverse people for the huge effect they've had on how we view and practice our craft.

As we wrote this book, we had wonderful discussions about the ideas and tips about literatures we should read from an array of thoughtful colleagues and students. Our most helpful Stanford colleagues have included Charles A. O'Reilly III, Tom Byers, Chip Heath, Kathleen Eisenhardt, Bill Barnett, Pamela Hinds, Diane Bailey, Steve Barely, Debra Gruenfeld, George Kembel, Randy Komisar, James March, David Kelley, Tina Seelig, and Deborah Stipek. Robert Sutton was also fortunate to serve as a Fellow in Residence at the Center for Advanced Study in the Behavioral Sciences at Stanford in 2002–2003, where he drafted several chapters of this book and had charming conversations with fellow scholars about the emerging ideas, especially with Tony Bryk, Frank Dobbin, Anders Ericsson, Debra Gruenfeld, Steve Levitt, and Alan Ryan. Sutton taught a doctoral seminar on evidence-based management in 2004 in the Department of Management Science and Engineering, and received great suggestions—and troubling criticisms—from the students in that seminar Rosalind Chow, Yosem Companys, Liz Gerber, Gael LeMens, Paul Leonardi, Carlos Lluesma, Ingrid Marlies, Renee Rottner, and Olivia Williamson, as well as from other Stanford doctoral students including Tsedal Beyene, Jan Chong, Ralph Maurer, Nathan Furr, Emily Cox, Nick Switanek, and Dana Wang. We also would like to give special thanks to several especially insightful master's students for their comments on the prospects and challenges of developing evidence-based management, Cliff Redeker, Albert Lee, Dr. Albert Chan, Parnav Goel, and Dr. Roni Zeiger. We received inspiring and constructive comments from colleagues outside of Stanford including Sally Baron, Max Bazerman, Rob Cross, Tom Davenport, Amy Edmondson, Fabrizio Ferraro, Katherine Klein, Julia Kirby, Sheila Puffer, Larry Prusak, Kelley Porter, Denise Rousseau, Siobhan O'Mahony, Rakesh Khurana, Tom Stewart, Victor Seidel, and Mark Zbaracki. Robert Sutton would also like to give special thanks to James Plummer, the Dean of the Stanford Engineering School, and to Senior Associate Deans Laura Breyfogle and Channing Robertson, who make the Engineering School such a great place to work. These leaders care deeply about people, are selfless, and always put the needs of the institution above all else. It is a privilege to work with them.

The ideas, evidence, and stories in this book were shaped by literally thousands of interactions that we've had over the years with engineers and other professionals, consultants, managers, and executives, as well as the many wonderful frontline people who do the work that makes their organizations successful. These interactions ranged from brief informal conversations, to structured and unstructured interviews, to quick observations, to long-term ethnographic studies, to speaking and consulting engagements, to serving on advisory boards and boards of directors. We wish we could thank all these people, but we can't remember them all, and even if we could, it would take up an entire book! But we would like to thank some of the most influential people, and to ask for forgiveness from those we have omitted. We thank Paul Saffo from the Institute for the Future; Gary Loveman of Harrah's; Joe Mello and Kent Thiry and their many teammates of DaVita; Dennis Boyle, Brendan Boyle, Duane Bray, Tim Brown, Jane Fulton-Suri, Kathleen Hughes, Cliff Jue, David Kelley, Tom Kelley, Whitney Mortimer, Diego Rodriquez, Roby Stancel, Rickson Sun, and Scott Underwood from IDEO; past IDEO employees including Gwen Books, Dave Lyons, Alex Kazaks, Peter Skillman, Larry Schubert, and every other IDEO employee past and present; John Reinertsen of McDonald's; John Lilly, formerly of Reactivity (now at the Mozilla Corporation); Libby Sartain, Nitin Sharma, and Usama Fayyad from Yahoo!; a host of former HP managers and executives including Don Schmickrath, Mei-lin Cheng, and especially Corey Billington; Dennis Bakke, formerly of AES and now CEO of Imagine Schools; Jim Goodnight, David Russo (now at Peopleclick), Jeff Chambers, and John Dornan of SAS Institute; Dr. Laura Esserman of the University of California at San Francisco;

Joey Altman of the (now defunct) Wild Hare; Spencer Clark of Cadence; Sonia Clark; Steve Dow of Sevin Rosen; Richard Kovacevich of Wells Fargo Bank; Jan Benson, Hallie Kintner, Bill Jordon, and Jan Aase of General Motors; Steve Ciesinski, former CEO of Resumix and now CEO of Laszlo Systems; George Zimmer of The Men's Wearhouse; Bill Crown of CC Industries; Peter Ebert, Anamarie Franc, Michael Heinrich, Erin Liman, Matthew Holloway, Zia Yusuf, and the rest of the members (and founders) of SAP's Design Services Team; Tim Tomlinson of Tomlinson, Zisko; Kevin Goodwin and his colleagues at SonoSite; and Vance Ikezoye, Jim Schrempp, Mike McTeigue, and the rest of the people at Audible Magic. Robert Sutton also thanks Ellen Pearlman, Marcia Stepanek, and Edward Baker for their help in publishing his "Organizational Behavior" column in *CIO Insight*, where the first glimmer of some of the ideas in the book were first published.

Robert Sutton was provided financial support from several generous groups and organizations as we wrote this book, including the Stanford/General Motors Collaborative Research Laboratory, the Center for Advanced Study in the Behavioral Sciences, the Stanford Technology Ventures Program, Stanford's Center for Work, Technology, and Organization, the IBM Services Sciences, Management and Engineering Faculty Award, the John & Daryl Lillie Fund at the Stanford Engineering School, and the MacArthur Foundation Research Network on Teaching and Learning. Jeffrey Pfeffer has been generously supported by the Stanford Business School and its many donors. We appreciate this support for our work. We never take for granted the wonderful colleagues and infrastructure of Stanford that makes what we do possible. Daphne Chang in the business school library has been a hero in helping with the references.

We are especially indebted to Donald Lamm, who is officially our literary agent, but is much more than that. Don worked in the business for over 40 years, eventually rising to CEO of W.W. Norton before "retiring" from that job and becoming a literary agent. Don has been involved in this project before we ever wrote the first word, giving advice, helping us with the title, editing, fighting for us and with us, and pushing us gently along the way. He is among the most gracious and smart people we know. And when someone tells us "I've been in the publishing business for 20 years, and I can tell you . . . ," Don always has the same reply, "I've been in the publishing business for almost 50 years, and the only thing I can tell you is that no one can predict what will happen." We also give our thanks to Christy Fletcher of FletcherParry, who teamed with Don at key points along the way. Her brilliance and tenaciousness are something to behold.

Robert Sutton also wishes to thank Les Tuerk and Tom Neilssen of the BrightSight Group for their support during the long process of producing this book, for booking him so many speeches over the years, and for being so fun to work with.

We have also been simply delighted with our experiences with Harvard Business School Press. We especially thank Melinda Merino, who is imaginative, enthusiastic, and relentless—qualities that have made this a better book at every stage. We also thank marketing manager Zeenat Potia for her great work (especially for being open to the initial cover designs done by the amazing Elizabeth Gerber), Marcy Barnes-Henrie for getting the manuscript into production so quickly and so well, Monica Jainschigg for caring about the language and flow of the book as much as we do, and Erin Brown for exceptional help with book publicity. Moreover, we would like to thank everyone in the different parts of Harvard Business School Publishing—including Harvard Business School Press, the Harvard Business Review, HBSP Conferences, HBSP Newsletters, and HBSP eLearning—for exceptional cooperation on this book. In a world where dysfunctional internal competition reigns in so many organizations, the cooperation we've seen among these groups—and benefited from—has been most impressive.

Finally, we want to thank those closest to us for supporting us at every turn. Robert Sutton thanks his mother Annette Sutton and his late father Lewis Sutton for all their love and support over the years, and his sweet, loving, and loud children, Eve, Claire, and Tyler. We dedicate this book to the smart, patient, and beautiful Kathleen Fowler and Marina Park Sutton, the loves of our lives.

Index

About the Authors

Jeffrey Pfeffer is the Thomas D. Dee II Professor of Organizational Behavior in the Graduate School of Business, Stanford University, where he has taught since 1979. He received his BS and MS from Carnegie-Mellon University and his PhD in business from Stanford. Pfeffer has served on the faculties at the University of Illinois, the University of California at Berkeley, and as a visiting professor at the Harvard Business School. He has taught executive seminars in 27 countries throughout the world. He serves on the board of directors of Aubidble Magic, Unicru, and SonoSite, as well as on numerous editorial boards of scholarly journals. He is writes a monthly column for *Business 2.0* and is the author or coauthor of 11 books, including *The Knowing-Doing Gap, The Human Equation, New Directions for Organization Theory, Competitive Advantage Through People, Managing with Power,* and *The External Control of Organizations,* as well as more than 100 articles and book chapters.

Robert I. Sutton is Professor of Management Science & Engineering in the Stanford Engineering School, where he is codirector of the Center for Work, Technology, and Organization, and a cofounder of the Hasso Platner Institute for Design at Stanford. He received his PhD in organizational psychology from the University of Michigan and has served on the Stanford faculty since 1983. Dr. Sutton was a Fellow at the Center for Advanced Study in the Behavioral Sciences and has served as an IDEO Fellow since 1996. He has given many executive seminars, consulted to numerous corporations, and currently directs the Leadership for Strategic Execution executive program for the Stanford Engineering School. His honors include the award for the best paper published in the *Academy of Management Journal,* the Eugene L. Grant Award for Excellence in Teaching, the McCullough Faculty Scholar Chair, credit for two "breakthrough" ideas in *Harvard Business Review,* and selection by *Business 2.0* as a leading business "guru." He has served as an editor and editorial board member of numerous scholarly publications, and published more than 100 articles and book chapters. He is coauthor of *The Knowing Doing Gap* and author of *Weird Ideas That Work,* which *Harvard Business Review* selected as one of the 10 best business books of the year.